CUTTING EDGE

INTERMEDIATE

photocopiable resources by Chris Redston

TEACHER'S RESOURCE BOOK

Longman

sarah cunningham   peter moor

Contents

Introduction — page 3

Teacher's tips
Making tasks work — page 8
Responding to learners' individual language needs — page 10
Working with lexis — page 12
Making the most of the *Mini-dictionary* — page 14
Using a discovery approach in the teaching of grammar — page 15

Module 1 — page 16

Module 2 — page 23

Module 3 — page 29

Module 4 — page 35

Module 5 — page 42

Module 6 — page 49

Module 7 — page 55

Module 8 — page 62

Module 9 — page 68

Module 10 — page 74

Module 11 — page 80

Module 12 — page 87

Resource bank
Index of activities — page 94
Instructions — page 96
Activities — page 104
Tests — page 161
Answer key — page 171

Introduction

Cutting Edge Intermediate is a course aimed at young adults studying general English at an intermediate level. It provides material for up to 120 hours' teaching, according to how much photocopiable material is used from the *Teacher's Resource Book*. It is suitable for students studying in either a monolingual or multilingual classroom situation.

STUDENTS' BOOK **CLASS CASSETTES**	*Cutting Edge Intermediate Students' Book* is divided into twelve modules, each consisting of approximately 8–10 hours' worth of classroom material. Each module is divided into two parts – **Part A Language** and **Part B Task**. **Part A Language** This is based around the input of new language and consists of: • **grammar** – two *Language focus* sections, one including a *Mini-task*, practice activities, integrated pronunciation work • **vocabulary** – including a *Wordspot* section, looking at some of the most common words in English (*have, time, place*, etc.) • **reading and/or listening** – with integrated speaking activities **Part B Task** This is based around a communicative task and consists of: • **Preparation for task** – listening and/or reading and useful phrases for the task • **Task** – extended speaking, often with an optional writing component • **Task link** – vocabulary, phrases and minor structures arising from the task • **Real life** – speaking and writing activities based around everyday situations related to the task (making a social arrangement, writing 'thank you' letters, etc.) **Mini-dictionary**: in the back cover pocket of the *Students' Book* is the *Cutting Edge Intermediate Mini-dictionary*, which contains definitions and examples for more than 2,000 words and phrases from the *Students' Book*. A detailed **Language summary** and **Tapescripts** for material on the *Class Cassettes* can be found at the back of the *Students' Book*.
WORKBOOK **STUDENT'S CASSETTE**	*Cutting Edge Intermediate Workbook* is divided into twelve parallel modules, consisting of: • **grammar** – consolidation and extension of main language points covered in the *Students' Book*; *Grammar snacks* focusing on typical problem areas such as articles and prepositions • **vocabulary** – additional practice and input • **skills work** – regular *Improve your writing* and *Listen and read* sections • **pronunciation** – focus on problem sounds and word stress There is an **Answer key** at the back of the *Workbook*. The optional **Student's Cassette** features exercises on grammar and pronunciation.
TEACHER'S RESOURCE BOOK	*Cutting Edge Intermediate Teacher's Resource Book* consists of three sections: • **Introduction** and **Teacher's tips** on: – Making tasks work – Responding to learners' individual language needs – Working with lexis – Making the most of the *Mini-dictionary* – Using a discovery approach in the teaching of grammar • **step-by-step teacher's notes** for each module – including alternative suggestions for different teaching situations, particularly for tasks, detailed language notes and integrated answer keys • photocopiable **Resource bank** – including learner-training worksheets, communicative grammar practice activities and vocabulary extension activities The teacher's notes section is **cross-referenced** to the *Resource bank* and the *Workbook*.

Introduction

The thinking behind *Cutting Edge Intermediate*

Cutting Edge Intermediate Students' Book has a multi-layered syllabus, which includes a comprehensive grammar and vocabulary syllabus, incorporating systematic work on listening, speaking, reading and writing. It takes an integrated approach to pronunciation, and includes learner-training and revision. However, it has three distinctive features:
- it has a task-based element
- it places particular emphasis on lexis
- it employs a 'discovery' approach to the teaching of grammar.

As these features are likely to be of greatest interest to teachers familiarising themselves with the course, they are dealt with first below.

Task-based element

WHAT DO WE MEAN BY A 'TASK'?

It is an oral or written activity, in which the primary goal is to achieve a particular outcome or product. The tasks in this course all involve an extended oral phase, often followed up with an optional written phase. They include interviews, story-telling, mini-talks, problem-solving and ordering discussions.

WHAT DO WE MEAN BY A 'TASK-BASED APPROACH'?

The important elements of the task-based approach in *Cutting Edge Intermediate* are as follows:

1 **The task is treated as an end in itself rather than an opportunity to 'practise' specific language.** It should be intrinsically motivating and be relevant to 'real life'.

2 **The tasks are central to the course, not just incidental speaking activities.** For this reason, much of the language input in the course relates to the tasks, and students are carefully prepared for tasks with a model or stimulus and time to plan. After the task, teachers can provide feedback on students' performance and further input if required before the writing stage (if there is one).

3 **Learners are provided with the language needed in order to perform the task.** This can only be anticipated to some extent – it will partly depend on what the individual student wants to say. However, in *Cutting Edge Intermediate* we anticipate it in a number of ways:
- the grammar and/or lexis in Part A of the module is useful (to a greater or lesser extent) for the performance of the task in Part B.
- each task is accompanied by a *Useful language* box with a range of phrases and structures of immediate use for students as they perform the task.
- each task is accompanied by a *Personal vocabulary* box for students to write in the individual words and phrases that they need to perform the task.
- specific lexical/functional areas leading out of the task are developed afterwards in the *Task link* sections.

4 **Learners use the best language they can to achieve the task, and are encouraged to 'raise their game'.** For this reason planning and rehearsal time is built into the preparation stages, with the intention of encouraging students to be more ambitious in what they try to say. It is sometimes suggested that the teacher should deliberately put students under more pressure to improve their performance.

5 **Tasks provide students with just the right amount of challenge.** Students use what they already know, developing their confidence and fluency, and at the same time creating a need for further new input. However, learners should not be over-stretched, or they will resort to 'pidgin-English' (or their own language) to perform the task. In *Cutting Edge Intermediate* we start with simpler personalised tasks and gradually move on to simulations and more complex discussions as students' knowledge and confidence increases.

WHAT ARE THE ADVANTAGES OF A TASK-BASED APPROACH?

1 Students have regular and structured opportunities to speak and are given an opportunity to practise skills and language that they may well need to use in the 'real world'.

2 It contributes to progress at this critical stage, by encouraging students to plan and be more ambitious in the language they use, rather than just saying the first thing that comes into their heads.

3 Because learners are striving to express what they want to say, they are more motivated to absorb the language needed – either new language that they ask you for, or language that they have already met, but not acquired properly so far. In this way, students have their 'own syllabus' as well as the one in the *Students' Book*.

4 The tasks offer variety of pace, especially when combined with a more traditional syllabus, as in this course.

5 Tasks provide a natural opportunity for revision and recycling and give teachers the opportunity to assess learners' progress

(See *Teacher's Tips: making tasks work* on pages 8–9 and *Responding to learners' individual language needs* on pages 10–11.)

Introduction

Lexis

SELECTION CRITERIA

A good vocabulary is vital to communicative success, so new lexis is introduced at every stage in the *Students' Book* and recycled wherever possible. We have paid particular attention to the selection of useful, high-frequency lexis, and have kept in mind the fact that words and phrases will be used and understood in an international context. To help us, we have used information from the *British National Corpus*.

MINI-DICTIONARY

The accompanying *Mini-dictionary* includes references and examples for words and phrases in the *Students' Book* that students are unlikely to know (a full outline of which words and phrases have been included appears at the front of the *Mini-dictionary*). Students are referred to the *Mini-dictionary* at appropriate points throughout the *Students' Book*.

THE IMPORTANCE OF PHRASES AS WELL AS INDIVIDUAL WORDS

These days it is recognised that in order to communicate fluently we make extensive use of 'pre-fabricated chunks' of language. There are thousands of these and they operate as single units of meaning, just as individual words do. They consist of:
1 **collocations** (common word combinations) including:
   - nouns + verbs *(work long hours, have a drink)*
   - adjectives + nouns *(old friends, bad news)*
   - adverbs + verbs *(work hard, will probably)*
   - verbs + prepositions/particles, including phrasal verbs *(think about, grow up)*
   - adjectives + prepositions *(famous for, jealous of)*
   - other combinations of the above *(go out for a meal, get to know)*
2 **fixed phrases**, such as: *Never mind!, On the other hand ... , If I were you ... , Someone I know,* etc.
3 **semi-fixed phrases** (that is phrases with variations), such as: *a friend of mine/hers/my brother's; both of us/them/my parents; the second/third/tenth biggest in the world,* etc.
4 **whole sentences which act as phrases**, such as: *How are you?, He's gone home, I'll give you a hand, I agree to some extent.*

This kind of lexis is incorporated in the *Students' Book* in a number of different ways:
- alongside single-word items in vocabulary slots.
- in the *Wordspot* sections, which focus on the most useful collocations of very high-frequency words like *get*, *think* or *time*.
- in the *Useful language* boxes which accompany the task.
- in the *Real life* sections, where we focus on typical situational language.
- alongside related grammar structures.

PERSONALISED INPUT

What can be considered as useful vocabulary is partly individual – different students have different vocabulary needs. A task-based approach provides the opportunity for students to ask for the words and phrases they need in order to express what they want to say – for this reason there are *Personal vocabulary* boxes on the task pages. At other points throughout the *Students' Book* we encourage students to ask their teacher for language they need in order to express what they really want to say.

(For practical suggestions see *Teacher's tips: making the most of the Mini-dictionary* on page 14 and *Working with lexis* on pages 12–13.)

Approach to grammar

GENERAL PRINCIPLES

- Our grammar syllabus includes work on tenses and other verb forms, as well as areas such as quantifiers and relative clauses. It aims to provide thorough coverage and practice.
- The new language in Part A of each module is generally useful for the task in Part B, although how much it is needed depends on the task in question, as well as how much the individual student chooses to use it.
- We have tried to bring the criteria of frequency and usefulness to bear on grammatical input too, and traditional areas of grammar have been extended to include high-frequency lexical phrases. For example, work on superlatives includes phrases like *one of the biggest in* and *by far the biggest*; work on 'future predictions' includes *may well* and *it's likely to*.
- We have sometimes chosen to emphasise the 'base' meaning of forms such as the Present Perfect, rather than give learners lists of disparate 'uses', which we believe can overwhelm and confuse them.

METHODOLOGY

All new language is introduced in context, via listenings, readings and quizzes, and learners arrive at the new language and its rules via a 'discovery' approach, which involves the following:
- *Mini-tasks*: one of the *Language focus* sections in each module is preceded by a *Mini-task*, which gives students a natural opportunity to use the language without previous input. These *Mini-tasks* allow the teacher to monitor students' existing knowledge and the errors they make, and to adjust their lesson accordingly.
- *'Test-teach' language awareness activities*: these focus more explicitly on the target language – students are expected to draw on existing knowledge to hypothesise about new language.

5

Introduction

- **Analysis sections**: these accompany each *Language focus* section and take students step-by-step through the main problems that they need to consider. Rules are summarised in more detail in the *Language summary* at the back of the book.

All new language is practised in meaningful contexts, often through communicative pairwork activities. Further practice is provided both in the *Workbook* and via the photocopiable activities in the *Resource bank*.

(For practical suggestions see *Teacher's tips: Using a discovery approach in the teaching of grammar* on page 15.)

Other important elements in *Cutting Edge Intermediate*

Listening

Cutting Edge Intermediate places strong emphasis on listening. Listening material includes:
- short extracts and mini-dialogues to introduce and practise new language.
- words and sentences for close listening and to model pronunciation.
- longer texts (interviews, stories and conversations), often in Part B of the module as a model or stimulus for the task.
- regular *Listen and read* sections in the *Workbook* to further develop students' confidence in this area.

Speaking

There is also a strong emphasis on speaking, as follows:
- the tasks provide a regular opportunity for extended and prepared speaking based round realistic topics and situations (for example, recommending places to visit to a foreign visitor, telling a story about something unusual that happened to you, discussing and solving problems).
- the topics and texts in Part A of each module provide opportunities for follow-up discussion.
- much of the practice of grammar and lexis is through oral exercises and activities.
- there is regular integrated work on pronunciation.
- most of the photocopiable activities in the *Resource bank* are oral.

Reading

There is a wide range of reading material in the *Students' Book*, including newspaper articles, factual/scientific texts, stories, quizzes, forms, notes and letters. These texts are integrated in a number of different ways:
- extended texts specifically to develop reading skills.
- texts which lead into grammar work and language analysis.

- texts which provide a model or stimulus for tasks and models for writing activities.

Note: for classes who do not have a lot of time to do reading in class there are suggestions in the teacher's notes section on how to avoid this where appropriate.

Writing

Writing skills are developed through:
- writing activities in the *Real life* sections, such as writing letters, filling in an application form, etc.
- *Optional writing* sections following on from many of the tasks – these give students an opportunity to write about what they have discussed, with the benefit of more time to think. (The teacher's notes section also provides suggestions on how to vary the original task for the writing stage.)
- exercises on linkers and other areas which are particularly important for writing.
- regular *Improve your writing* sections in the *Workbook*, which deal with a large range of sub-skills including spelling, punctuation, avoiding repetition, linkers, time words, etc.

Pronunciation

Pronunciation work in *Cutting Edge Intermediate* is integrated with work on grammar and lexis, and is presented in 'pronunciation boxes' so as to stand out clearly. In the *Students' Book* the focus is mainly on stress, connected speech and intonation, while the *Workbook* focuses on problem sounds and word stress. A range of activity types are used, including discrimination exercises and dictation, and there is an equal emphasis on understanding and reproducing. Pronunciation sections in both the *Students' Book* and the *Workbook* are generally accompanied by exercises on the cassette, which provide models for students to copy.

Revision

The *Students' Book* revises and recycles material in the following ways:
- a *Do you remember?* quiz at the end of eight modules includes a variety of quick questions focusing particularly on areas of confusion.
- a *Consolidation* spread at the end of Modules 4, 8 and 12 combines grammar and vocabulary exercises with listening and speaking activities, recycling material from the previous four modules.
- three photocopiable tests in the *Resource bank* for use after Modules 4, 8 and 12.

In addition, the task-based approach offers constant opportunities for students to re-use what they have learnt, and for teachers to remind them of important points.

Introduction

Learning skills

Cutting Edge Intermediate develops learning skills in a number of ways as follows:
- the discovery approach to grammar encourages learners to experiment with language and to work out rules for themselves.
- the task-based approach encourages learners to take a pro-active role in their learning.
- looking words and phrases up in the *Mini-dictionary* gives students constant practice of a range of dictionary skills.
- the *Resource bank* contains five learner-training worksheets aimed at developing students' awareness of the importance of taking an active role in the learning process.

Teacher's tips

Making tasks work

❶ Treat tasks primarily as an opportunity for communication

Some of the tasks in this course may be familiar: the difference is in how they are treated. The main objective is for students to use the language that they know (and if necessary learn new language) in order to achieve a particular communicative goal, not to 'practise' specific language. Although it is virtually impossible to perform some of the tasks without using the language introduced in Part A of the module, in others students may choose to use this language only once or twice, or not at all. Do not try to 'force-feed' it. Of course, if learners are seeking this language but have forgotten it, this is the ideal moment to remind them!

❷ Make the task suit your class

Students using this course will vary in age, background, interests and ability. All these students need to find the tasks motivating and 'do-able', yet challenging at the same time. Do not be afraid to adapt the tasks to suit your class if this helps. The teacher's notes contain suggestions on how to adapt certain tasks for monolingual and multilingual groups, students of different ages and interests, large classes, and weaker or stronger groups. There are also ideas for shortening tasks, or dividing them over two shorter lessons. We hope these suggestions will give you other ideas of your own on how to adapt the tasks.

❸ Experiment with where you use the task within the module

We have placed the tasks at the same place in each module, but this does not mean that teachers always need to follow this order when doing the tasks. Other possibilities are:
- *to do the task before the 'language' part of the module*: this is particularly appropriate if students claim that they 'already know' the grammar, and will help you to assess for yourself whether they need any more input on the language point being covered. You may find that you can omit some of the *Language focus* sections, pick out certain parts of them, or just set some practice exercises or reading through the appropriate section of the *Language summary* for 'revision' homework.
- *to do the* Task link *before the task*: the *Task links* focus on phrases or minor structures that relate directly to the task (for example, *Making recommendations* for the task in which students plan a tour of their country/region). Often a few phrases relating to the language area covered in the *Task links* are included in the *Useful language* boxes, but you may prefer to look at the language area in more detail before students do the task.

There may be other ways in which you wish to change the order of the material in each module – the important thing is to do the task at a point when you feel your students will be most motivated and best able to do it.

❹ Personalise it!

All the tasks in *Cutting Edge Intermediate* have a model or stimulus to introduce them. Sometimes these are recordings of people talking about something personal, such as a childhood memory or an object of value to them. However, finding out about you, their teacher, may be more motivating for some students, so you could try providing a personalised model instead. If you do this, remember to:
- plan what you are going to say, but do not write it out word for word, as this may sound unnatural.
- bring in any photos or illustrations you can to help to bring your talk alive.
- either pre-teach or explain as you go along any problematic vocabulary.
- give students something to do as they are listening (the teacher's notes give suggestions on this where appropriate).

This approach may take a little courage at first, but students are likely to appreciate the variety it provides.

❺ Set the final objective clearly before students start preparing

Do not assume that students will work out where their preparations are leading if you do not tell them! Knowing, for example, that their film review will be recorded for a class radio programme may make a big difference to how carefully they prepare it.

❻ Give students time to think and plan

Planning time is very important if students are to produce the best language that they are capable of. It is particularly useful for building up the confidence of students who are normally reluctant to speak in class. The amount of time needed will vary from task to task, from about five to twenty minutes.

This planning time will sometimes mean a period of silence in class, something that teachers used to noisy, communicative classrooms can find unnerving. Remember that just because you cannot hear anything, it does not mean that nothing is happening!

Teacher's tips

It may help to relieve any feelings of tension at this stage by playing some background music, or, if practical in your school, suggest that students go somewhere else to prepare – another classroom if one is available.
Students may well find the idea of 'time to plan' strange at first, but, as with many other teaching and learning techniques, it is very much a question of training.

❼ Respond to students' individual language needs

As students are preparing, it is important that you make it clear that they can ask you about language queries, so that when they perform the task they are able to say what they personally want to say.

(See *Teacher's tips: responding to learners' individual language needs* on pages 10–11.)

❽ Feed in 'useful language'

Although the task should not be seen as an opportunity to 'practise' discrete items, you may find that there is specific language that would be useful in order to perform the task successfully. One way of deciding whether this is the case is to do the task yourself first (without any preconceptions of what language you 'should' use) and noticing what language you use. You may be surprised to find that it is language not usually taught in English-language courses.

USEFUL LANGUAGE BOXES

Each task is accompanied by a *Useful language* box containing phrases which can be adapted by individual students to express different ideas and opinions, rather than anything very specific. The phrases included were selected after trying out the tasks a number of times with 'real' classes. Sometimes the *Useful language* boxes include structures which have not yet been covered in the grammar syllabus. However, the examples used can be taught simply as phrases – it is not intended that you should launch into major grammatical presentations here!
The phrases in the *Useful language* boxes can be dealt with at different points in the lesson:
- before students start their preparation for the task.
- during the preparation phase on an individual basis.
- after the task in the feedback stage.

(See *Teacher's tips: responding to learners' individual language needs*, number 8 on page 11.)

❾ Give students an opportunity to 'rehearse'

This will not be necessary for the simpler tasks, but for more complicated tasks, or with less confident students, it can make a big difference. It will help fluency, encourage students to be more ambitious with their language, and possibly iron out some of their errors. This rehearsal stage can take various forms:
- students tell their story, etc. in pairs before telling it in groups or to the whole class.
- students discuss issues in groups before discussing them as a class.
- students go over what they are going to say 'silently' in their heads (either during the lesson, or at home if the task is split over two lessons).

❿ Insist that students do the task in English!

It may not be realistic to prevent students from using their own language completely, but they should understand that during the performance of the task (if not in the planning stage, where they may need their mother tongue to ask for new language) they must use English. At the beginning of the course, it may be useful to discuss with your class the importance of this, and the best ways of implementing it.
(See *Learner-training worksheet 1* on pages 104–105 of the *Resource bank*.)
Students will be more tempted to use their own language if they find the task daunting, so do not be afraid to shorten or simplify tasks if necessary. However, planning and rehearsal time will make students less inclined to use their first language.

⓫ Try increasing the 'pressure' on students

A teacher's first priority is to improve students' confidence with the language. At the beginning of the course, this may mean putting students under as little pressure as possible (for example, by doing tasks in groups rather than in front of the whole class). As time goes on, however, a certain amount of pressure can sometimes improve the quality of language students produce. This can be done in the following ways:
- by getting students to give their talk, report, etc. standing up in front of the whole class.
- by recording or videoing their performance of the task and re-playing it to them later.
- by making it clear that you will be correcting any errors they make at the end of the task.

⓬ Make notes for further input and correction after the task

Before or during the performance of the task, you may notice errors and gaps in students' knowledge that you want to look at. It is usually best not to interrupt the flow of the task, but be prepared to make a note of these points to cover later on.

(See *Teacher's tips: responding to learners' individual language needs* on pages 10–11.)

9

Teacher's tips

Responding to learners' individual language needs

At appropriate points throughout the *Students' Book*, during the tasks, mini-tasks and speaking activities, students are instructed to ask their teacher about any words or phrases they need. The ability to respond to students' individual language needs is central to a task-based approach, and you may find yourself doing this during pair/group/individual work and during preparation stages. The following suggestions are designed to help teachers who may feel daunted by the idea of unplanned, unpredictable input.

❶ Encourage students to ask about language

Students who take an active approach to their own learning are far more likely to succeed than those who sit back and expect the teacher to do it all for them. It is important to make students aware of this (see *Learner-training worksheet 1* on pages 104–105 of the *Resource bank*), and to convey to them your willingness to deal with their queries. Circulate during pair and individual work, making it clear that you are available to answer questions. Even if you cannot answer a query on the spot, let students know that you are happy to deal with it.

❷ Be responsive, but do not get side-tracked

One danger of this approach is that a teacher may get side-tracked by dominant students who want all their attention, leading to frustration and irritation among others. If you feel that this is happening, tell these students that you will answer their questions later, and move quickly on. Make sure that you keep moving round during pair/group/individual work. Keep a 'bird's-eye' view of the class, moving in to help students if they need it rather than spending too much time with one pair/group/individual.

❸ Encourage students to use what they already know

There is also a danger that students will become over-dependent on you, perhaps asking you to translate large chunks for them, which they are very unlikely to retain. Always encourage students to use what they know first, only asking you if they <u>really</u> have no idea.

❹ Have strategies for dealing with questions you cannot answer

Have at least one bilingual dictionary in the classroom (especially for specialised/technical vocabulary) for students to refer to, although you may still need to check that they have found the right translation. If students ask for idioms and expressions, make sure you keep it simple – in most cases you will be able to come up with an adequate phrase even if it is not precisely the phrase the student wanted. Finally, if all else fails, promise to find out for the next lesson!

❺ Note down important language points to be dealt with later

Note down any important language points that come up during tasks and discussions and build in slots to go over these later on. Write the errors onto the board or OHT, and invite students to correct them/think of a better word, etc. Remember that it is also motivating (and can be just as instructive) to include examples of <u>good</u> language used as well as errors. Feedback slots can either be at the end of the lesson, or, if time is a problem, at the beginning of the next.

❻ Select points for these correction slots carefully

Students are more likely to retain a few well-chosen points in these correction slots rather than a long list of miscellaneous language points. The following are useful things to bear in mind:
- *Usefulness*: many items may only be of interest to individual students – only bring up <u>general</u> language with the whole class.
- *Quantity/Variety*: try to combine one or two more general points with a number of more specific/minor ones, including a mixture of grammar, vocabulary and pronunciation as far as possible.
- *Level:* be careful not to present students with points above their level or which are too complex to deal with in a few minutes.
- *Problems induced by students' mother tongue:* correction slots are an excellent opportunity to deal with L1 specific errors (false friends, pronunciation, etc.) not usually mentioned in general English courses.
- *Revision:* the correction slots are a very good opportunity to increase students' knowledge of complex language covered previously, as well as to remind them of smaller language points.

Teacher's tips

❼ Don't worry if you can't think of 'creative' practice on the spot

If students encounter a genuine need for the language as they try to achieve a particular goal, it is more likely to be remembered than if it is introduced 'cold' by the teacher. In many cases, elaborate practice may be unnecessary – what is important is that you are dealing with the language at the moment it is most likely to be retained by the student. With lexis and small points of pronunciation, it may be enough to get students to repeat the word a few times and write an example on the board, highlighting problems.

❽ Some simple 'on the spot' practice activities

If you feel more work is needed, the box opposite includes some well-known activities which are relatively easy to adapt 'on the spot' (you can always provide a more substantial exercise later). A few examples should be enough for students to see how the structure is formed, and to increase awareness of it. These activities are also useful for practising phrases in the *Useful language* boxes.

a **Choral and individual drilling**

b **Questions and answers**: ask questions prompting students to use the language item in the answer. For example, to practise the phrase *famous for* ask questions such as:
What's Monte Carlo famous for? > It's famous for its Casinos.
What's Loch Ness famous for? > It's famous for the Loch Ness Monster.
Alternatively, give an example, then prompt students to ask questions to each other, like this:
'Monica, ask Henri about Venice.' > What's Venice famous for, Henri?

c **Forming sentences/phrases from prompts**: for example, to practise the construction *it's worth ... -ing* provide the example: *The National Gallery is worth visiting*, then give prompts like this:
ROYAL PALACE/SEE > The Royal Palace is worth seeing.
THIS DICTIONARY/BUY > This dictionary is worth buying.

d **Substitutions**: give an example phrase/sentence, then provide prompts which can easily be substituted into the original. For example, to practise the non-use of the article, start with *I hate cats*, then prompt as follows:
LOVE > I love cats.
BABIES > I love babies.
DON'T LIKE > I don't like babies.

e **Transformations**: these are useful if there is another construction with almost the same meaning. Give one construction and get students to say the same thing using another. For example, to practise *although*:
He's rich, but he's very mean. > Although he's rich, he's very mean.
She's over eighty, but she's very active. > Although she's over eighty, she's very active.

f **Combining shorter sentences/phrases**: give two short sentences and ask students to combine them with a more complex construction. For example, to practise *too ... to*:
She's very young. She can't do this job. > She's too young to do this job.
He's too old. He can't drive a car. > He's too old to drive a car.

g **Dictate sentences for students to complete**: dictate a few incomplete sentences including the phrase or structure, which students complete themselves, then compare with other students. For example, to practise *it takes ... to*, dictate:
It takes about three hours to get to ... It only takes a few minutes to ... It took me ages to ...

Teacher's tips

Working with lexis

❶ Become more aware of phrases and collocations yourself

Until recently, relatively little attention was given to the thousands of phrases and collocations that make up the lexis in English, along with the traditional one-word items. If necessary, spend some time looking at the list of phrase-types on page 5 of the *Introduction*, and start noticing how common these 'pre-fabricated chunks' are in all types of English. They go far beyond areas traditionally dealt with in English-language courses – phrasal verbs, functional exponents and the occasional idiom, although of course they incorporate all of these.

Such phrases blur the boundaries between 'vocabulary' and 'grammar' – in teaching these phrases you will find that you are helping students with many problematic areas that are traditionally considered to be grammar, from the use of articles and prepositions, to the use of the passive and the Present Perfect. Many common examples of these structures are in fact fixed or semi-fixed phrases. We are not suggesting that a 'lexical approach' should replace the traditional grammatical approach to such verb forms, but that it is a useful supplement.

❷ Make your students aware of phrases and collocations

Students should also know about the importance of such phrases. They may look at a phrase like *leave home* and assume that they know it (because the two constituent words look 'easy'), although in fact they are unable to produce the phrase for themselves when appropriate. *Learner-training worksheet 4* on page 109 of the *Resource bank* aims to develop students' awareness of such collocations.

❸ Keep an eye on usefulness and be aware of overloading students

It is easy to 'go overboard' with collocations and phrases as there are so many of them. Also, perhaps because they often consist of such common words, they can be more difficult for students to retain, so limit your input to high-frequency, useful phrases as much as possible. As you teach lexis, ask yourself questions like: *How often would I use this phrase myself? How often do I hear other people using it? Can I imagine my students needing it? Is it too idiomatic, culturally specific or complex to bother with?*

❹ Feed in phrases on a 'little but often' basis

To avoid overloading students and ensure that your lexical input is useful, teach a few phrases relating to particular activities as you go along. For example, in a grammar practice activity, instead of simple answers such as *Yes, I do* or *No, I haven't*, feed in phrases like *It depends, I don't really care, I would probably, I've never tried it*. The same is true of discussions about reading/listening texts and writing activities.

❺ Introduce phrases in context, but drill them as short chunks

Phrases can be difficult to understand and specific to certain situations, so it is important that they are introduced in context. However, students may retain them better if you drill just the phrase (for example, *badly damaged, go for a walk*) rather than a full sentence with problems which might distract from the phrase itself. Alternatively, use a very minimal sentence (*It's worth visiting* rather than *The National Gallery is worth visiting*). The drilling of such phrases can be a valuable opportunity to focus on pronunciation features such as weak forms and linking.

❻ Point out patterns in phrases

Pointing out patterns will help students to remember phrases. Many do not fit into patterns, but you can often show similar phrases with the same construction, like this:

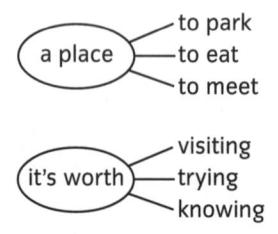

```
            ┌── to park
a place ────┼── to eat
            └── to meet

              ┌── visiting
it's worth ───┼── trying
              └── knowing
```

❼ Be ready to answer students' questions briefly

One possible problem with a more lexical approach is that students may ask a lot of questions beginning *Can you say ...?, What about ...?* Although students should be encouraged to ask questions, there is obviously a danger of overload – and it may also be the same student who is asking all the questions! Unless you feel that it is really important, answer briefly 'yes' or 'no' and move quickly on. If you are not sure, the best answer is probably *I've never heard anyone say it myself*. If the student is still not satisfied, say that you will give them an answer the following lesson.

Teacher's tips

❽ Keep written records of phrases as phrases

One simple way to make your students more aware of collocation is to get into the habit of writing word combinations on the board wherever appropriate, rather than just individual words. The more students see these words together, the more likely they are to remember them as a unit. Rather than just writing up *housework* or *crime*, write up *do the housework* or *commit a crime*. In sentences, collocations can be highlighted in colour or underlined – this is particularly important when the associated words are not actually next to each other in the sentence. Remind students to write down the collocations too, even if they 'know' the constituent words.

❾ Reinforce and recycle the phrases as much as you can

This is particularly important with phrases which, for the reasons given above, can be hard to remember. Most revision games and activities teachers do with single items of vocabulary can be adapted and used with phrases. You may find the following useful in addition:

- *Making wall posters*: many of the *Wordspot* sections in the *Students' Book* include making a wall poster with a diagram like that in the *Students' Book*. Seeing the phrases on the wall like this every lesson can provide valuable reinforcement. There are many other areas for which wall posters would be effective, for example common passive phrases, or common offers with *I'll ...* . Always write the full phrase on the poster (*get married* not just *married*) and remove the old posters regularly as they will lose impact if there are too many.
- *A phrase bank*: copy the new words and phrases from the lesson onto slips of card or paper (large enough for students to read if you hold them up at the front of the room) and keep them in a box or bag. This is a good record for you as well as the students of the phrases that you have studied – you can get them out whenever there are a few spare moments at the beginning or end of a lesson for some quick revision. Hold them up, and as appropriate, get students to give you:
  - an explanation of the phrase
  - a translation of the phrase
  - synonyms
  - opposites
  - the pronunciation
  - situations where they might say this
  - a sentence including the phrase
  - the missing word that you are holding your hand over (for example, *on* in the phrase *get on well with*)
  - the phrase itself, based on a definition or translation that you have given them.

13

Teacher's tips

Making the most of the Mini-dictionary

❶ Build up students' confidence with monolingual dictionaries

Some students may never have used a monolingual dictionary before. *Cutting Edge Intermediate Mini-dictionary* is designed to help students make the transition from bilingual to monolingual dictionaries. The explanations are graded to intermediate level, and the dictionary focuses on the meanings of words as they are used in the *Students' Book*, so students should have little difficulty in finding the information they are looking for. (See the introduction to the *Mini-dictionary* for a detailed explanation of which words and phrases have been included.) If students lack confidence, the following ideas may help:

- discuss with them the value of using a monolingual dictionary. Point out that they will avoid misleading translations, that it may help them to 'think in English', and that they will be increasing their exposure to English.
- look up words together at first, reading out and discussing the explanations as a class. Use the *Mini-dictionary* 'little and often' for limited but varied tasks (for example, for finding the word stress or dependent preposition of a new item of vocabulary).
- encourage students to use the *Mini-dictionary* in pairs and groups as well as individually so that they can help each other to understand the explanations and examples. Circulate, making sure that they understand definitions.

❷ Explain the different features of the Mini-dictionary

Many students do not realise how much information they can find in a dictionary, so point out all the features given, such as parts of speech, phonemic script, irregular verb forms, etc. *Learner-training worksheet 2* and *3* on pages 106–108 of the *Resource bank* introduces students to these areas.

❸ Discourage over-use of the Mini-dictionary

There are many other important strategies for improving vocabulary as well as dictionary skills, such as guessing meaning from context, sharing information with other students and listening to the teacher. Encourage your students to use a balance of approaches.

Discourage over-use of the *Mini-dictionary* during reading activities, by focusing students' attention initially on 'key' words in the text, rather than 'anything they don't understand'. If students are really keen to look up other words, you can allow time for this at the end.

❹ Vary your approach

If you always use the *Mini-dictionary* in the same way, students may get tired of it before long. Try using the *Mini-dictionary* in the following ways instead for a change:

a *Matching words to definitions on a handout*: make a worksheet with the new words in column A and their definitions from the *Mini-dictionary* mixed up in column B. Students match the words with the definitions.

b *Matching words to definitions on cards*: the same idea can be used giving each group two small sets of cards with definitions and words to match.

c *I know it/I can guess it/I need to check it*: write the list of new words on the board, and tell students to copy it down marking the words xx if they already know it, x if they can guess what it means (either from context, or because it is similar in their own language) and ? if they need to look it up. They then compare answers in pairs to see if they can help each other, before looking up any words that neither of them know.

d *Student–student teaching*: write out (either on the board or on a handout) the list of words you want to introduce, and allocate one to each student. Tell students to look up the word and find the meaning, the pronunciation and a good example of how it is used to help other students to understand it. Circulate, helping individuals, particularly with pronunciation problems. Students then mingle and find out the meaning and pronunciation of other words on the list they did not know. Go through any problems/questions at the end.

e *Look up the five words you most need to know*: instead of pre-teaching the vocabulary in a reading text, set the first (gist-type) comprehension activity straightaway, instructing students not to refer to their *Mini-dictionary* at this point. Check answers or establish that students cannot answer without some work on vocabulary. Tell them that they are only allowed to look up five words from the text – they have to choose the five that are most important to understanding the text. Demonstrate the difference between a 'key' unknown word in the text and one that can easily be ignored. Put students in pairs to select their five words, emphasising that they must not start using their *Mini-dictionary* until they have completed their list of five. After they have finished, compare the lists of words that different pairs chose and discuss how important they are to the text, before continuing with more detailed comprehension work.

f *True/False statements based on information in the Mini-dictionary*: write a list of statements about the target words on the board, then ask students to look them up to see if they are true or false, for example: *The phrase ... is very informal – true or false? ... means ... – true or false?*

Using a discovery approach in the teaching of grammar

Cutting Edge Intermediate uses a 'discovery' approach to grammar input because:
- we believe that students absorb rules best if they work them out for themselves.
- students of this level often have some previous knowledge of the language.

This knowledge is often difficult for the teacher to predict. The *Mini-tasks*, 'test-teach' exercises and *Analysis* boxes are designed so that students can utilise this knowledge, and so that teachers can adjust their approach to take account if it.

❶ Use Mini-tasks to assess students' existing knowledge

In Part A of each module there is a *Mini-task* designed to give students the opportunity to use the target language if they can, allowing you to assess what they already know. For this reason, it is best not to focus on the target language explicitly before doing the *Mini-task*, but to make a note of how well or otherwise students use it. Errors collected as students perform the *Mini-task* can be looked at with the whole class after the *Analysis* or practice activities.

❷ Be prepared to modify your approach as you discover what students know

It is unlikely that you will discover that all students are using the target language perfectly and need no further work on it at all. However, you may realise they only need brief revision, that you can omit certain sections of the *Analysis* or go through some or all of it very quickly. Alternatively, you may decide to omit some of the practice activities, or set them for homework.

On the other hand, you may discover that many students know less than you would normally expect at this level. In this case spend more time on the basic points, providing extra examples as necessary, and leave more complex issues for another day.

❸ Encourage students to share what they know and to make guesses

It is useful to do 'test-teach' exercises (like the one on page 111 of the *Students' Book*) in pairs or groups. In this way, stronger students can help weaker ones, and you do not have to provide all the input. If neither student knows, encourage them to guess – sometimes they have internalised rules without realising. This can be checked as you go over the answers together.

❹ Give students time to adjust to this approach, but be flexible

The idea of such exercises is that learners form their own hypotheses about new rules, which they then check and refine – a learning skill that hopefully they will carry outside the classroom. Students not used to this approach may take time to adapt, but this does not mean that they will never get used to it. Some students get anxious if they do not have things explained immediately. In such cases, do not leave them to become more frustrated – either answer their questions briefly on an individual basis, or make it clear that you will be dealing with them later.

If there are language areas that you think your class will be unable to tackle without previous input, you can change the whole approach, presenting the rules at the beginning of the *Language focus*, and setting 'test-teach' exercises and *Mini-tasks* as controlled and less controlled practice activities.

❺ Use Analysis boxes in different ways

Questions in the *Analysis* boxes can be tackled in different ways, depending on the ability/confidence of your students and the relative difficulty of the language point in question. Here are some possible approaches:

a **Answer the questions individually/in pairs then check them together as a class**: this a good way of encouraging a more independent attitude in the students. Make sure that students understand what they have to do for each question, and monitor carefully to see how they are coping – if they are obviously all stuck or confused, stop them and sort out the problem. As you check answers, write up examples to highlight any important problems of form, meaning etc. The *Language summary* can be read at the end, either individually or as a class.

b **Answer the questions together as a class**: with weaker classes, or for areas that you know your students will find difficult it may be best to read out questions to the whole class and work through them together, with examples on the board. Alternatively, set more straightforward questions for students to answer in pairs, and do more complicated ones together as a class. As students gain more confidence, you can set more and more questions for them to do on their own.

c **Students work through the questions individually/in pairs and check their answers themselves in the Language summary**: stronger, self-sufficient students may be able to take most of the responsibility for themselves. Most classes should be able to do this with the simpler *Analysis* boxes. It is still important that you monitor carefully to make sure that there are no major problems, and check answers together at the end to clear up any remaining doubts.

module 1

Part A Language

Language focus 1 (PAGE 6)
Questions and answers

See *Teacher's tips: using a discovery approach in the teaching of grammar* on page 15.

Mini-task

Check the meaning of *to have something in common*. If the class already know each other, suggest other topics, for example birthdays, height, last holiday, etc. As students are talking, make a note of how well they are using question forms. Do not focus on this explicitly, but make notes for correction after the *Analysis*. Write up and explain the phrases: *both of us ..., we both ..., neither of us ...* before students feed back to class. If students have been working in groups, write up: *we all ..., all of us ..., none of us ...* .

[1.1] Emphasise that students only need to make notes. Pause briefly after each question to allow students time to write. Tell them to leave a blank if they do not understand any of the questions. Circulate as they are doing the exercise, to help you assess their listening skills, and to identify weak students.

Analysis

All the tenses dealt with here are looked at in more detail later. Most students should at least be familiar with the form, but if there are serious difficulties with the use, it is probably best to leave this until the later modules where these are covered.

1 Ask students to do this quickly to help you assess their level. With enough time, all but the weakest students should be able to form the questions; good students should be able to form the questions quickly.

ANSWERS
(See tapescript for recording 1 on page 153 of the Students' Book.)

2 Point out that the tense and person of the auxiliaries must agree with the question.

ANSWERS
a Yes, I do.
b My brother does, but my parents don't.

PRACTICE

1 Check the meaning of *whose* before students make the questions individually or in pairs. Check answers with the whole class.

ANSWERS
a How do you get here from your house?
b Have you got / Do you have any special reason for learning English?
c How long have you been in this class?
d Whose class were you in last year (term, month)?
e Did you do anything special last night?
f What sort of music do you like?
g Does / Do all your family live in the same town as you?

2 Students might benefit from some repetition drilling of the question forms before asking each other. Make it clear that they can ask questions of their own if they want to. Point out that if you want to repeat a question that has been asked to you, it is more natural to say *How about you?* rather than repeating it.

Pronunciation

1 [1.2] Students work individually before checking answers with the whole class.

ANSWERS
b Did you <u>do</u> anything <u>special</u> last night?
  <u>No</u>, I <u>didn't</u>.
c Do you <u>come</u> from <u>Spain</u>?
  No, I <u>don't</u> – I come from <u>Argentina</u>.
d Do <u>all</u> your family live here?
  My <u>parents</u> and <u>grandparents do</u>, but my <u>sister</u> doesn't any more.
The stressed words are the ones most important to the speaker's meaning.

2 Re-play the cassette or provide a model yourself before getting students to repeat. Isolate the weak forms before practising the whole sentence.

ANSWER
These words are said very quickly so they sound weak and short.

16

module 1

Helping students with stress and weak forms

Focus on stress first – the following techniques might help students to hear stress patterns:
- reading out the sentences yourself, exaggerating the stressed syllables
- clapping / tapping on the stressed syllables as students listen and repeat
- mumbling the stress pattern like this: *mm-mm-MM-MM-mm*
- marking the stressed syllables on the board with blobs, colours, etc.

Once you have established the stress pattern, move on to weak forms. Again it helps to exaggerate, so model them as even weaker than they are on the cassette. (Be careful that in drawing students' attention to weak forms you do not accidentally stress them!) If students are having difficulty, it helps to start with a stressed syllable, and gradually build in the weak forms, like this: *live near here? > you live near here? > Do you live near here?*

Do not go on for too long if students do not pronounce the sentences perfectly, as they may find this frustrating. Focus on this little and often, ideally whenever you introduce a new phrase or structure involving weak forms.

3 [1.3] The exercise can be oral or written. When checking answers from the cassette, students may have difficulty catching the exact words used. Encourage them to listen again, several times if necessary, rather than giving them the answer yourself. This is very useful in developing their ability to listen closely to the language used.

ANSWERS
(For possible answers see tapescript for recording 3 on page 153 of the Students' Book.)

4 Making a wall poster will be useful in future lessons to remind students of how to ask classroom questions in English. Teach and practise any additional questions that may be relevant to your class, for example: *When's the library open?*, *Who's teaching us on Friday?*, etc.

ADDITIONAL PRACTICE

RB Resource bank: 1B *Three person snap* (short answers with *do, have, be*), page 113, Instructions page 97

Workbook: Making questions, page 6; Short answers, page 6; Question tags, page 7

Vocabulary (PAGE 8)

People around you

See *Teacher's tips: making the most of the Mini-dictionary* on page 14.

1 a) Introduce students to the mini-dictionary for the first time. Practise the new words by repetition drilling, marking the stressed syllables on the board. The pronunciation of the following words may need particular attention: *acquaintance* /əˈkweɪntəns/, *colleague* /ˈkɒliːg/, *mother-in-law* /ˈmʌðəɪnlɔː/, *niece* /niːs/, *neighbour* /ˈneɪbə/, *parent* /ˈpeərənt/, *stranger* /ˈstreɪndʒə/, *cousin* /ˈkʌzən/, *relative* /ˈrelətɪv/.

b) When brainstorming other vocabulary to add to the columns, discourage vocabulary that is too simple (*mother*, *father*, etc.), and focus on items that students may not know, for example *nephew*, *manager*, etc.

ANSWERS
family: cousin, niece, mother-in-law, parent, relative, step-mother
friends: best friend, (classmate), flatmate, partner
work: colleague, partner
school: classmate, headteacher
other: stranger, acquaintance, ex-boyfriend, neighbour

2 [1.4] Emphasise that students can write their answers in any shape they want to. Pause the cassette after each instruction to give students time to think and write. Alternatively, dictate the sentences yourself.

3 Do an example or two using students' own answers.

ADDITIONAL ACTIVITY

RB Resource bank: 1C *Vocabulary extension* (phrases for talking about people around you), page 114, Instructions page 97

Speaking and reading (PAGES 8–9)

1 Give students a minute or two to read the sentences. Check the meaning of any unknown words. The pronunciation of the following may need drilling: *marriage* /ˈmærɪdʒ/, *divorce* /dɪˈvɔːs/, *career* /kəˈrɪə/, *average* /ˈævərɪdʒ/, *birthrate* /ˈbɜːθreɪt/.

2 Students read the article and check answers in pairs.

ANSWERS
All of the topics are mentioned, except for the first and the third.

17

module 1

3 Students work in pairs before checking answers with the whole class. For each statement, get students to read out the parts of the text which show whether or not it is true.

> **ANSWERS**
> Statement d) is not true, all the others are.

4 Make sure everyone is clear which text they are reading. Discuss the differences between the two families with the whole class.

> **ANSWERS**
> The main differences are:
> – that Nathalie Guérin is separated from her husband
> – she has a part-time job, while Mi-ran has no plans to return to work

5 The pairwork activity in Exercise 4 should lead on naturally to a group / whole class discussion of these questions.

Language focus 2 (PAGES 10–11)

Present Simple and Continuous

See *Teacher's tips: using a discovery approach in the teaching of grammar* on page 15.

1 [1.5] Play the cassette and go through the answers with the whole class.

> **ANSWERS**
> a step-father b brother (Dan) c Mum (Carol)
> d granny e younger brother (Tom)

2 Students work individually before checking in pairs and as a whole class.

> **ANSWERS**
> b Christmas lunch c mother d abroad
> e brothers f aunt and uncle / computer course / after that g growing up h go out / old

Analysis

1 Write up an example verb in the Present Simple and Continuous, highlighting common problems. (Full tables showing these forms are on page 140 of the *Language summary*). Although this should be revision, many students may need to be reminded of the following problems:

Present Simple
- the third person singular *s* in the affirmative form
- the use of *do / does* in the question form
- the use of *don't / doesn't* in the negative form

Present Continuous
- the use of the contracted form of the auxiliary *be*

2 If necessary translate the key words for the students before getting them to do this in pairs or groups.

> **ANSWERS**
> Those on the left are usually associated with the Present Simple. There is some overlap between the different uses, but the following examples are clearest:
> a habit: *She doesn't go out much.*
> b permanent: *The granny lives with Erica's family, ...*
> c describing a state: *Erica looks very much like her mother.*
>
> Those on the right are usually associated with the Present Continuous. Again there is some overlap between the different uses, but the following examples are clearest:
> d in progress now: *Erica is showing her friend a family photo.*
> e temporary: *Erica's older brother is living with his aunt and uncle in Manchester, ...*
> f describing a changing state: *Her younger brother is growing up very fast.*

3 Students discuss the questions in pairs or groups.

> **ANSWERS**
> a None of these four verbs would normally be found in the Present Continuous form, because they describe states (they are 'stative').
> b *Having lunch* describes an action not a state – it is 'dynamic'. (Other examples are: *have a shower, a walk*, etc.) *Have two brothers* describes a state. (Other examples are: *have a lot of money, brown hair, a cold*, etc.)
> c Other examples of stative verbs include: *believe, understand, like, love, hate, seem, remember.* (There are more examples in the *Language summary* on page 141.)

PRACTICE

1 a) Students work individually before checking answers with the whole class.

> **ANSWERS**
> 2 is reading   3 smokes*   4 likes   5 knows**
> 6 understands   7 wants
>
> * *is smoking* is also possible if you want to show that this is a temporary situation, for example because you are worried at the moment
>
> ** the capital of Venezuela is Caracas

b) Practise a few example questions by repetition drilling, for example: *How many brothers and sisters do you have?*, *Are you reading a good book at the moment?* Do this exercise as a mingle drill, possibly making it into a competition to see who can find all the people first.

18

module 1

2 Check the meaning of: *to lose weight*, *to go grey*, *to improve*. It may be useful to feed in opposite verbs here: *to put on weight*, *to get worse*.

3 a) Give students 5–10 minutes to think about what they want to say. Encourage them to ask you about any difficult / very specific vocabulary they need.

b) Encourage students to ask each other questions. If possible, put them in groups with people they do not normally work with.

ADDITIONAL PRACTICE

RB Resource bank: 1D *Something in common* (Present Simple and Continuous), page 115, Instructions page 97

Workbook: Present Simple or Continuous, pages 7–8; Word order (adverbs of frequency), pages 8–9

Alternative approach to the Present Simple and Continuous

A more task-based approach may be more challenging here (although this approach will require you to 'think on your feet' quite a lot during the lesson!)

- Play the cassette or give a short talk of your own about your family and friends. If possible, illustrate your talk with photos. Try to make it sound natural rather than scripted.
- Briefly check basic comprehension.
- Move straight on to Practice Exercise 3, getting the students to talk about their family / friends in the same way that you / Erica did. Do not do any specific input on present tenses, but emphasise that you want them to talk about these people's lives as they are at the moment. Write up the following prompts to encourage this: *their jobs / studies, where they live, anything else important in their lives at the moment*.
- Give students time to plan what they will say and feed in any necessary vocabulary. Put students in small groups and get each one to give a short talk. Circulate and note down any errors you hear with the use of the Present Simple and Continuous (these can be errors of form, meaning or pronunciation – it may help to divide your notes into these three sections).
- Write up the errors, and get students to correct them. Go over the problems on the board yourself, or direct them to the *Language summary* page 140 of SB. Select exercises from the *Students' Book* (Practice Exercises 1 and 2) or the *Workbook* on the areas they need to practise.
- If you do not feel confident about selecting material on the spot like this, spread this approach over two lessons, allowing you to analyse students' errors and needs more carefully.

Wordspot (PAGE 11)

have (and *have got*)

See *Teacher's tips: working with lexis* on pages 12–13.

1 [1.6] Students work individually or in pairs. Play the cassette before checking answers with the whole class.

ANSWERS
a lunch   b look   c accident   d rest   e problems
f great time   g baby girl

2 Ask students to copy the diagram into their notebooks, so that there is enough room to write.

ANSWERS
(section in brackets)
have lunch (f); *have a look* (e); *have an accident* (g); *have a rest* (g); *have problems* (g); *have a great time* (g); *have a baby* (a)*

*Note: you may need to contrast *have a baby* here (= *give birth*) with *have a baby* (= *She's got a lovely baby*).

3 If you feel that your students have already had enough, do not feed in these additional phrases.

ANSWERS AND LANGUAGE NOTES
a (section in brackets)
 have a broken leg (d); *have a party* (g);
 have fun (g); *have a lot of energy* (b);
 have a holiday (g); *have a meeting* (g);
 have a strange feeling (c); *have a wash* (e)

b *Have* can be used in all of the phrases. The diagram is divided into two halves: on the left, *have* = *do* – *have got* cannot be used; on the right, *have* = *possess* – *have got* can be used. Note that where *have* = *possess*, *have* is a 'state' verb, so the Present Continuous form is not possible. (*I am having brown hair.*) Where *have* = *do*, *have* is a dynamic verb, so the continuous form is possible. (*We are having a break.*)

Notice that many verbs can be replaced by *have* + noun: *have a swim / have a shave / have a think / have a talk / have a try / have a cry*.

4 This exercise focuses particularly on *have* meaning *do*, which is likely to be less familiar to students. Give a couple of examples first to illustrate the exercise.

5 Prepare this in advance by copying the diagram onto a poster-size sheet of paper. Answers to Exercises 2 and 3 can be copied onto the poster when checking answers.

19

module 1

Part B Task

See *Teacher's tips: making tasks work* on pages 8–9 and *Responding to learners' individual language needs* on pages 10–11.

Preparation for task (PAGE 12)

1. Students work in pairs or groups, looking at the photos and talking about the activities in the box.

2. [1.7] Before listening, emphasise that students do not need to understand everything at this stage.

> **ANSWERS**
> Philip – 1; Sonia – 3.
> They talk about: *working long hours, doing a course of some kind, staying in in the evening, watching / playing sport, studying hard*

3. First spend some time familiarising students with the idea of the pie-charts. Ask them what they think they show and what kind of information might go in the gaps. Ask if there are any words in the pie-charts they don't understand.

> **ANSWERS**
> b working very long hours at the moment; works in import / export; does a lot of business with Italy
> c doesn't travel much, but hopes to travel more in the future (to Europe and the US)
> d likes football; watches it on TV
> e goes to the theatre occasionally; sometimes sees a musical
> f loves travelling; has travelled quite a lot round Europe, but wants to go to the US
> g doing a course in textile design; really likes it; has to spend a lot of time on project work, also essays and reading
> h the thing she likes most in London; goes at least once a week
> i plays football in women's team every Sunday

Task (PAGE 13)

1. Give students 5–10 minutes to prepare on their own. Encourage them to ask you for any special vocabulary they need, and draw their attention to the *Personal vocabulary* box. Their interviews may be more focused if they write down a few questions in advance, but emphasise that they do not have to stick to these questions if others seem more appropriate.

2. Explain that students are going to draw a pie-chart for their partner, like the ones in Exercise 3. Emphasise that the idea is to represent what is generally important in their partner's life, rather than the exact amount of time they spend on it. As students perform the task, feed in any language they need in an informal way, so as not to interfere with communication. Do not correct at this stage unless absolutely necessary. Note down errors / useful language for analysis at the end of the task.

3. Explain the task and give students a few minutes to think about what they will say. There are two purposes here, which you should explain:
   - for them to focus on the most important information.
   - for them to plan / practise the exact language they will use.

4. As students speak, note down errors / useful language to look at later together. One possibility is just to focus on errors relating to grammar in this module, that is question formation / use of auxiliaries and the Present Simple and Continuous.

> **Task: alternative suggestions**
>
> a *If you want to make the material more personal:* instead of (or as well as) using the listening material, give a short talk about yourself based round a pie-chart, inviting students to ask you questions about your interests, etc.
>
> b *If you want to do more language input before the task:* do the *Task link* on page 14 before the task to give students a wider range of phrases to use when talking about their interests, etc. Omit Exercise 4, however, as this may pre-empt the task.
>
> c *If students already know each other well or do not like talking about themselves:* get students to choose a famous person they know / admire and to spend their planning time imagining what this person's pie-chart would look like. Then conduct the interview as a role play. As a possible follow-up, other students could listen and try to guess which famous person is being interviewed.
>
> d *If you have a large class:* stages 3 and 4 of the task could become very long and boring. To avoid this do one of the following:
>   - divide the class into groups of about 8–10 for this stage.
>   - split up the introductions over several lessons, but remember to ask students to bring their pie-charts to the next few lessons.
>   - pick just one student from each pair to be introduced.

module 1

Task link (PAGE 14)

How you spend your time

1 Students work individually before checking answers as a whole class.

> **ANSWERS**
> a 5 b 7 c 4 d 3 e 6 f 2 g 1 h 8

2 Ask students to memorise the phrases individually, or use repetition drilling. Students may do this more effectively if you practise just the phrases rather than whole sentences. (See *Teacher's tips: working with lexis* on pages 12–13.)

> **ANSWER**
> They are followed by the *-ing* form of the verb (gerund).

3 Students can do this as a spoken exercise in pairs rather than as a written exercise.

4 Give a couple of examples first to illustrate the activity, before students stand up and mingle.

ADDITIONAL PRACTICE

RB **Resource bank:** 1E *Who am I?* (expressions of liking and disliking), page 116, Instructions page 97

Real life (PAGES 14–15)

Writing an informal letter

1 Check the meaning of: *an accountant*, *to be engaged*, *an opportunity*, *to be retired*.

> **ANSWERS**
> a 14 years ago / when Adam was 12
> b Adam is now an accountant / he's engaged to a girl called Patti / he likes mountain-climbing / he has two sisters called Sofia and Magda / his father is retired
> Janus is married to a woman called Barbara / he has two sons / he likes mountain-climbing
> c Because his company is sending him to the Warsaw office for about four months.
> d meet all his Polish relatives / go mountain-climbing / He wants to improve his Polish.

2 Highlight the way in which a letter is laid out in English, pointing out the following features:
- the address is in the top right-hand corner
- the date is beneath the address
- we always open the letter with *Dear* + name followed by a comma *Hello Janus / My dear friend*, etc. are not usual in English.

> **ANSWERS**
> - *Love, Jane:* friends / less close relatives
> - *Lots of love, Sue and Dave:* close friends / relatives
> - *Best wishes, Mark:* acquaintances / 'friendly' business letters
> - *All my love, Simon:* close friends / relatives / boyfriend and girlfriend

3 Students work in pairs or groups before checking answers with the whole class.

> **ANSWERS**
> (general guidelines only)
> a beginning b either c end d either e end
> f beginning g beginning h end

4 Spend some time explaining the two options. Students can do this writing activity for homework.

Do you remember?

> **ANSWERS**
> 1 a 's b Does c Did d 'm e –
> 2 a How many pets does he have?
>   b How often do you see your cousins?
>   c How much money have you got with you?
>   d Does his mother-in-law live with them?
>   e Are all your brothers and sisters married?
> 3 a Present Simple = generally, who can play the piano
>   Present Continuous = now (for example, because you can hear some music)
>   b Present Simple = permanently
>   Present Continuous implies that it is temporary (for example, during the summer holidays)
>   c Present Simple = the normal way to describe a nice person
>   Present Continuous = at the moment / temporary (this may be unusual for him / he has some reason for being nice, etc.)
> 4 Sentences c) and e) are wrong in the Present Continuous form because the verb is describing a state (it is a 'stative' verb).
> 5 Sentences b) and c) can be re-written with *have got* because they describe a state / possession.
> 6 a *a classmate* is a person in the same class as you / *a flatmate* is a person you share a house or flat with
>   b *visiting friends* is going round to see them at their house / *entertaining friends* is usually at your own home (or possibly taking them out to a restaurant)
>   c your *step-brother* is the son of your father or mother's new husband or wife / your *brother-in-law* is your husband or wife's brother

module 1

  d *to rise* (*go up*) is the opposite of *to fall* (*go down*)
  e *an acquaintance* is a person you know but not close enough to be called a friend / *a neighbour* is a person who lives next to or near you

7 a My girlfriend's very good <u>at</u> drawing.
  b I'm not very interested <u>in</u> sport.
  c I know quite a lot <u>about</u> DIY.
  d My flatmate isn't going <u>out</u> much at the moment ...
  e I stayed <u>in</u> last night, ...
  f My boyfriend and I eat <u>out</u> about twice a week.

8 have a lovely time; work long hours; do a college course; look after children; do the housework; stay in for the evening; have a broken arm; bring up your children

module 2

Part A Language

Vocabulary and speaking (PAGE 17)

Remembering and forgetting

1 Before discussing the questions, check any unknown vocabulary. (Note that *facts and figures* is a set phrase used to describe factual information, dates, statistics, etc.)

2 Students work individually before checking with the whole class. As you check the answers, elicit / write up examples of full sentences with the correct forms, highlighting possible constructions, using the examples.

> **ANSWERS**
> The following are wrong:
> b *learn* – someone how to use a computer
> c *remind* – to phone someone
> d *forget* – of something
> e *recognise* – to do something
> f *lose* – a bus

Reading (PAGES 17–18)

1 Set the task for the groupwork. Circulate, making sure students understand what is shown in each picture.

> **ANSWERS**
> *top left*: he is forming a visual image; *top right*: he is inventing a story; *bottom left*: he is making a list; *bottom right*: he is forming a word from the first letter of each thing

2 Before reading, check the meaning of: *to prove something, a prayer, training, to be effective, to lose your memory, to recognise someone or something, to pat, to confuse two things, to pretend, to be blind.* As you check the answers, get students to read out the part of the text where the six techniques are mentioned.

> **ANSWERS**
> repeating things, 'chunking', forming a mental picture, inventing a story, asking yourself questions, reading and re-reading things

3 Students work in pairs or groups before checking with the whole class. Again, ask students to locate the part of the text in which each answer is found.

> **ANSWERS**
> a) *remembering things for a few seconds* – repeating things; *remembering foreign words* – forming a mental picture; *remembering long numbers* – 'chunking'; *remembering long lists of words* – inventing a story; *remembering information you are studying* – asking yourself questions
> b) people forget their identity and wander the streets; the man who lost his memory for faces and thought a stranger was watching him each time he looked in the mirror; the man who lost his visual memory and could not recognise everyday objects.

4 Put students into pairs and check they know where to find their instructions. Check briefly the meaning of all the words from Module 1 before they do the quiz.

5 After students have compared results, do some brief feedback to find out who was the most successful in various pairs and whether or not the results bear out what the text said about memory techniques.

ADDITIONAL ACTIVITY

[RB] **Resource bank:** *Learner-training worksheet 5* (recording and remembering vocabulary), pages 110–111, Instructions page 97

Language focus 1 (PAGES 19–20)

Past Simple and Continuous

See *Teacher's tips: using a discovery approach in the teaching of grammar* on page 15.

Mini-task

Give students a few minutes to think about language they need to tell their anecdote – do not highlight the need to use the Past Simple here as this will give you a better idea of how well they use it 'naturally'. Make a note of students' problems with the use and form of the two past tenses, without correcting or commenting at this stage. Use your notes to assess how much time and attention needs to be given to the Analysis *and practice that follows. For example:*

- *Is it necessary to revise the form of the Past Simple and Continuous?*
- *Would students benefit from a homework on irregular verbs?*
- *Do they need work on the pronunciation of -ed endings?*
- *Are they aware that the Past Continuous cannot be used with state verbs?, etc.*

Any useful errors you collect can be corrected after the Analysis.

23

module 2

1 [2.1] Focus students' attention on the pictures. Introduce the characters, asking students to guess what their first impressions of each other were, etc.

ANSWERS
In the picture: it is a rainy day, not a hot day; she looks animated, he looks embarrassed; she is wearing a red dress.

2 Students work individually or in pairs. Students should have studied these forms before and be able to attempt the exercise, but if they clearly have no idea, move straight on to the listening stage. Pause the cassette after each verb to check students heard the answer correctly.

ANSWERS
1 met 2 was spending 3 was doing 4 decided
5 arrived 6 started 7 thought 8 were having
9 began 10 told 11 were talking 12 thought
13 hated 14 liked 15 was wearing
16 didn't suit 17 didn't tell

Analysis

1 As you elicit answers from students, write up the full form of the Past Simple and Continuous using an example verb (see tables in *Language Summary* on page 141). Highlight the following:
   - that in the Past Simple, regular verbs are followed by *-ed*.
   - that irregular verbs have to be learnt individually (point out that there is a list on page 152).
   - that questions and negatives are formed with *did* and *didn't* in all persons.
   - that the question and negative forms in both cases are with the 'bare' infinitive (*Did they start ...?* not ~~*Did they started?*~~, *We didn't start* not ~~*We didn't started*~~.)
   - that the form of the Past Continuous is the same as the Present Continuous, except that *was / were* is used.

ANSWERS
a examples of irregular Past Simple verbs: *met, thought, began, told*
b examples of regular Past Simple verbs: *decided, arrived, started, hated, liked*
c examples of the Past Continuous: *was spending, was standing, were talking*

2 As you elicit / check the answers, contrast the uses of the Past Simple and Continuous with the help of a 'time-line' on the board. As you check the answer to c), remind students that this is the same as with the present tenses (and all other tenses).

ANSWERS
a Past Simple (examples: *I met Julia ... / I started talking to her ...*)
b Past Continuous (examples: *She was standing there ... / I was spending a few months in Britain ...*)
c Past Simple (examples: *She actually thought I was a bit rude / I liked her immediately ...*)

PRACTICE

1 [2.2] Check the meaning of: *to have a lot in common, a coincidence, to get on well, to fall in love, to get engaged*. Students work individually or in pairs before listening to the cassette to check answers.

ANSWERS
1 met 2 were travelling 3 started 4 discovered
5 had 6 lived 7 were going 8 were training
9 was working 10 talked* 11 fell 12 decided
13 reached 14 were 15 was 16 are

* both forms are possible, but the Past Continuous suggests that this is not permanent

Pronunciation

1 Discuss the questions together before checking answers on the cassette.

ANSWERS
a talked – 1 syllable
b started – 2 syllables
c reached – 1 syllable
d decided – 3 syllables
-ed is pronounced /ɪd/ when the verb ends in either *t* or *d*

2 Put the students in pairs to discuss this before checking answers as a whole class.

ANSWERS
- waited – (2 syllables) /ˈweɪtɪd/
- helped – (1 syllable) /helpt/
- liked – (1 syllable) /laɪkt/
- travelled – (2 syllables) /ˈtrævəld/
- arrived – (2 syllables) /əˈraɪvd/
- invited – (3 syllables) /ɪnˈvaɪtɪd/

3 [2.4] Play the cassette and focus students' attention on the weak forms.

4 Drill the story in short sections first. Ask students to take turns to read aloud sentences to the whole class or to a partner, or to read aloud the whole passage individually.

module 2

> **Helping students with stress and weak forms**
>
> a *Regular past forms:* if students have difficulty in hearing the number of syllables, break them down slowly like this: *tra – velled*. Count the number of syllables on your fingers at the same time.
> b *Past Continuous was and were:* to help students stress the correct words, practise the weak forms using 'back chaining'. Students repeat the phrases in the following way: ... <u>working</u> ... was /wəz/ <u>working</u> ... Mum was <u>working</u> ... Mum was <u>working</u> for the <u>Times</u>.

2 Give students a few moments to select a topic. Check the meaning of: *(birthday) present, to celebrate, a flight, a destination, to get somewhere on time.* Remind students briefly how Past Simple questions are formed, giving an example or two. Give them a few moments to think about how to form the questions, but emphasise that you do not want them to write the questions down (unless they are a very weak group). Pre-teach and practise the phrase *I'm afraid I can't remember.* Emphasise that this is a competition to see who has the best memory, and remind students to keep a tally of their partners' scores.

> **Practice Exercise 2: alternative suggestions**
>
> a Get one student to choose a topic and send him / her outside to try and remember everything he / she can about it. Allocate one question from the memory card for each student to construct and memorise. Bring in the student from outside. The rest of the class takes turns to ask him / her the questions to see how many answers he / she gets right. Repeat this procedure with each of the cards.
> b Instead of (or as well as) using the cards in the book or as additional practice, students write memory cards of their own about, for example: *last Christmas, their last shopping trip, their first day in this school,* etc. (Do not talk about the topic of childhood, as this comes up later in the module.) Ask students to include a mixture of simple and harder questions and help students to construct any difficult questions. Feed in any vocabulary they need.

ADDITIONAL PRACTICE

RB Resource bank: 2A *Past tense pelmanism / What about you?* (irregular Past Simple forms), page 117; 2B *Alibi* (Past Simple and Continuous), pages 118–119, Instructions page 98

Workbook: Past Simple or Continuous, pages 13–14

Language focus 2 (PAGES 20–21)

Comparing past and present

See *Teacher's tips: using a discovery approach in the teaching of grammar* on page 15.

Focus students' attention on the photos. Students work individually or in groups before checking answers with the whole class.

> **ANSWERS**
> a T b T c F d F e T *(or possibly false, according to opinion)* f T

Analysis

1 Students answer the questions in pairs or as a whole class. As you check answers, highlight:
  • the forms of *used to*
    – *used to* + verb for all persons
    – the question form *Did you use to*, etc.
    – the negative forms *I didn't use to*, etc.
  • the pronunciation of *used to* – /ju:stə/
  • that there is no equivalent present form (this is particularly important in languages where an equivalent form does have a present tense, for example Spanish).
2 Point out that:
  • *not ... any more / not ... any longer* have the same meaning.
  • *any more* and *any longer* always come after the verb.
  • we can also say *no longer*, but this is more formal.
3 Point out that *still* comes before most verbs, but after *be*.
  They still live in the same house.
  He is still at school.

> **ANSWERS**
> 1 a We use *used to* to talk about habits in the past.
>   b Instead of *used to* we can always use the Past Simple.
> 2 *not ... any more / not ... any longer*
> 3 *still*

PRACTICE

1 Give an example of your own first, based on the pictures. Go round checking and correcting if necessary as students write their sentences.

2 Give students a few minutes to think about what they are going to say before they discuss the differences in pairs. It might help if you give some examples from your own childhood first. Alternatively, write up some more prompts, for example: *food, animals, school, visiting relatives, going to the beach,* etc.

25

module 2

ADDITIONAL PRACTICE

RB Resource bank: 2C *School reunion* (*used to, still, not ... any longer / more*) pages 120–121, Instructions page 98
Workbook: *used to*, pages 14–15; *still, not any more / longer*, page 15

Wordspot (PAGE 21)

time

See *Teacher's tips: working with lexis* on pages 12–13.

1 Students work individually or in pairs before checking answers with the whole class. Most of the phrases on the diagram should be familiar, but *a waste of time* may need explaining with an example sentence (*It's such a waste of time sitting in traffic jams for hours.*) If *time* is translated in a number of different ways in the students' own language, it may be useful to translate the phrases to show all the different meanings of *time* in English.

2 [2.5] Pause the cassette after each mini-dialogue and elicit the answer orally before getting students to write it down. Get students to practise the phrases with some repetition drilling. For further oral practice, students could read the dialogues aloud in pairs.

> **ANSWERS**
> (section in brackets)
> a *for a long time* (b)   b *a great time* (c)   c *haven't got time* (f)   d *by the time* (e)   e *on time* (e)   f *all the time* (b)   g *in two days' time* (e)

3 Put students in pairs and refer them to the correct pages. Ask them to answer the questions in full sentences to make sure they are practising the *time* phrases. Students feed back briefly to the whole class what they found out.

4 Prepare this in advance by copying the diagram onto a poster-sized sheet of paper. Answers to Exercise 2 can be copied directly onto the poster when checking through.

Part B Task

See *Teacher's tips: making tasks work* on pages 8–9 and *Responding to learners' individual language needs* on pages 10–11.

Preparation for task (PAGE 23)

1 [2.6] Focus students' attention on the pictures and ask them to predict what the stories will be about. Check the meaning of the 'key' words, particularly *field*, *bury* and *half-brother*. Play the cassette and discuss whose predictions were most accurate.

> **ANSWERS**
> T = a big sister, a field / going shopping / burying, a chocolate bar, stealing, the police
> A = Czechoslovakia, a rose, 1988, 1968, a five-year old-son, a half-brother, two little girls

2 This re-telling stage is intended to help give students the confidence to tell their own stories, but if time is short it could be omitted.

> **Exercises 1 and 2: alternative suggestion**
>
> As both these stories are quite long, you may prefer to select just one, whichever you think will most interest your students. Focus their attention on the relevant pictures, and adapt the listening task by telling them that only some of the 'key' words will appear in the story. They should listen and tick the ones that do.

Task

1 a) Explain that students are going to tell the story of a childhood memory of their own. Emphasise that it does not need to be something serious or sad – a story of something silly or amusing might be more appropriate.

b) Emphasise that students do not need to write the story, but just make notes and think about how they will tell it. Write up an example: *shopping with mother – saw favourite chocolate, put it in mother's shopping bag*, etc. Go round the class supplying any special vocabulary that students need. Give students about fifteen minutes to plan their stories.

2 As students tell their stories, encourage the others in the group to ask questions or respond to what they hear. Remind students that they may need to explain unknown words in their stories, but encourage them to do this in English.

module 2

Optional writing

This can be done as homework. If you feel students may be fed up with their story, they can write a different one.

> **Task: alternative suggestions**
>
> a *If you want to make the task more personalised:* tell a story yourself about a childhood memory. (See number 4 of *Teacher's tips: making tasks work* on page 8.)
>
> b *Helping students to think of a story:* visualisation techniques may help students to remember a specific story. Get students to close their eyes and think of the time, for example, when they were at primary school. Tell them to try and visualise where they lived, what their house was like, what their school was like, who their teachers were, what they liked, etc. Then give them the specific suggestions for types of stories from the *Students' Book*.
>
> c *If personal memories of childhood are not suitable:* students may not wish to talk about incidents which are personal to them. If so, suggest the following alternatives:
> - a funny / interesting / unusual story about someone else's childhood / children
> - a family anecdote that is often re-told
> - something funny / adventurous / frightening, etc. that happened to them as adults.
>
> d *Alternative for the story-telling stage:* if you feel that your students will not work well in groups, get them to tell their stories to the whole class. Unless your class is very small, one of the following approaches will probably work better to avoid this becoming monotonous:
> - select a few of the most interesting stories to be told to the class; get the other students to write their stories for homework and display on the wall.
> - spread the story-telling out over a few lessons, with two or three students telling their stories each time as a warmer or 'filler' at the beginning or end of lessons.
>
> e *Recording students' stories:* if you do not have time to listen to everyone's story in class, this is a useful way of ensuring that some students do not miss out on the 'performance' stage of the task. Many students (particularly teenagers who are shy about performing in front of the class) may find this a motivating alternative to written homework. Collect and correct students' cassettes as with normal homework, attaching corrections on a piece of paper, with additional comments on pronunciation. The recording of the task is also ideally suited to language laboratory work, since this enables you to correct and help students before they work on the final product.

Task link (PAGE 24)

Short questions

1 [2.7] Focus students' attention on the picture to establish the context (people arriving in an office first thing in the morning). Check the meaning of: *a file, apparently, annoying / annoyed, to be cancelled*. Play the cassette, pausing after each mini-dialogue to allow students time to write. Check answers with the whole class.

> **ANSWERS**
> See tapescript Module 2, recording 7 on page 155 of the *Students' Book*.

2 Use the examples in the book to highlight the following points:
- short questions are formed using just the auxiliary verb.
- the auxiliary verb matches the first sentence in tense, person, negative form, etc.
- use example b) to point out that if the auxiliary is not in the first sentence (as in Present Simple / Past Simple affirmative form) we use the auxiliary in the related question form.

3 Do an example together first. Students work in pairs before checking answers with the whole class.

> **ANSWERS**
> a Isn't he? b Does she? c Can it? d Did you?
> e Doesn't she? f Was it? g Didn't she? h Is it?

> **Pronunciation**
> **Helping students with stress and intonation of short questions**
>
> - Ask students if the second speaker sounds interested in what the first person is saying. Ask them how they know this and whether or not this is the same in their language. Emphasise that, in English, if your intonation is very flat you may sound bored and rude. Focus on the intonation curves in the example, modelling the pattern yourself (possibly exaggerating), or re-playing the first couple of examples on the cassette. Humming or exaggerating the intonation pattern may well help students to hear this more clearly. If students produce flat intonation, pulling an exaggeratedly bored face may help to reinforce the importance of intonation.
> - Highlight that the stress in these short questions is on the auxiliary verb – emphasise this by clapping on the stressed words as you model or re-play the cassette.

module 2

Do you remember?

ANSWERS

1. a was snowing / came (*was coming* – in this case the journey is not seen as complete)
   b met / were (*were meeting* – implies repeated meetings)
   c came / was cooking
   d dropped / was shopping
   e tried / were (*was trying* – implies that he tried repeatedly / for a long time)
   f arrived / went home

2. thought, fell, grew, brought, stole, slept, got, wore, read, hid

3.
A	B	C
●	● ○	○ ● ○
used	happened	remembered
closed	started	imagined
tried	wanted	decided
		invented

4. a remember when something happened, remember to do something, etc.
   b in a year's time, in three months' time, etc.
   c last time, the first time, for a long time, etc.
   d lose your car keys, lose your glasses, etc.
   e have black hair, have a cold, have a drink, etc.

5. Sentence b) is wrong.

6. a on time   b remind me   c Did you?
   d buried him   e trained

28

module 3

Part A Language

Speaking and listening (PAGE 26)

1 Introduce the quiz by asking students how good their knowledge of geography is, etc. Check the meaning of: *densely populated, area, further, island, coastline*. Emphasise that the exercise must only be discussed in English (you could deduct 'penalty points' if students use their mother-tongue!).

2 [3.1] Before playing the cassette, check the meaning of: *square kilometres, approximately, a continent*. Emphasise that students will hear a lot of extra information in addition to the answers. (The answers are presented in this way to give students practice in picking out relevant information. However, if time is short you could simply give them the answers.)

ANSWERS
1 The Nile is the longest; the Amazon is the second longest.
2 The Vatican city is the smallest; Monaco is the second smallest.
3 Monaco 4 Ukraine 5 Tokyo-Yokohama, Mexico City, São Paulo, Seoul, New York 6 New York to London 7 Greenland 8 the Andes
9 China 10 Canada

Language focus 1 (PAGE 27)

Comparatives and superlatives

See *Teacher's tips: using a discovery approach in the teaching of grammar* on page 15.

Mini-task

The first option is intended for mono-cultural classes. If your country has several neighbours, allocate different ones to different groups. The second option is intended for multi-cultural classes. If possible, put students into mixed-nationality pairs. Check the meaning of: scenery, climate and cost of living. If there are other obvious differences between their country and neighbouring ones (for example, size), add further prompts of your own. Before they start discussing, give students a minute or two to think whilst you circulate, supplying any vocabulary they need.

Make a note of how well students are using comparative forms, but do not comment at this stage. Useful errors can be corrected after the Analysis.

Analysis

Revision of basic comparatives and superlatives

Check that students understand the questions, including grammatical terminology such as *comparative, syllable,* etc.

ANSWERS
1 big – bigger / biggest
   friendly – friendlier / friendliest
   crowded – more crowded / most crowded
   popular – more popular / most popular
   far – farther / further / farthest / furthest

2 one-syllable words: adjective + -er / -est
   two-syllable words
   ending in -y: adjective + -er / -est*
   other two or three-
   syllable words: more / the most + adjective
   other irregular forms: good / better / best
                            bad / worse / worst

*spelling rules:
 – in one-syllable adjectives with short vowel sounds, the final consonant doubles
 (big > big**g**er > big**g**est)
 – adjectives ending in -e, add -r / -est
 (nice > nic**er** > nic**est**)
 – adjectives ending in -y, -y changes to -i-
 (pretty > pr**etti**er > pr**etti**est)

Big and small differences

Do the first example in Exercises 1 and 2 together. (It is best not to do Exercise 3 until you have checked the answers to 1 and 2.) Highlight the following points:

1 • *much higher / a lot higher* have the same meaning
  • the pronunciation of *slightly* /ˈslaɪtli/
2 • the opposite of *the most* is *the least*
  • *by far* + superlative shows a big difference between this and the rest
  • we also say *the fourth / fifth / sixth*, etc. *biggest*
  • *one of the biggest* means there are several big ones, but we are not saying it is the biggest of all

ANSWERS
1 a – *X is slightly higher than Y; X is a little higher than Y.*
   b – *X is far, far higher than Y.*
   c – *X is much higher than Y; X is a lot higher than Y.*
   Phrases used for showing big / small differences are: *slightly higher than, much higher than, a little higher than, a lot higher than, far, far higher than.*

2 a *by far the biggest / the biggest ... of all*
   b *the second biggest, one of the biggest / one of the least populated*

29

module 3

    c by far the biggest / the biggest ... of all / one of the biggest / the third biggest

3 Possible answers are:
The Amazon is slightly shorter than the Nile; The Amazon is one of the biggest rivers in the world; The Amazon is the second biggest river in the world; Monaco is the second smallest country in the world; Monaco is by far the most densely populated country in the world; New York is the fifth biggest city in the world; Tokyo-Yokohama is by far the biggest city in the world; Ukraine is the second biggest country in Europe.

Analysis: alternative suggestions

a *If you are short of time:* set the revision of basic comparatives and superlatives as homework in advance of the lesson.

b *If you have a strong group:* omit the basic revision and put students in pairs to work through the rest of the *Analysis* and read the *Language summary*. Deal with any outstanding problems as you check the answers with the whole class.

c *If you have a weak group:* provide additional practice of the basic forms before / instead of moving on to the more complex forms in 'Big and small differences'. Use students in the class to talk about height, age, etc. or choose other countries in the world to compare size, population, etc.

PRACTICE

1 Emphasise that students should use the phrases from the 'big and small differences' section in the *Analysis* table. (If you have a very weak class, the exercise will still work with just the basic comparative forms.) This can be done as either a spoken or written exercise – in both cases, students will need to work with a partner.

2 a) Explain that students have to draw a plan of their home (if they live in a house, it might be better to draw an outside view). Emphasise that a rough plan with names of rooms written on is all that is needed. Circulate, making sure they are drawing their plans big enough. Draw your own plan on the board.

b) [3.2] Check the meaning of: *sunny, messy, to relax, furniture*. Show students on your own plan how you would mark the first item on the cassette. Emphasise that they do not need to write anything but the number, but they should remember why they marked the things / places.

Practice Exercise 2: alternative suggestion

Instead of drawing a plan of their homes, get students to draw a map of their country. Emphasise that this needs to be quite large, but not particularly accurate. (This activity will only work if students have a reasonable geographical knowledge of their country – check factual information in advance, such as the second / third largest city, etc.)

Read out the following phrases and get them to mark the appropriate place names on the map. Tell students to write down the first place that comes into their mind: *the second biggest city, one of the most industrialised parts of the country, one of the prettiest parts of the country, the most beautiful city of all, the best place to go shopping, one of the most peaceful areas, one of the least interesting towns, the worst place to go on holiday,* etc.

Students then exchange maps and ask each other why they have marked particular places.

ADDITIONAL PRACTICE

RB **Resource bank:** 3A *The best place in the world* (superlatives and Present Perfect), pages 122–123, Instructions page 98

Workbook: Comparatives and superlatives, pages 20–21; Comparative and superlative adverbs, page 21

Language focus 2 (PAGE 28)

Comparing things in different ways

See *Teacher's tips: using a discovery approach in the teaching of grammar* on page 15.

1 Focus students' attention on the pictures, by asking them whether they like the rooms, why / why not, etc. Students find the objects in pairs. Check the pronunciation of: *mirror* /mɪrə/, *stool* /stuːl/, *cushion* /kʊʃən/.

2 Do the first example together, before getting students to work individually or in pairs. Do not pre-teach the comparative forms, but encourage students to work out the meanings from the context.

ANSWERS
a T/T b T/T c T/F d T/T e T/T

Analysis

1 Write up the sentences and underline the comparative phrases with students' help. Check answers as you go along, explaining the differences below. Highlight and drill sentences with *as*. Highlight the weak forms.

ANSWERS
a They mean exactly the same – it is just a different way of saying the same thing.
b *fewer ... than / less ... than:* they mean the same, but *less* is used with uncountable nouns, whereas *fewer* is used with countable nouns.

30

c *not as ... as*: they do *not* mean the same – *not as ... as* does not simply mean *is not the same as*; it means *is less than*. This may be different in the students' own language and difficult for students to understand.
d These mean the same, but *just* here emphasises that they are exactly the same.
e These mean roughly the same thing, but *exactly* is more similar than *more or less* – it may be subjective as to which best represents the pictures.

2 Students work individually before going through the answers with the whole class.

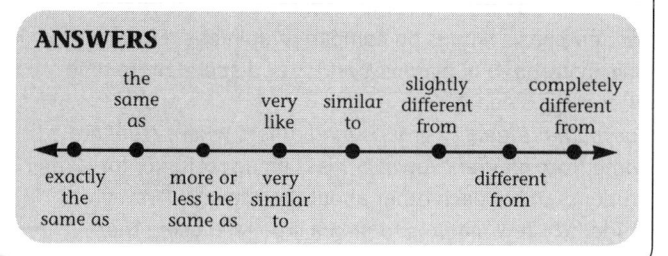

ANSWERS

```
     the                    slightly    completely
     same           very  similar different  different
     as             like    to      from       from
 ●────●──────●──────●──────●──────●──────●────▶
exactly      more or  very                different
  the        less the similar                 from
same as      same as   to
```

PRACTICE

1 Emphasise that students should use the phrases from the *Analysis*, and also those from *Language focus 1* to express the differences as precisely as possible. Make this into a competition by saying that the winner will be the person / pair / group who find(s) the most differences. The focus here is on accuracy, so go round checking and correcting sentences. When feeding back, check that the meaning is also correct by referring to the pictures.

ANSWERS
(the same ideas can obviously be expressed in a number of different ways)
There are fewer plates on the wall in A; there are fewer photographs on the table in B; the vase in A is completely different from the vase in B; the shade in A is more or less the same as the shade in B; the rug in B is slightly different from the rug in A; the mirror in A is exactly the same as the mirror in B; etc.

2 a) 📼 [3.3] Ask students what they know about Hungary and when it changed from being a communist country (1989). Students then read the information in the box. Refer them to prompt ideas before playing the cassette.

ANSWERS
prices: they have gone up a lot; **people**: they are better dressed / there are a lot more foreigners now; **general atmosphere**: this is similar in many ways; **shops**: they have a lot more things in them; **cars and traffic**: there is more traffic, and the cars are a lot better than before; **public transport**: this is still very good but it is much more expensive.

b) Emphasise that these are not the exact words Judit uses – they summarise the points she makes. (If students are having difficulty in remembering what she said, refer them to the tapescript on page 155 of the Students' Book.) Students work in pairs or groups before checking with the whole class.

ANSWERS
1 completely; from   2 the; as   3 much / a lot; than   4 one; the most; in   5 just as; as
6 less; than; just as; as   7 very; to

Pronunciation

1 📼 [3.4] Play the cassette as many times as necessary, pausing after each sentence for students to write, or read out the sentences yourself. (Keep to a natural speed, with natural use of weak forms and linking – maintain this speed however many times students ask you to repeat the words.)

ANSWERS
a 7   b 7   c 6   d 10   e 9   f 9

2 Make sure that students are familiar with the schwa sound. Read out the phrases yourself, exaggerating the /ə/ sounds slightly and getting students to copy. Alternatively, get students to guess where the /ə/ sounds are themselves before playing the cassette to check. Drill the phrases, before getting students to repeat the whole sentences from the cassette.

ADDITIONAL PRACTICE

Workbook: Comparing things in different ways, page 22

Wordspot (PAGE 29)

place

See *Teacher's tips: working with lexis* on pages 12–13.

1 With a mono-lingual group, you could translate the phrases into the students' own language rather than paraphrasing them in English. This is probably easier and more effective in showing the different meanings of *place*.

place: **notes on use**

The point of this exercise is to show students that *place* has a number of meanings, often as a way of describing things rather vaguely or casually (*a place to stay*). There may be no equivalent of such phrases in the students' own language. Point out that there is a tendency in English to use vague rather than precise language, a point picked up on in Exercise 3.

module 3

> **ANSWERS**
> a vacancies / spaces   b town   c hotel
> d point / exact position   e instead of her
> f happened   g an off-licence   h everywhere
> i correct position   j house / flat / home

2 Students work in pairs or groups before checking with the whole class.

> **ANSWERS**
> (section in brackets)
> no places left (f); a place called (a); a cheap place to stay (b); the place (e); in her place (g); took place (g); a place to buy wine (b); all over the place (g); put it back in its place (c).

3 Put students in pairs and refer them to the appropriate page at the back of the book. Do at least one example to ensure that they understand. Note that: *a place for ... + -ing* (*a place for parking*, etc.) is equally acceptable in many of the phrases.

Reading (PAGES 30–31)

1 Do this as a race to see which group finds the six things which don't fit first. Discuss what else students know about life in Ancient Rome or other ancient cities.

> **ANSWERS**
> a toy aeroplane; a newspaper; a cigarette; a bicycle; a rifle; a mobile phone

2 Check the pronunciation of: *vehicle* /ˈviːɪkəl/, *plumbing* /ˈplʌmɪŋ/, *Empire* /ˈempaɪər/. (See *Teacher's tips: making the most of the Mini-dictionary* on page 14.)

3 Emphasise that students only have to find this information – they do not need to understand each word in the text. Students work in pairs to find the information as quickly as possible.

> **ANSWERS**
> a women and slaves   b Rome   c 30   d Jericho
> e writing and plumbing / drains   f Peking
> g crime / traffic congestion

4 Students work individually before comparing answers in groups.

5 Students discuss the questions in groups or with the whole class. The discussion can be brief or quite lengthy, depending on time and interest level.

ADDITIONAL ACTIVITY

RB Resource bank: 3B *Amazing cities!* vocabulary extension (word building), page 124, Instructions page 98

Vocabulary (PAGE 31)

Describing towns and cities

1 Students work individually or in pairs checking the meaning of the words. (Note that *docks* always has an 's' on the end, but can be a singular noun – *a docks*). Give students 5–10 minutes to answer the questions individually.

2 *For students who come from the same town:* the emphasis here is on comparing opinions. They can run quickly through questions 1 and 2, and spend more time discussing 3 and 4.
For multi-nationality groups (and others where students come from different towns): this is an opportunity for students to tell each other about their towns. First, give students a few minutes to plan a little talk, using the vocabulary in the questions. Encourage them to ask each other questions. This will probably take some time, so keep feedback quite brief.

> **Vocabulary: alternative suggestion for students who all come from the same town / city**
>
> - Students think of another town from their own country, but do not tell anyone which town they are thinking of. They then read through questions 1 and 2 and decide how they would answer them for the town they have chosen.
> - Choose one student to answer 'twenty questions' about the town he / she has chosen, without saying which town it is. He / she can only answer *yes / no* questions (*Is it on the coast?*, etc.)
> This activity could either be done as a whole class, or in large groups. Questions 3 and 4 could then be discussed together as a class, in relation to the towns students have talked about.

Part B Task

See *Teacher's tips: making tasks work* on pages 8–9 and *Responding to learners' individual language needs* on pages 10–11.

Preparation for task (PAGE 32)

1 Focus students' attention on the pictures and ask if anyone has visited Ireland before going through the questions. If students do not know much about Ireland, encourage them to tell you anything at all they know.

2 [3.5] Focus students' attention on the map and check that they can see all the places mentioned on the cassette (see tapescript on page 156). Check the pronunciation of: *Killarney* /kɪˈlɑːniː/, *Killorglin* /kɪˈlɔːglɪn/, *Blarney* /ˈblɑːniː/, *Croagh Patrick* /krəʊˈpætrɪk/.

> **ANSWERS**
> a In Cork.
> b/c Cork (1 night); Blarney (0 nights); Killarney/the Ring of Kerry (including Killorglin, Dingle Bay and Kenmare) (2–3 nights); Limerick (1 night); possibly Westport or Waterford (1 night)

Task (PAGE 33)

1 *If you have a multi-nationality class*, it is probably most motivating if students prepare the tour for each other, either in nationality groups or individually. It is particularly important that they draw a map of their countries, as other students may be unfamiliar with the basic geography. Each student will need to draw their own map.

If you have a mono-nationality class (unless they all happen to be familiar with different regions), designing the tour for one of the groups in the pictures will probably work better. This can be done in pairs or groups of four, to facilitate the role play stage later.

Talk students through the decisions they have to make, then give them time to think. If this is done in class, they will need about half an hour – stress that this time is for planning, map-drawing and note-making (both the tour itself and the language needed). Students do not need to write out the tour in full.

2 Circulate, answering vocabulary questions, and helping students to plan the tour itself. If necessary, ask or prompt questions, for example: *How long do you think they should stay in ...?*, etc. Remind students to look back at the phrases in the tour of Ireland and in the *Useful language* box to use in their own tours if appropriate.

3 If students have prepared carefully, this stage could take from between twenty to forty minutes, so make sure that you allow enough time.

- *The first option is for multi-nationality classes* – students will need to be re-grouped so there is a mix of nationalities in each group.
- *The second option is for mono-nationality classes*, who have been preparing for a role play. In both cases, encourage students to ask each other questions. Students can report back briefly about what appeals / doesn't appeal about each tour.

Optional writing

The focus here is on accuracy, so go over any corrections from the spoken tours that you have. Remember only to select the most useful errors, and to limit the number of points to a maximum of ten.

Task: alternative suggestions

a *If you want to provide a model yourself*: it may be more motivating for students if you present a tour of an English-speaking country / region that you have visited. If you are an English native speaker, students may be very interested in your own region and town.
Plan briefly what you will say, incorporating some of the useful phrases in the Ireland tour (*It's worth visiting*, etc.). If possible, take a map of the country to refer to, marking the places you talk about with stickers. Encourage students to ask any questions they have as you present your tour.

b *If you are short of time or have short lessons*: do the model for the task (either the Ireland model or your own) on one day, then set the planning stage (*Task*, Exercise 1) as homework. Students can talk through their tasks in the next lesson, after asking you about any vocabulary they need.

c *Making the role play option more motivating*: if your students all come from the same country and perhaps only know the same region, there is a danger that they will all choose the same places, and that there will be no genuine communication. This is why we have included the option to choose a group of people illustrated. The idea is that these groups of people would look for a different kind of holiday, encouraging students to prepare different tours. Instead of using the photos in the book, you could:

- bring in photos of your own of foreign friends or relatives. Explain that they are coming to the students' country for a week and want to see as much as they can. Give brief details of their ages, interests, budget, etc. and ask students to design a tour for them.

- bring in some photos of famous foreigners likely to interest students, or get them to think of someone themselves (actors / rock stars, etc.) Tell students that this person is coming on holiday to their country, and that they are going to be his / her personal guide for a week, and that they must plan a tour for them.

Once the tour is organised, tell them to imagine they are having lunch with the person they organised the tour for. Students talk through the tour in a conversation similar to that between Helen, Bob and Isobel. At this role play stage, some students will have to take the part of the visitor. They can either stay in the same pairs to do this or be mixed up, so that they are not seeing the same tour that they themselves planned.

module 3

Task link (PAGE 34)
Recommending and advising

1 [3.6] Introduce Zelda and the situation she is in by focusing on the pictures. Ask students to guess what kind of advice her friends gave her. Emphasise that students will hear extracts from four separate conversations and that, for now, they only need to identify the topics being discussed. After listening, see how much of the advice students can remember.

> **ANSWERS**
> 1 cheap places to stay
> 2 the best things to eat and drink
> 3 the best ways to travel about
> 4 money

2 Emphasise that students should tell you when to stop the cassette, but be ready to stop it yourself if they miss the important phrases. See if students can remember the phrases by themselves, rather than immediately giving them the answers.

> **ANSWERS**
> **Asking for recommendations:** *What about the ...?; What should I ...?; What do you suggest?; Have you got any other tips?*
> **Giving recommendations:** *You must ...; You should definitely ...; It's probably best to ...; I would recommend ...*
> **Recommending not to do something:** *Be careful with ...; It's probably best ...; Personally, I wouldn't ...; Don't ... (if you can help it)*
> **Responding to recommendations:** *Thanks. I'd really appreciate that; Right – I'll remember that; Thanks for telling me.*

Pronunciation

1 [3.7] Stop the cassette after each pair of sentences to see if students can hear which one sounds friendly/interested. Ask students why this is.

> **ANSWERS**
> b speaker 2   c speaker 2   d speaker 2   e speaker 1

2 Highlight the stressed words by clapping on the stressed syllable, exaggerating, etc. Get students to copy the intonation on the cassette.

> **ANSWERS**
> The stressed words are:
> a must   b definitely   c personally   d I'd   e really

3 The first option is intended for multi-nationality groups. They can talk about their own countries, but make sure they work with a different student from the one in the *Preparation for task / Task*. The second option is intended for mono-nationality groups. In both cases remind students of the topics to be covered, and give them a few minutes to prepare. Circulate, supplying vocabulary. Make a note of any errors, particularly with the language for recommending, to look at later.

ADDITIONAL PRACTICE

RB **Resource bank:** 3C *The City Language School* (recommending and advising), pages 125–126; 3D *How do I get to ... ?* (asking for and giving directions), page 127, Instructions page 98–99

Do you remember?

> **ANSWERS**
> 1 Sentences b) and f) are correct, the others need to be corrected as follows:
>   a He's <u>taller</u> than his brother.
>   c He's not as old <u>as</u> me.
>   d It's the <u>most</u> interesting book I've read for a long time.
>   e He's one of <u>the</u> kindest people I know.
>   g New York is one of the biggest <u>cities</u> in the world.
> 2 a *island* (the other two are very similar to each other)
>   b *pollution* (it has nothing to do with vehicles, getting around)
>   c *border* (it's not by the sea)
>   d *carnival* (it's not a place to shop)
>   e *forest* (the other two are similar)
>   f *cushion* (the other two are pieces of furniture to sit on)
>   g *peaceful* (the other two are negative adjectives)
> 4 c<u>a</u>stle Emp<u>e</u>ror fav<u>ou</u>rite g<u>u</u>ard is<u>l</u>and cush<u>i</u>on plum<u>b</u>ing sc<u>e</u>nery ve<u>h</u>icle sli<u>gh</u>tly
> 5 a the ... as   b a ... than   c on the   d to   e in the   f take   g seat   h place

34

module 4

Part A Language

Vocabulary (PAGE 36)

Life experiences

See *Teacher's tips: working with lexis* on pages 12–13.

1 Focus students' attention on the picture and check that they understand what it represents. Elicit some ideas about what happens at these stages in a person's life. Students will be familiar with most of the words in the box, but may not be able to use the full phrases correctly. Note that certain phrases could go at any stage (for example *fall in love*), although students may well disagree about which. Do some repetition, drilling the phrases, rather than complete sentences.

> **ANSWERS**
> **as a child:** learn how to read
> **in your teens:** leave home / pass your driving test / leave school / fall in love / go to university
> **in your twenties:** leave home / start work / move house / settle down / pass your driving test / get married / get a degree / fall in love / get engaged / have an affair
> **in your thirties:** move house / settle down / get married / get divorced / bring up your children / have an affair
> **later in life:** retire / get divorced / get married / have an affair

> **Vocabulary (life experiences): language notes**
>
> As you check the answers highlight the following important features of the phrases:
> - the non-use of the article in phrases like *move house / go to university / leave home*, etc.
> - the fact that *settle down* is inseparable, while *bring up (your children)* is separable
> - the use of *get* in *get engaged / married / divorced*
> - the meaning of *pass an exam* (to be successful) if you have students for whom this is a 'false friend'
> - the stress / pronunciation of: *engaged* /ɪnˈgeɪdʒd/, *married* /ˈmærid/, *divorced* /dɪˈvɔːst/, *to retire* /rɪˈtaɪə/.

2 To encourage students to remember the phrases, write up the four categories and tell students to close their books whilst they are discussing their answers in pairs.

Reading (PAGES 36–37)

1 Check the meaning of: *twins, to affect, your personality*. Students discuss the questions in pairs, groups or with the whole class.

2 Emphasise that students only need to scan the text for the relevant information, they do not need to understand everything.

> **ANSWERS**
> b photo 3 (Grace and Virginia Kennedy)
> c photo 1 (June and Jennifer Gibbons)
> d photo 2 (Terry Connolly and Margaret Richardson)
>
> *Caption e does not go with any of the pictures.*

3 Before students read the text in more detail, check the meaning of: *to be separated, closeness, to be capable of, to be adopted, to trace someone, identical, a coincidence, a similarity, genetic*. Students discuss the questions in pairs before checking with the whole class.

> **ANSWERS**
> a Tom Bouchard is a professor at the University of Minnesota. He wanted to find out if there are still similarities between twins even if they are separated at birth. He traced sixteen pairs of twins adopted by different families at birth.
> b They had the same tastes / hobbies / phobias; suffered the same illnesses and accidents; they dressed in the same kind of clothes and jewellery; some of them had had children at the same time and called them the same names.
> c Because the coincidences between them were so incredible.
> d It may be partly genetic, but partly just coincidence.

4 This discussion can be brief or lengthy, depending on time and interest level. Feed in phrases for describing similarities, for example: *both of us are ..., all of us are ..., I ... whereas my mother ...* .

ADDITIONAL ACTIVITY

RB Resource bank: 4A *Twin lives* vocabulary extension (dependent prepositions), page 128, Instructions page 99

35

module 4

Language focus 1 (PAGES 38–39)

Present Perfect Simple (and Past Simple)

See *Teacher's tips: using a discovery approach in the teaching of grammar* on page 15.

Mini-task

Give an example to make sure that students understand what to do, for example: I've broken my leg twice. Anna, have you ever broken your leg? – No, okay and what about you Daniel? – No, okay that's one thing I've done that the other two haven't.

Give students a minute to think of things that they've done which their partners are unlikely to have done. Listen carefully to the language students use, and whether or not they are able to use the Present Perfect. If so:

- *is this: a few set phrases I've been to ... / Have you ever ...?*
- *are they using have / has / haven't / hasn't properly?*
- *do they have a good knowledge of past participles or are they only using a few high frequency ones properly?*
- *are they using the Present Perfect where they should be using the Past Simple?*

Make a note of any useful errors for correction after the Analysis section.

1 If students have already read the twins text, ask them to close their books and see how much they can remember about who the Jim Twins were and why they became famous.

2 Check briefly that students understand the basic difference between the Present Perfect and Past Simple (verb + *-ed*, *have / has* + past participle). Students work in pairs. If they are not sure, encourage them to guess. However, if they seem to have no idea at all, move quickly on to checking the answers with the whole class. With each answer, ask students to explain why they have chosen each form – the *Analysis* should act as a summary of what has been discussed with the *Language summary* providing further detail. It may help to draw timelines on the board to help students to understand the differences, as follows:

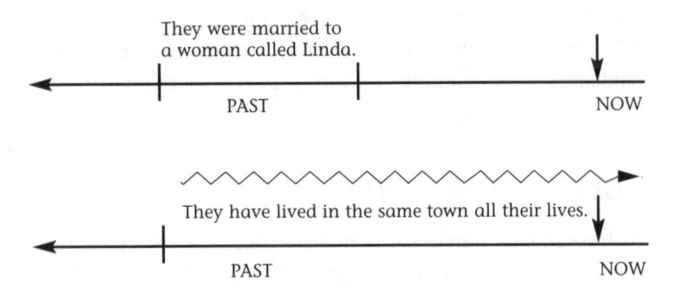

They were married to
a woman called Linda.
← PAST ———|————————|→ NOW

They have lived in the same town all their lives.
← PAST ~~~~~~~~~~~~~~~~~~~~~~ NOW

Language focus 1: alternative suggestion (without doing the *Twin Lives* reading text first)

If you do not have time or do not wish to do the reading in class, you can still do *Language focus 1*.

Either: give students the reading to do for homework. Ask them very briefly what it was about, then focus on the Jim Twins, what happened to them when they were babies and what they discovered when they finally met up. Ask which coincidences they found the most amazing and whether they know any other stories of amazing coincidences. Then proceed with the *Language focus* as normal.

or: without opening books, introduce the students to the Jim Twins, and what happened to them when they were babies. Explain that they eventually met up in their forties, and put students into pairs or groups to discuss briefly what they think happened. Do some brief feedback then tell them to open their books and show them the Jim Twins' pictures. Ask if they think they look alike, and get them to read the box describing the coincidences. Discuss briefly which coincidences they find most remarkable, and which ones are not really surprising. Then proceed with the *Language focus* as normal.

ANSWERS

a *were born* (because this is clearly finished / in the past – a definite time is given)
b *owned* (this is clearly in the past, they are not children now)
c *were married* (this is finished because they are now divorced)
d *have both lived* (this is still continued and therefore related to the present)
e *have suffered* (this is still continuing – point out that sentences with *since* are in (the Present Perfect)
f *have had* (this refers to their whole lives, which have not finished – they could have another heart attack)

Language focus 1: notes on the approach to the Present Perfect

In many courses / student grammars it has been customary to divide the Present Perfect into several 'uses'. However, we believe that there is essentially only one 'use' of the Present Perfect – that it connects the present and the past, so that the past action is still part of the present in some way or another. As such, it should be regarded as a present tense, not a past tense, and has much in common with other perfect forms which are studied later in the course. We believe that it is more helpful for students to see this basic element that all Present Perfect verbs have in common rather than learning a list of apparently disparate 'uses'. In the *Analysis* and *Language summary*, although we have referred to rules that students may already be familiar with, we have tried to draw them together so that students can see this overall pattern.

Analysis

Students work individually or in pairs before discussing answers with the whole class. As well as checking meaning it may be necessary to check form. In particular, highlight the following points:

- Present Perfect – formed with *have / has* + past participle
- *have* and *has* are often shortened to *'ve* and *'s*
- regular past participles are verb + *-ed*, irregular ones have to be learnt individually (see list on page 152 of the *Students' Book*)
- in questions *have / has* and the pronoun are inverted
- negatives are formed with *haven't / hasn't*

ANSWERS
(example sentences given in brackets)
a Past Simple (a, b and c)
b Present Perfect (d, e)
c Present Perfect (f)

Note: there is an overlap between b and c – elements of both ideas can be seen in all the sentences where the Present Perfect is used.

PRACTICE

1 Put students into pairs or groups to check who the famous people are. Ask them briefly what they know about any who may be less well-known to them, before getting students to do the exercise. Emphasise that they may need to use the same ending twice, or some endings not at all.

ANSWERS
a Steven Speilberg made *Jaws* in 1975. / Steven Speilberg has made a new film.
b Jack Nicholson played the Joker in *Batman*. / Jack Nicholson played a mental patient in *One Flew over the Cuckoo's Nest*.
c Julia Roberts starred in *Pretty Woman*. / Julia Roberts has starred in more than twenty films.
d Bruce Willis and Demi Moore have been married for several years. / Tom Cruise and Nicole Kidman have been married for several years.
e Marilyn Monroe was married several times. / Elizabeth Taylor has been married several times.
f Jane Fonda hasn't made any films for many

years. / Brigitte Bardot hasn't made any films for many years.

Note: if any of the people in the exercise have died / got divorced since this book was published, Present Perfect answers will change to Past Simple. Discussion about this will help students to understand the Present Perfect better.

2 Check that students know who the famous people are. Students work individually or in pairs before checking answers with the whole class.

ANSWERS
a Arnold Schwarzenegger has just made a new film.
b James Dean died in a car crash when he was only twenty-four.
c As well as being an actor, Robert Redford has directed several films.
d Clark Gable's last film was with Marilyn Monroe – it was also her last film.
e Michael Jackson became a star when he was still a young child.
f Tom Hanks has won several Oscars.

3 a) [4.1] Focus students' attention on the pictures and discuss the questions with the whole class.

b) Students complete the gaps individually or in pairs before checking answers with the whole class.

ANSWERS
a 1b 2d 3e 4c 5a
b 1 've finished 2 haven't finished 3 've changed 4 've lost 5 's just gone 6 's / gone 7 Have / seen 8 've lost 9 have / met

Pronunciation

1 Stop the cassette after each *have / 've* and write up the verb, getting students to tell you whether or not *have* is weak or strong. (It may be useful to write up the phonemic spellings /hæv/ and /həv/.)

ANSWERS
a *Have* is strong if it stands alone without a main verb. It is weak in the question form.
b It is often contracted in the affirmative if it is followed by a main verb.

Point out these rules are true for all auxiliary verbs, not just *have*.

2 Get students to repeat the pronunciation chorally and individually. Start with the stressed word in each phrase, which should help students to get the weak forms and contractions right. The other phrases can be 'back chained' in a similar way.

module 4

ADDITIONAL PRACTICE

RB Resource bank: 4B *Find someone who ... lied!* (Present Perfect Simple for experience), page 129, Instructions page 99

Workbook: Present Perfect Simple and Past Simple, page 26; Present Perfect + *just / yet / already*, page 27

Language focus 2 (PAGES 40–41)

for, *since* and *ago* (and Present Perfect Continuous)

See *Teacher's tips: using a discovery approach in the teaching of grammar* on page 15.

1 [4.4] Focus students' attention on the photo of Montse and check that they know where Tarragona and Barcelona are (*in Catalonia, Northern Spain*).

> **ANSWERS**
> a She works in a **travel agency**; **Pablo** is her boyfriend; she was born in **Tarragona**; she lives in **Barcelona**.
> b a 1977 b 11 c three months d 16

2 Check that students understand what the lifeline is. Students work individually or in pairs before checking answers with the whole class. All the verb forms can be completed on the basis of what students have already studied in *Language focus 1*.

> **ANSWERS**
> a twenty (*in 1998, at the time of publication*)
> b has lived c met d has known e three years
> f three months g 's been h a child
> i nine years

Language focus 2: notes about the approach to the Present Perfect Continuous

It is not our intention to introduce the students to all 'uses' of the Present Perfect Continuous. For example, we do not focus on the 'activity / result' contrast between Present Perfect Simple and Continuous, which we consider to be more suitable for Upper Intermediate students. Instead we have chosen to focus on a very common use for the Present Perfect Continuous with *for* and *since*, which:

– students are likely to have at least heard already.
– can be drawn into their existing knowledge of continuous versus simple aspect.
– will form a confidence-building basis for understanding other contexts in which the Present Perfect Continuous is used.

Analysis

Verb forms

Focus mainly on the difference in form here, as the difference in meaning is dealt with later. The form of the Present Perfect Continuous (*have / has been* + verb + *-ing*) should cause few problems, but it would be useful to highlight the following on the board:

- in the question form only *have* is inverted, *been* doesn't change position
- the negative form
- the use of *has / hasn't* in the 3rd person singular
- the fact that *been* never changes form
- the contracted forms of *have / has*
- the weak form of been /bɪn/ (see below)

> **ANSWERS AND VERB FORMS**
> 1 a sentences a, c and e   b sentences b, d, f and g
>   c sentences h and i
>
> 2 a *They are long / repeated actions.* Point out that this is one of the most important distinctions between Present Perfect Simple and Continuous. (You could draw a parallel with the Past Simple and Continuous, if you think students will find this useful.)
> *They are not complete.* This is similar to the Present Perfect Simple, but different from the Present Perfect Continuous.
>
> b Sentences b and f can be changed to Present Perfect Continuous – this emphasises the duration of the action; sentences d and g cannot be changed into the Present Perfect Continuous because they describe states (this is the same as with other tenses).

Note: in both cases, this could also suggest that the action is temporary, as this is another implication of continuous aspect. Be careful about overloading students with too much information here, however – this distinction is very fine.

Time words: *for*, *since* and *ago*

> **ANSWERS**
> 1 *ago, when, for*: point out that *ago* and *when* can only be used with the Past Simple; *for* can be used with both Past Simple and Present Perfect. Check that students can see the difference between the use of *for* in e and f. The following time lines may be useful:
>
> FINISHED
> She studied tourism for three years at university.   NOW
> ← PAST

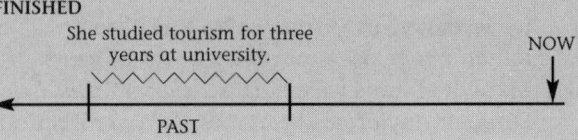

38

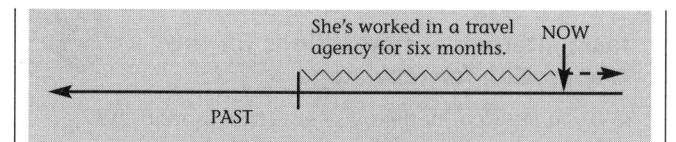

module 4

> She's worked in a travel agency for six months.
>
> PAST ←——————|~~~~~~~~~NOW~~~→
>
> 2 _For_ is used with periods of time: _twenty years, five minutes, ages and ages_; _since_ is used with points in time: _six o'clock, I was a child, 1965_

- Write up the most useful examples you have collected, and ask students which are correct and which aren't. As you correct the mistakes, elicit / point out the differences between the Present Perfect Simple and Continuous. Read the _Language summary_, either individually or as a class.
- Follow this up with Practice Exercise 1 or exercises from the _Workbook_, as necessary.

PRACTICE

1 a) [4.5] Stress that students only need to write a phrase with _for_, _since_ or _ago_ not a complete sentence. Stop the cassette after each sentence, re-playing if necessary.

b) Use the cassette to check answers and work on pronunciation as you go along. Insist on the correct use of the verb forms in the reconstructed questions – if students are having problems, remind them of the appropriate rules. Use the cassette to correct their answers focusing on the pronunciation of weak forms at the same time.

2 a) Remind students of the kind of information on Montse's lifeline (where she lives / used to live, her studies, job, languages, hobbies, relationships, etc.) Give them ten minutes to prepare their own lifeline.

b) Circulate giving help, suggestions and vocabulary. To make the practice more controlled / accuracy-oriented, or if you have a weaker class, get them to write sentences about themselves similar to the ones in Exercise 2 on page 40. Check and correct them as you go round. Students then spend a few minutes memorising the correct forms before the next stage.

c) Circulate and note down both good and bad examples of the use of the verb forms / time words. Write up the sentences (about ten) and ask students to identify the correct ones, and correct those that are wrong.

> _Language focus 2:_ **alternative suggestion**
>
> If your class is of a higher level than the average intermediate class, you could take a more 'task-based' approach here, as follows:
>
> - Do the _Montse_ listening as in the book or alternatively present your own 'lifeline', but instead of moving on to the _Analysis_, move straight on to Practice Exercise 2.
> - Get students to do the activity as in the book, but take careful notes of the way in which they use _for_ and _since_, and whether or not they are using the Present Perfect Continuous correctly. If students are using _for_, _since_ and _ago_ well, you may decide not to focus on these, but you will still probably need to do work on the Present Perfect Continuous.

ADDITIONAL PRACTICE

RB **Resource bank:** 4C _How long have you had it?_ (Present Perfect Simple and Continuous for unfinished past), page 130, Instructions page 99
Workbook: _for_, _since_ and _ago_, page 27; Present Perfect Continuous, page 28

Wordspot (PAGE 41)

get

See _Teacher's tips: working with lexis_ on pages 12–13.

1 Check the meaning of _obtain_ before students do the exercise individually or in pairs.

> _get:_ **language notes**
>
> - _get_ is only used to mean _become_ when followed by an adjective (you cannot for example say _He got a doctor_).
> - note the two different meanings of _get on well with_:
>   to progress well: _She's getting on well with her driving._
>   to have a good relationship with: _She gets on well with her driving instructor._

2 [4.6] Give students time to guess the answers before playing the cassette. Stop the cassette after each dialogue to check answers, re-playing the cassette rather than giving students the answers. Students can then practise reading the dialogues aloud in pairs.

> **ANSWERS**
> a taxi b cold c worse d home e rid of
> f on okay with g the message

3 Students write their dialogues in pairs – the best ones can be acted out for the whole class.

4 Prepare this in advance by copying the diagram onto a poster-sized sheet of paper.

module 4

Part B Task

See *Teacher's tips: making tasks work* on pages 8–9 and *Responding to learners' individual language needs* on pages 10–11.

Preparation for task (PAGE 42)

1 Students work in groups of three or four. Encourage students to discuss each person as fully as they can. Direct students to the extracts at the back of the book if they want more information.

2 Check / drill the pronunciation of: *principles* /ˈprɪnsɪpəls/, *talented* /ˈtæləntɪd/, *courageous* /kəˈreɪdʒəs/, *to achieve* /əˈtʃiːv/ *an achievement* /ənəˈtʃiːvmənt/, *to admire* /ədˈmaɪə/.

Task (PAGE 43)

1 Check the meaning of *committee* and *set of stamps* and make sure students understand the situation. Check the list of possible titles, and suggest alternatives that your students may find more appealing (*the greatest footballers in the world today / great rock guitarists*, etc.) Put students with similar interests together in a group and give them three minutes to choose a title.

2 It is important for students to have time to think about their individual choices before discussing it together. Emphasise that they should rank the four people they choose, as this will give them more to discuss later. Tell students to think carefully about the language they need to justify their choices – they can use the phrases in Exercise 2 of the *Preparation for task* and ask you for any other phrases they need. They will need about ten minutes.

3 Students work in their groups again. It may be helpful to appoint a chairperson. Draw students' attention to the *Useful language* box.

4 If you have a large class, select just two or three groups to report back fully to the whole class (the other groups could just quickly list the people that they have chosen). Make sure that each group gives the title of their set of stamps, before reporting back. Encourage the others to ask questions – these could either be 'information' questions (*Who is ....? Why is he famous?*), or questions about why they have selected these people.

Optional writing

Students can either write about someone famous or someone they know personally (a relative, a friend, etc.). Check through the details to be included, giving examples of each. These topics can form the basis for paragraphing the piece of work.

> **Task: alternative suggestions for the *Preparation for task* stage**
>
> a *If you are short of time:* ask students to read the extracts on the famous people before the lesson. Alternatively, discuss the pictures during the lesson and talk about any of the people they don't know. They then read the extracts at the end of the lesson or for homework.
>
> b *If you want to make the reading exercise into an information exchange:* give each student a different famous person to read about at the back. Tell them to memorise three facts about that person that the other students might not know. Tell each student to take a blank piece of paper, and write on it the names of the other nine famous people, leaving enough space to take notes about them. Give them a few minutes to decide what questions they want to ask about these people. Students mingle, finding out what they need to know – give a time limit of about five minutes. Feedback as a class briefly, focusing on any unanswered questions.

Task link (PAGE 44)

Describing people

> **Task link: notes about the selection of language**
>
> The examples here are based on real descriptions of people given by native speakers. Traditional adjectives for describing people form only a small part of what they say. Far more common are sentences with verbs which describe the person's typical behaviour. Phrases like *He's the sort / kind of person who ..., She's someone who ...* are far more generative and easier to use. The verb phrases added will often be very individual to that person, but may well be easily constructed from language students already know.

1 Students work individually or in pairs / groups before checking answers with the whole class.

ANSWERS
positive: a, b, d, f, h; negative: c, e, g

2 [4.7] Focus students' attention on the pictures and get them to speculate about the kind of people they are. Explain what the students are going to hear – emphasise that the people in the pictures are the ones being described, not the speakers.

module 4

> **ANSWERS**
> man – 2; woman with horse – 3; woman on phone – 1

3 Students work in pairs / groups before discussing answers with the whole class.

> **ANSWERS**
> 1 she just **goes on and on about her problems** …, she really **gets on my nerves** sometimes
>   The general attitude is negative.
> 2 he always seemed to **have lots of confidence in himself**; he's always been **a good talker** …
>   The general attitude is positive.
> 3 she's so **positive and enthusiastic** about everything …, she always **sees the good side of things** …, she used to **really annoy** me …, and still be so **cheerful**
>   The general attitude is positive.

4 Go over the possibilities with the whole class. When students have finished, discuss what they have written in groups / with the whole class.

Real life (PAGE 45)

Filling in an application form

1 Focus students' attention on the photo of Ahmet and get students to scan the form to find out what kind of course he is applying for. Students work in pairs before checking answers with the whole class.

2 Check the pronunciation of: *male* /meɪl/, *female* /fiːmeɪl/, *signature* /ˈsɪɡnətʃə/, *qualifications* /ˌkwɒlɪfɪˈkeɪʃənz/.

Real life: suggestions for role play

a *If you don't get the students to fill in the second application form for themselves:*

- Divide the class into two groups, As and Bs. The As are Ahmet, and the Bs are the head of the Journalism Department at the college – they are going to interview Ahmet to decide whether or not to offer him a place on the course.

- Explain that in a few minutes they are going to conduct an interview to see whether or not Ahmet will get a place on the course. The As and Bs should first work together in groups of three or four to prepare the interview. The As should memorise the information about Ahmet, and try to think of other questions they might be asked in the interview (perhaps requiring information that is not given on the form). The Bs should think of questions to ask. Encourage them to ask about other things not mentioned on the form.

- Reorganise the class into pairs consisting of one A and one B, and tell the students not to look at Ahmet's form in the book. Elicit from the students how they think the interview should start (*Hello. How do you do? / Do sit down. / Did you have any trouble getting here?*, etc.) Then get them to act out the interview in pairs. Circulate, noting down any errors, useful phrases, items of vocabulary to be discussed later.

b *If you do get your students to fill in the second form for themselves:* the role play can be done using themselves, rather than Ahmet, as the interviewees. In this case make sure that B gets A's form in advance to study, and make sure that they have understood which course A has applied for. Otherwise the role play can be done as above.

Consolidation modules 1–4

> **ANSWERS**
> A 2 a Do you speak any other languages?
>   b How long have you been here?
>   c What are you doing at the moment?
>   d Did you have a good holiday?
>   e Where were you born?
>   f How often do you go swimming?
>
> B 1 voted 2 was having 3 later 4 has grown
>   5 came 6 stands 7 has only been 8 since
>   9 leave 10 was 11 still wait 12 once missed
>   13 was playing 14 is becoming 15 still come
>   16 have been 17 died
>
> C Martin talks about: his friends, his hairstyle, his character, his clothes, his appearance
>   *his friends:* he is no longer engaged.
>   *his hairstyle:* he used to have long hair, now it is shorter.
>   *his character:* he is a lot more relaxed, laid-back, not as arrogant or self-confident as he used to be.
>   *his clothes:* he wears clean clothes now and has to be quite well-presented.
>   *his appearance:* he used to be a bit dirty; he used to have a beard.
>
> E acquaintance; bring up; classmate; driving test; ex-boyfriend; florist's; get rid of; harbour; increase; light; mother-in-law; niece; old-fashioned; partner; retire; stool; trouble; underground; vehicles; wide

Students can now do *Test one (modules 1–4)* on pages 161–163.

module 5

Part A Language

Speaking and reading (PAGES 48–49)

1 Give students 5–10 minutes to discuss the questions. Before they read the text check the meaning of: *well-organised / badly-organised / disorganised, to plan something in advance / carefully, to make plans, to be flexible / inflexible, to prioritise, to be spontaneous / spontaneity, to achieve a goal*. (See *Teacher's tips: making the most of the Mini-dictionary* on page 14).

2 Emphasise that students should not answer the questions yet. Students work individually before checking answers with the whole class.

> **ANSWERS**
> (question numbers in brackets)
> attending a meeting (6), packing for a holiday (7), filling in an important form (1), arranging a night out with a friend (2), winning money (3), booking a holiday (4), giving someone a message (5)

3 Students work in pairs. Get students to predict the conclusions, and do some brief feedback on this.

4 Get students to add up their scores then direct them to the conclusions at the back of the book. Ask students whether or not they agree with the quiz conclusions, and get them to explain why.

ADDITIONAL ACTIVITY

RB Resource bank: 5A *How organised are you?* vocabulary extension (phrasal verbs), page 131, Instructions page 100

Language focus 1 (PAGES 49–50)
Future plans and intentions

See *Teacher's tips: using a discovery approach in the teaching of grammar* on page 15.

> **Language focus 1: notes on the approach to future forms**
>
> - *will* versus *going to*: we have chosen not to contrast *will* for 'spontaneous decisions' with *going to* for 'plans' for several reasons. Research suggests that *will* is the most common way of talking about the future, and that the most common use of *will* is the one described here. *Will* for 'spontaneous decisions' is far less frequent. When it does occur, it is often in the communicative context of 'offers'

or 'on the spot' responses. This has therefore been dealt with separately in Module 7 within the context of polite social behaviour.

- **Present Continuous versus *going to***: students may find the difference between these two forms difficult to see. This is partly because there is a genuine overlap: *going to* can almost always be used instead of the Present Continuous. However, Present Continuous cannot be used where there is just a vague intention, there must be some kind of arrangement. For example: *You're going to start phoning travel agents in the next week or two* cannot be put into the Present Continuous.

1 Get students to underline the verb forms used and ask what the three forms are. All three forms should be familiar, but it may be useful to remind students briefly of the following points:

- contraction of *will* (*'ll*) and *will not* (*won't*)
- the difference in form between Present Continuous and *going to* (with *going to* the main verb is in the infinitive)

> **ANSWERS**
> a it'll take   b you're doing   c You're going to start phoning

2 Explain or translate the following: *to predict, to be inevitable, an intention*.

> **ANSWERS**
> *will*; *going to*; Present Continuous
>
> Other examples are:
> **will:** *That'll give you time to read it through; you know you probably won't even get down to it; you know it'll take you at least thirty minutes; you definitely won't be late*
> **going to:** *you're going to pack after that*
> **Present Continuous:** *you're going out tonight*

3 Discuss this with the whole class. Check the meaning of the verbs and phrases, especially *about to* and *due to*. Point out which constructions are followed by a gerund and which are followed by an infinitive with examples. Highlight the following:

- the use of prepositions with these verbs / phrases.
- that *due to* can be used either with an infinitive (as in the example given) or without (*You're due at a meeting ...*).

module 5

> **ANSWERS**
> you **intend to do** it tomorrow; you're **due to be** at a meeting; you'**d like to have** enough time to; you'**re thinking of going to** Greece
> Other constructions you could mention are:
> I've decided to ...; I hope to ... / I'm hoping to ...; I want to ... ; I'm planning on + gerund

PRACTICE

1 [5.1] **a)** Check the meaning of *a domestic task* and *good intention*. Emphasise that students should just write notes. Play the cassette, pausing after each instruction to give students time to write.

b) As students write the complete sentences, circulate and help with any extra vocabulary they need. Note down any errors with the use of the future forms for analysis and correction later on.

2 [5.2] Check the meaning of: *to sort out your notes, to be lazy, I can't afford it*. As well as providing reinforcement of the future forms, this exercise is intended to give students practice in listening closely, and breaking down strings of words effectively. It is therefore important to get them to work out the answers for themselves by re-playing the cassette as often as necessary, rather than giving the answers yourself.

> **ANSWERS**
> a really want to go / probably won't go / 'll probably go
> b 'll probably watch / 'll phone
> c 'm going to sort
> d 'm not going to do / 'm going to lie
> e 're thinking of going
> f 'd like to have

Pronunciation

[5.3] Play the cassette or read out the phrases, pausing to highlight likely problems, and drilling them as you go along.
- the dark /l/ in *I'll*: to help students make this sound, encourage them to insert an extra /j/ (y) sound /aɪl/ > /aɪ-y-l/
- the vowel sound in *won't*, which may be difficult to distinguish from *want*.

3 **a)** Focus students' attention on the photo and get them to speculate about what they think the people's plans are. Check the meaning of: *vague plans, a business studies course, personnel management, to study law / a lawyer, a glossy magazine, to be desperate to do something, auditions, the odd one out*. Students work individually or in pairs before checking with the whole class.

> **ANSWERS**
> 1 him to become   2 to go   3 happen   4 to work
> 5 to be   6 to work   7 to go   8 to become
> 9 to be   10 of going   11 to miss

b) Before starting the interview get students to make notes under the headings about themselves to make sure that they have something to say. Pre-teach / write up useful questions such as:
– *Have you got any holiday plans?*
– *Are you planning to buy anything soon?*
– *Have you got any special plans for your career?*
– *Have you got any other long-term plans?*
As students interview each other, circulate and supply any vocabulary they need. Note down examples of correct and incorrect use of future forms for analysis and correction.

c) This could be set for homework. Ensure that at least one person is writing about each member of the class.

ADDITIONAL PRACTICE

Workbook: *will* and *won't*, page 32; *going to*, page 32; Present Continuous for future arrangements, page 33; Other ways of talking about the future, page 33

Wordspot (PAGE 51)

work

See *Teacher's tips: working with lexis* on pages 12–13.

1 Emphasise that not all of the sentences have a word missing, and that not all of the prepositions in the box are needed.

> **ANSWERS**
> Sentences b, d and j are correct (sentence j could also read *worked out*).
> Words missing are: c to work <u>in</u>   e worked <u>as</u>
> f <u>off</u> work   g <u>out of</u> work   h <u>from</u> work   i work <u>out</u>

2 Get students to copy the diagram into their notebooks to allow space to write in the phrases. Drill the phrases before getting students to work in pairs. Check answers with the whole class.

> **ANSWERS**
> (sections in brackets)
> *work of art* (e);   *office work* (a);   *work for a company* (b);   *doesn't work* (c);   *work as* (b);   *off work* (b);   *out of work* (b);   *get home from work* (b);   *work out how much it cost* (e);   *work out perfectly* (d)

3 Check the meaning and pronunciation of: *a funeral* /ˈfjuːnərəl/, *to complain* /təkəmˈpleɪn/, *unemployment* /ˌʌnɪmˈplɔɪmənt/, *a plumber* /ˈplʌmə/, *to be ridiculous* /rɪˈdɪkjələs/. Students work in pairs before checking answers with the whole class.

43

module 5

> **ANSWERS**
> a 3 b 8 c 6 d 7 e 4 f 1 g 5 h 2

4 Give an example yourself first with a good student so that students understand what they have to do.

5 Prepare in advance by copying the diagram on to a poster-sized sheet of paper. Add new phrases as you check answers to Exercise 2.

Vocabulary (PAGE 52)

Training and work

See *Teacher's tips: making the most of the Mini-dictionary* on page 14.

1 Students work individually or in pairs. Emphasise that there isn't necessarily a right or wrong answer, but encourage them to say why they think they are positive or negative. At the feedback stage, check the meaning and pronunciation of: *challenging* /ˈtʃæləndʒɪŋ/, *talented* /ˈtæləntəd/, *qualifications* /ˌkwɒləfəˈkeɪʃəns/, *responsibilities* /rɪˌspɒnsəˈbɪlətis/, *opportunities* /ˌɒpəˈtjuːnətis/, *physically* /ˈfɪzɪkli/.

> ***Training and work:* additional language notes**
>
> Students may have difficulty distinguishing between *training*, *qualifications* and *skills*.
>
> - *training* is education / courses aimed at teaching you to do a particular job (*training to be a doctor*, *teacher-training*, etc.)
> - *qualifications* are exams / certificates you get, especially those which enable you to do a particular job
> - *skills* is a general word for abilities you have in a particular area; you get them from training courses, experience or have them naturally. This word is often used in the plural – *people skills*, *management skills*, *communication skills*, etc.

> **ANSWERS**
> **positive:** well-paid, challenging, talented, special training and qualifications, good people skills, job satisfaction, a lot of variety, a lot of responsibility, a lot of opportunities
> **negative:** badly-paid, stressful, work long hours
> **positive or negative:** hard work physically, work shifts, a lot of responsibility

2 Check that students understand what the jobs are before doing the exercise individually or in pairs. Check answers with the whole class and discuss possible answers for Exercise 3 at the same time.

ADDITIONAL ACTIVITY

RB **Resource bank:** 5C *Vocabulary extension* (talking about work and training), page 134, Instructions page 100

Listening (PAGE 52)

Working in something different

1 Focus students' attention on the photos and check that they know what each job is. Check the meaning of *to be suited to* a job. Students discuss the questions in pairs.

2 [5.4] Emphasise that students only have to identify who is speaking at this stage. If your class have difficulties with listening, pause after each extract and work out together who is talking.

> **ANSWERS**
> 1 Pat – bank manager
> 2 Dave – nursery school teacher
> 3 Debbie – engineer
> 4 Kevin – house husband

3 Before playing the cassette again, collect all the information students remember on the board. Listen again and add further information to the questions.

> **ANSWERS**
> a) **bank manager:** she was persuaded by her boss to take her job seriously. She did a course at evening school to get qualifications
> **nursery school teacher:** no real plans for the future
> **engineer:** interested in science at school and applied for apprenticeship in electrical engineering
> b) **bank manager:** variety, dealing with people, challenging
> **nursery school teacher:** job satisfaction, watching children develop, very stressful, no career structure or chances of promotion
> **engineer:** gets on with people at work
> **house husband:** spending time with kids, hard work

4 Check that students understand the questions / statements. Students discuss the questions in groups whilst you circulate and supply any vocabulary needed.

44

Language focus 2 (PAGE 53)

Future clauses with *if*, *when*, etc.

See *Teacher's tips: using a discovery approach in the teaching of grammar* on page 15.

Mini-task

Focus on the examples, and show in note form what they should do (sister – professional dancer, Danuta – USA, etc.) Do not highlight time clauses at this point, as this will give you a better understanding of students' existing knowledge. Students work in pairs. Circulate, supplying any vocabulary and noting down errors with time clauses for correction after the Analysis.

Check the meaning of: *to apply for a job, to be fully qualified, to fail an exam, to retire, to do something professionally*. Students discuss the answers briefly in pairs, before checking with the whole class.

> **ANSWERS**
> a Pat   b Dave   c Kevin   d Debbie   e Anita

Language focus 2: alternative suggestion

If you want to do the *Language focus* without doing the listening first, focus students' attention on the photos and check that everyone understands what jobs the people do. Put the students in groups and get them to discuss briefly the following questions:

- Are they surprised to see any of these people doing these jobs?
- What do they think the advantages and disadvantages of each job are?
- What future prospects / possibilities do these people have?

Feedback briefly with the whole class, then proceed with the *Language focus* as normal.

Analysis

1 Do the first example with the class and then get students to do the other examples individually before checking answers together.

> **ANSWERS**
> a retires; I'll probably apply
> b finishes; might try
> c starts; I'll go back
> d I'll be; I fail
> e I can't train; I've got

2 Discuss the questions with the whole class.

> **ANSWERS**
> The sentences refer to the future, but the verb after these words is in the present.
> Note: this is probably different in the students' own language – with a monolingual group it may be worth contrasting this with examples from their own language.

3 Students discuss this in pairs before checking with the whole class.

> **ANSWERS**
> A future form is used in the 'main' clause (*will* is most common here, but *going to* and modal forms are also used).

PRACTICE

1 Students work individually or in pairs before checking answers with the whole class.

> **ANSWERS**
> a will get / doesn't have   b becomes / will be
> c goes / will probably feel   d will not earn / finishes   e leaves / will really miss   f becomes / won't work

2 This exercise can be either spoken or written. Give some more personalised examples of your own first.

ADDITIONAL PRACTICE

RB **Resource bank:** 5B *The great diamond robbery* (future clauses with *if*, *when*, etc.), pages 132–133, Instructions page 100

Workbook: Future clauses with *if*, *when*, etc., page 34

Part B Task

See *Teacher's tips: making tasks work* on pages 8–9 and *Responding to learners' individual language needs* on pages 10–11.

Preparation for task (PAGE 54)

1 Focus attention on the advertisement and get students to scan it to answer the questions. Ask if students would be interested in applying to this agency. Check the meaning of: *employment agency, to recruit, staff, nanny, an applicant, an application form, an interview, suitable*. Discuss answers with the whole class.

module 5

> **ANSWERS**
> *Horizons Unlimited* is an employment agency offering jobs abroad – nannies, office staff, etc.

2 Students read the information and answer the questions in pairs. Ask the first question and get students to predict the skills and duties required before checking in the information. Once students have read the job description, spend some time discussing which skills are essential for the job, and which are useful. Check / Pre-teach the following items of vocabulary which occur both in the job description and the candidates' notes: *remote, computer skills, a driving licence, a chambermaid, salary, to be absent on business, to have excellent references, to be enthusiastic, to be capable, to be efficient, to have a very strong personality*.

> **ANSWERS**
> a assistant hotel manager / part-time childminder
> b *the duties are:* to organise hotel reception / office, to organise part-time staff, to help in kitchen / bar when necessary, to look after owner's children when he is away, to look after premises, organise cleaners
> c essential skills: hotel experience, computer skills, good French
> d useful skills: good skiing, driving licence, other languages (especially German and English)

3 [5.5] Introduce Marion O'Neill and Monsieur Bertrand, and check that students know who they are. Focus students' attention on Marion's notes. Tell them that they will listen to Marion talking to Monsieur Bertrand, and emphasise that they only have to listen for his answers to her questions. Get students to compare answers in pairs, before going over the answers as a class.

> **ANSWERS**
> *How old are children?* – thirteen and eight
> *Why?* – person would feel isolated, wants them to take children to school
> *What will the person have to do?* – drive them to school, pick them up, give them supper, look after them at weekend
> *How important is this?* – quite important because of the children, but not as important as finding someone nice

> **Preparation for task: alternative suggestions**
>
> a *If you are short of time:* briefly introduce the job vacancy yourself, summarising the skills and qualities needed. You could also omit the listening stage, although it is important to tell the students the age of Monsieur Bertrand's children. Then move straight on to a discussion of the candidates.
>
> b *If you have short lessons:* spread the task over two lessons – the preparation stage could be done in one lesson, with students looking at the candidates for homework and deciding on their good and bad points. The task itself, together with feedback could then be done the next lesson.

Task (PAGE 55)

1 a) Divide students into groups of five and allocate each student a candidate. (If you don't have the correct number of students, put weaker students together in pairs, or allocate strong students two candidates). Give students a few minutes to read the notes at the back of the book, and help with any comprehension problems.

b) Explain that the task is to find the best candidate for the job. Ask students to make notes about the strengths and weaknesses of their candidate.

2 Give students 5–10 minutes to think about what they will say about their candidate. Get them to close their books and remember, rather than reading the notes.

3 Students work in their groups again. It may be useful to appoint a chairperson for each group, to ensure that everyone gets a chance to speak. Emphasise that they need to listen and make notes about each candidate, asking questions about anything that is not clear. As they discuss the candidates, circulate and make notes of errors / useful language for analysis and correction later on.

4 Give students a few minutes to think about how they will express their decision to the class. Each group presents their decision to the rest of the class. If there is disagreement (and enough time) encourage further discussion to see if the class can agree on the one most suitable candidate.

> **Task: alternative suggestions**
>
> a *Role play:* the task can be done as a role play with interviewers and candidates, as follows:
>
> - Divide the class into two groups, the interviewers and the five candidates. The interviewers should make a list of questions they want to ask the candidates, while the five candidates read and memorise the information at the back of the book. They should spend time thinking about how they can express these personal details in English.
>
> - The candidates are then interviewed one by one (you may need to set a time limit of five minutes per candidate).
>
> - The interviewers then discuss who they think is most suitable for the job. Whilst this is going on, the five candidates can either 'drop' their roles and join in the discussion, or remain in their roles and be available to answer any further questions that interviewers might have.

If you have a larger class, the groups of interviewers and candidates can be duplicated and final decisions on the best candidate compared.

b *Using the feedback / correction stage of the task for revision purposes:* this task brings together much of the language that students have studied in the first five modules of this book. Whilst performing the task, students will almost certainly need to use: present tenses, past tenses, Present Perfect Simple and Continuous, comparatives and superlatives, future time clauses.

Collect errors in these five categories, as a lead into a revision session. Copy these onto the board and give them to students to correct in pairs. Refer students to the appropriate rules and *Language summary* for revision where necessary.

Real life 1 (PAGE 56)

Writing a covering letter

1 Focus students' attention on the photo of Louisa and make sure that everyone understands what a CV (*curriculum vitae*) and covering letter (*a letter you write enclosing something else*) are. It would be useful to contrast this briefly with the conventions for this in their own language if these are different.

ANSWERS
Louisa's address goes in the top right hand corner, with the date below it. The name and address of the person she is writing to go below it on the left. This is always the rule for formal letters in English.

2 Ask students to guess what they think she might write in her covering letter. Check the meaning of: *an advertisement, to be available, to be qualified, to be bilingual*. Students order the letter individually or in pairs before checking answers with the whole class. Point out / elicit any differences between a formal letter in English and the students' own language.

ANSWERS
h, g, f, a, i, b, e, c, d, j
The letter will probably contain three paragraphs.

Writing a formal letter: alternative suggestion for controlled practice stage

- As you are checking the answers to Exercise 2, write the letter in order onto the board. Students close their books and read through the whole letter on the board, aloud or silently, trying to remember the important phrases.
- Rub one of the important phrases out of the letter, replacing it with dots. Get a student to read out the letter, supplying the missing phrase at the appropriate point.
- Rub out another phrase and get another student to read it out as before, supplying the missing phrase. Repeat this until the letter disappears and is replaced by dotted lines.
- When the letter has been reduced to no more than a few prompts, get students to write it out from memory, either in pairs or individually.

3 Discuss the questions with the whole class.

ANSWERS
Dear Sir or Madam; I am writing in reply to ...; I enclose ... (as requested); I look forward to hearing from you soon ...; Yours faithfully,

Point out that if you write the person's name (*Mrs Garcia*) you should then finish the letter *Yours sincerely*. Also, point out that it is not acceptable to use contracted forms in formal letters.

4 Refer students back to the job advertisement on page 54 and ask them to guess what other jobs the agency might have. Students can invent experience if necessary.

Real life 2 (PAGE 57)

Making a formal telephone call

1 [5.6] Explain that Louisa has had a job interview, but has not heard whether or not she has got the job. She is phoning to find out what is happening. Ask students to predict what she might say. Play the cassette and discuss the questions in class.

ANSWERS
a She is phoning because she has not heard from Marion O'Neill since her interview.
b She is going to pass on the message and ask Marion O'Neill to call back.

2 Get students to guess what the missing phrases might be before playing the cassette. Stop the cassette after each phrase for students to tell you the exact words used.

ANSWERS
1 I'd like to speak to
2 Just a moment. I'll put you through.
3 Could I speak to
4 Can I ask who's calling?
5 Can I take a message, or would you like her to call you back?
6 I'm just phoning because
7 I'll pass on the message and ask her to call you back
8 you can leave a message on the answerphone

47

module 5

9 Can I just take your number, please?
10 thanks for calling

Pronunciation

1 [5.7] Play the cassette, stopping after each phrase and pointing out the features of connected speech marked on the page. Point out that these help people to speak quickly, and that, even if they don't want to copy this themselves, it is important to practise understanding it.

2 [5.8] Get students to practise saying the phrases, either providing a model yourself, or re-playing the cassette. Do not spend too long on this if students are having difficulty in reproducing the linking and weak forms – even passive awareness of these features of connected speech is very valuable.

> **Making a formal telephone call: alternative suggestion for controlled practice**
>
> - Copy the dialogue onto slips of card – each line should be on a different card, and ideally each speaker should be a different colour. Either make large cards to stick on the board big enough for the whole class to read, or small cards, a separate set for each pair of students.
> - After Exercise 2 get students to close their books and give / show them the set of cards with the dialogue mixed up. Students put the dialogue in order using the cassette to check if necessary.
> - Get students to read aloud the dialogue from the cards – you could focus on the features of pronunciation above as you are going along.
> - Leaving the dialogue in the correct order, turn over one or more of the cards, preferably ones which include some of the useful phrases for making a formal telephone call. Get a pair of students to read it aloud, supplying the missing phrases. Repeat the process until students gradually memorise the dialogue. Correct pronunciation, focusing especially on the features of connected speech highlighted in the pronunciation section.

3 [5.9] Introduce the situation and get students to guess the sort of thing that each speaker might say. Divide the class into As and Bs. Focus students' attention on the flow-chart, and read through the instructions, checking that they understand them. *With a less confident group*, elicit a possible dialogue first as a class, then get them to practise it in pairs. *With stronger groups*, get students to try it in pairs straightaway. Circulate, supplying / correcting phrases as necessary, or noting down errors for work later on.

Play the cassette at the end for students to compare with their own conversations. Stop the cassette at appropriate points to correct errors students have made.

Do you remember?

ANSWERS

2   a if you work *shifts*, sometimes you work during the day, sometimes at night, but your hours change; if you work long hours, you work a lot of hours per day / night, probably starting early in the morning and finishing late at night / in the evening.
    b you acquire job *skills* through training and experience; *qualifications* are exams you have passed after completing a course of study.
    c if something is *challenging*, it is difficult but also interesting and worth doing; if something is *stressful*, it causes you worry and problems.
    d if a job offers plenty of *variety*, it is interesting because it means you will be doing different things; if a job offers plenty of *opportunities*, it offers you the chance in the future to do something you want or which will be good for you.

3 The wrong sentence is: *As soon as I will see her, I ask her.* The corrected sentence is: *As soon as I see her, I'll ask her.*

4   a Thanks for calling.
    b Just a moment – I'll put you through.
    c I'll pass the message on and ask her to call you back.
    d Can I just take your number, please?
    e I'd like to speak to Susan Daniels, please.
    f Can you leave a message on the answerphone?
    g I'm afraid she's on the other line.
    h I'll just see if she's available.

5 pack your suitcase; save up for a new car; apply for a new job; book your holiday in advance; fill in an application form; put your money in the bank; work out how much something costs

6   a of   b after   c to   d in / to   e off
    f to / from   g out   h from

48

module 6

Part A Language

Vocabulary and listening (PAGE 59)

Television

See *Teacher's tips: making the most of the Mini-dictionary* on page 14.

1 Students discuss the questions in groups or with the whole class. In addition to discussing the questions, students can make a list of types of programmes in groups, including all the words in Exercise 2 and: *a documentary, the news, the weather forecast, a drama series, cartoons, thrillers, sit coms* (= 'situation comedies'), *detective stories*.

2 Check the meaning and pronunciation of: *advertisement* /ədˈvɜːrtɪsmənt/, *campaign* /kæmˈpeɪn/, *coverage* /ˈkʌvərɪdʒ/. Students work individually before comparing answers in groups.

3 [6.1] Emphasise that students only need to identify the type of programme being discussed.

ANSWERS
Speaker 1: interviews with politicians; Speaker 2: government advertising campaigns; Speaker 3: murder mysteries / thrillers; Speaker 4: children's programmes which include violence

4 Ask students if they understand the basic meaning of the adjectives, but do not explain the difference between the *-ed* and *-ing* forms. If students cannot hear which form is being used, re-play the cassette.

ANSWERS
Speaker 1: annoyed; Speaker 2: shocking; Speaker 3: bored / annoying; Speaker 4: interesting / worried

Language focus 1 (PAGE 60)

-ed / -ing adjectives

See *Teacher's tips: using a discovery approach in the teaching of grammar* on page 15.

Language focus 1: notes on the approach to *-ed / -ing* forms

These adjectives have been put before the passive in this module in the hope that this will help students understand the passive better, since the *-ed* adjectives are, in origin, passive forms. It might be useful to point out that these adjectives are all formed from verbs: *I am depressed* means *something depresses me*.

It is probably best not to mention the passive explicitly at this point, however, unless students ask.

Analysis

1 Students work in pairs matching the adjectives.

ANSWERS
The man is *depressed*, the news on the television / in the newspaper is *depressing*.

2 Ask if anyone can explain the difference between the *-ed* and *-ing* forms of the adjectives. (With mono-lingual classes, this may be best done through translation.)

ANSWERS
-ed (past participle) adjectives describe how the person feels; *-ing* adjectives describe the thing that makes them feel like this.
Point out that *-ed* adjectives are in fact past participles – adjectives like *upset* are not exceptions, they are simply formed from irregular verbs.

PRACTICE

1 Check the meaning of the adjectives by describing typical situations in which you might feel *disappointed / embarrassed*, etc. Put students in pairs to think of other adjectives, and remind them of those that came up in the listenings on page 59. Other adjectives to mention which are high frequency are: *frightened / frightening, surprised / surprising*. If your class is of a high level: *amazed / amazing, fascinated / fascinating, irritated / irritating, disgusted / disgusting, horrified / horrifying*.

2 Students work individually or in pairs before checking answers with the whole class.

ANSWERS
a interesting / shocked   b pleased / worrying
c exciting / disappointed
d interested / embarrassing

3 Focus on the example and the suggested responses, highlighting the fact that:

- *I'd (I would)* is used because you are imagining this situation / it is hypothetical
- the *-ing* adjectives are very often used in the construction *I find ... boring / annoying*, etc.

49

module 6

Check the meaning of: *a thriller, a famine, third-world, a chat / to chat*. Students discuss their responses in groups, then do brief feedback as a class. For further controlled practice students could write sentences about their responses, starting: *In this situation, I'd feel ...* or *I'd find it ...* .

ADDITIONAL PRACTICE

Workbook: *-ed / -ing* adjectives, page 38

Reading (PAGES 60–61)

1 Put students in groups to think of possible topics for news stories (*disasters, elections, wars,* etc.) Circulate and supply any vocabulary they need.

2 Tell students they are going to read some real-life news items from English newspapers. Check the meaning of: *a glazier, to admit to a crime, to plead guilty to a crime, to set fire to, a natural disaster, thunder, a storm, flooding, a preacher, to beg, to be injured, to sneeze, an explosive device, to be operated on*.
Students match the explanations to the headlines in pairs. (As they are doing this it would be useful to copy the headlines onto the board for the next exercise.)

3 Tell students to close their books and look at the headlines on the board. In groups students try and predict what the articles are about. Feed back their suggestions to the whole class, noting them down underneath each headline on the board, without saying whether or not they are correct. Students read the articles, then go through the suggestions, saying whether they are true or false.

> **ANSWERS**
> Polish fireman and glazier – 3; natural disaster – 6; lucky escape – 2; man unhappy with love life – 5; serious nose-problem – 4; death of a very old man – 1

4 Go through the true / false questions with the whole class, eliminating those that have already been answered in Exercise 3. Put students in pairs to find the remaining answers.

> **ANSWERS**
> a T b T c F d T e T f F

5 Students discuss the questions in groups or with the whole class.

Language focus 2 (PAGES 62–63)
Passive forms

See *Teacher's tips: using a discovery approach in the teaching of grammar* on page 15.

Mini-task

Give students a few minutes to think about the mini-task and ask about any vocabulary they need. They are likely to need the passive, but do not highlight it specifically yet. If they ask for it, provide phrases without giving explanations. Put students into groups to compare lists. Circulate, supplying vocabulary, and making notes about student errors. If students do use the passive while performing the mini-task, consider:

– *whether this is limited to just a few common phrases or are they able to use it convincingly?*
– *are they forming the passive tenses correctly?*

If they do not use the passive, note down examples of where the passive could / should have been used for correction after the Analysis.

1 Students work individually or in pairs before checking answers with the whole class. This a good point at which to establish the basic form of the passive (*to be* + past participle). You do not need to go into the different tenses at this point as these are dealt with in the *Analysis*.

> **ANSWERS**
> a shot b (was carried) c have killed
> d (have been killed) e crashed f (were injured)
> g (are expected)

Analysis

Note: we have used the term 'doer' in preference to 'agent' because it seems more transparent, but if your students are likely to be familiar with the term 'agent' already, make it clear that this is what is meant.

1 Check (by translation if necessary) that students understand what the subject of a verb is. Write out the first two sentences, underlining the subject and verb in each. The 'doer' (agent) of the verb can be shown with arrows, like this:

   a vet   shot   the tiger
   (subject) (verb) (object)

   the injured man was carried to safety
         (subject)   (verb)

In the second sentence, the subject is not the 'doer' – the 'doer' is unknown.

If students are having problems with this concept it might be useful to go through a few more of the sentences, identifying the subject and 'doer' in a similar way.

50

_____ module 6

> **ANSWERS**
> 1 The vet is the subject in sentence a) and the injured man is the subject in sentence b). The vet is the 'doer' of the action (because this is an active sentence), the injured man is not the 'doer' of the action, we don't know who carried him (because this is a passive sentence).

2 Read through each explanation with the whole class before asking students to find other examples.

> **ANSWERS**
> a f)   b g)
>
> Note: inevitably these explanations overlap, but sometimes one can be seen more clearly than the other, so it is useful to have both.

3 Remind students of the basic form of the passive verb, then ask them to identify the tenses one by one, contrasting them with a similar active sentence, for example:
they <u>are expected</u> to survive / doctors expect them to survive
they <u>were taken</u> to hospital / an ambulance took them to hospital
70 people <u>have been killed</u> / <u>floods have killed 70 people</u>.
Point out also:
– the formation of the negative and question form in each case, particularly in the Present Perfect, where students have two auxiliary verbs to manipulate.
– the fact that contractions can be used with the passive as with other verb forms.
– the fact that the *be* + past participle rule for forming the passive is completely regular.
Students can guess how *will* or *can* sentences are formed in the passive. (For example: *someone will help him* ... > *he will be helped* ...; *you can use it to* ... > *it can be used to* ... . However, it is probably best not to extend this to continuous forms at this stage, as these are complex to form and relatively infrequent.

4 Students work in pairs looking back at the article.

PRACTICE

1 **a)** [6.2] Introduce the idea of a general knowledge quiz and check the meaning of: *to be assassinated*, *to be invented by*, *to be discovered by*. This quiz can be done in pairs, individually or as a team game. If you do it as a team game, you may prefer to play the relevant section of the cassette after each question / answer rather than waiting until the end to check the answers all together. After checking the answers, get students to underline the passive forms in each of the questions.

> **ANSWERS**
> 1 c   2 c   3 b   4 c   5 c   6 b   7 c   8 a (*true at publication date; the first time will be in 2002*)

> **Pronunciation**
> Tell students that they are going to listen to the answers again and to focus on the pronunciation of the passive forms. Write up the example sentence and ask students which words are most important (which are stressed). Underline the stressed syllables: *The <u>Statue</u> of <u>Liberty</u> was <u>built</u> in <u>France</u>.*
>
> Play the first sentence, and ask students if *were* sounds strong or weak. Practise the sentences with the weak form, 'back-chaining' from the stressed main verb.

b) Tell students that each question in the quiz must contain a passive phrase. Remind students of the passive phrases used in the quiz they have just done and check the meaning and pronunciation of the words / phrases in the box. Put students into groups of four or five and give them a number of questions to write. Put up categories of questions for them to include (*sport, music, art, writers, films, inventions,* etc.). Suggest that students follow the same format as the questions in the book (a question with three answers or a statement with three possible endings). Set a time limit of 10–15 minutes.

c) Students read out their questions in teams. Allocate points for each question answered correctly.

2 Check the meaning of: *a judge, a courtroom, to sentence, a prisoner, a tunnel, a burglar, an attack, to rescue, a towel*. Students read the stories quickly to see what happened in each one. Feed back briefly with the whole class, before getting them to complete the gaps. Point out that they should think about the *tense of the verb* as well as whether it is passive or active.

> **ANSWERS**
> 1 spent   2 came   3 were sentenced
> 4 were returned   5 was attacked   6 was talking
> 7 heard   8 phoned   9 were contacted
> 10 was sent   11 was rescued   12 happened
> 13 is stolen

> **Additional suggestion: working with passives as 'set' phrases**
>
> The passive is very often found in set phrases, for example: *it is made in ..., he was injured ..., it is used for ..., it was held in ...,* etc. Students may need to understand the passive from a grammatical point of view in order to generate sentences of their own, but much of the passive can be activated in these 'chunks'. To help reinforce this idea:

51

module 6

a drill them as passive phrases. This may be more effective if you drill just the phrase (*it's used for ...*).

b write them up as passive phrases rather than in the infinitive form (*to be injured* rather than *to injure*).

c get students to read back through the news stories, quiz and crime stories, and make a list of typical passive phrases, divided into these topic areas:

crimes / justice: for example, *to be stolen, to be attacked, to be killed, to be assassinated*

accidents / disasters: for example, *to be injured, to be made homeless, to be rescued*

science / inventions: for example, *to be invented by, to be discovered by, to be designed by*

arts / creativity: for example, *to be written / composed / painted / directed by*

Make a wall-poster, listing groups like those above and adding to them when appropriate.

ADDITIONAL PRACTICE

RB Resource bank: 6A *Passive dominoes* (passive forms), page 135; 6B *Vocabulary extension* (passive verbs often in the news), page 136, Instructions page 100

Workbook: The passive, pages 39–40

Wordspot (PAGE 63)

by

See *Teacher's tips: working with lexis* on pages 12–13.

1 Explain that there is a word missing from each of the sentences. Emphasise that in two of the sentences the word missing is *on* not *by*. Students work individually or in pairs before checking answers.

ANSWERS
b *by* phone   c *on* foot   d *by* seven o'clock
e *by* fifteen per cent   f *by* selling   g *by* the door
h *on* purpose   i *by* car exhaust fumes
j *by* Debussy   k *by* himself   l *by* accident

2 After checking the answers, draw a diagram onto the board with the categories listed, and ask students where each example with *by* in the exercise goes.

Wordspot (*by*): additional suggestion

Write up the following additional phrases, and get students to add them to the appropriate category: *gone down by twenty per cent, by cheque, increased by fifty per cent, by next week, by e-mail, multiplied by, by taxi, divided by, (to make money) by working hard, by Shakespeare, by the river, to be injured by, by fax, to be invented by.*

3 Put students in pairs and direct them to the appropriate page at the back of the book. Do the first example for each student together as a class, emphasising the need to use a phrase with *by* in the answer.

Part B Task

See *Teacher's tips: making tasks work* on pages 8–9 and *Responding to learners' individual language needs* on pages 10–11.

Note: in order for students to be able to do the entertainment guide option for the task, it is important to bring in a local entertainment guide / newspaper. This is for information only, and does not need to be in English.

Preparation for task (PAGE 64)

1 Introduce the topic by briefly asking students how often they listen to the radio, which stations / programmes they prefer and if there are any stations / programmes that they particularly dislike. Students work in pairs before checking answers with the whole class.

ANSWERS
a advert   b review   c phone-in
d entertainment guide

2 [6.5] Explain to the students they will hear four radio extracts, but they will not understand everything – they simply have to identify the programme type.

ANSWERS
a entertainment guide   b advert   c phone-in
d review

3 Read through the questions, then re-play the cassette. Students work in pairs before checking answers.

ANSWERS
a jazz, heavy metal, soul   b theatre   c thriller
d a rock concert   e a film / negative

Task (PAGE 65)

1 Talk through the two alternatives and give students two minutes to make their decision. For each option students can work either individually or in pairs.

Go through the instructions for each option with the whole class. Focus on the *Useful language* section for each option, and get students to read it through, and ask you about any phrases they do not know, any pronunciation problems, etc.

Give students at least fifteen minutes to prepare their reviews / guides. Make it clear that they do not need to write out a script for the review / guide, but make notes to remind themselves of what to say. (If, however, you have a very shy / unconfident class, it may help if they write it out first.) Circulate, supplying vocabulary and making a note of any useful phrases / errors to analyse later on.

2 If there is enough time, give students at least one opportunity to 'rehearse' their review / guide before presenting it to the rest of the class. This can be done either individually or in pairs – at this point you can feed in some of your corrections / alternative suggestions if appropriate.

Tell students that they are going to present their guides / reviews to the class, and listen to the other students. Ask students to make a note of what they would like to see most and any questions they would like to ask. As they give their talks, make a note of further errors for analysis and correction.

Task: alternative suggestions

a *Collecting your own radio extracts for the Preparation for task stage*: if you have access to an English-language radio station, compile your own set of extracts, including reviews of up-to-the-minute films, concerts, etc. Bear these points in mind:
– extracts should be no longer than about 30 seconds, with a maximum of 4–6 in total.
– include at least one or two reviews, etc. to provide a model for the task mixed in with other items, such as news and weather forecasts.
– include extracts with stylistic clues, which will help students to identify the programme type without necessarily understanding much (for example with a phone-in).
– set very simple tasks. The first task could simply be to identify from a list of possibles what type of programme it is. If you set comprehension questions, these should be very general (*Is the weather going to be good? Did the caller win the competition*, etc.).

b *If you are short of time / cannot fit the whole task into one lesson*: do the *Preparation for the task* in one lesson, and allow ten minutes at the end for students to decide which option they want to choose. Give students plenty of possible options, as well as suggestions about where to find any necessary information.
If you have time, give students a few minutes to start the task in class, but set the preparation of the review / entertainment guide for homework. (It will motivate students more to know that they are going to give their reviews or make a radio programme in the next lesson).

c *If a large number of students choose the entertainment guide option*: there is a danger of this becoming repetitive. To avoid this give students specific areas to look at (films, sporting events, etc.). Alternatively, give more specific profiles – entertainment for families with children, etc.

d *Alternatives for the 'presentation to the class' stage:* this is an opportunity to try a formal style of presentation, in which students stand up in front of the class. For confident, high-level students this is a good way to make the task more challenging. Get students to present their reviews / guides over a few lessons, grouping together similar types of presentation, for example book reviews. If time is short, or you have a large class, the presentations could be done in larger groups of about six students, rather than to the whole class. Alternatively, get students to record their reviews / guides onto a cassette.

e *If you want to make your own student radio programme, follow this procedure:*

• Make it clear that you will be recording students later to make a class radio programme, so they understand what they are preparing for.

• Appoint a presenter to introduce and link together the items. This could be yourself or a strong student, with plenty of initiative. The following tips are useful:
– get the 'presenter' to circulate amongst the rest of the class and make a list of what items to include and in what order.
– give him / her the following useful phrases:
Hello and welcome to ...
Later in the programme we have ...
First of all on today's programme we have ...
And next we have ...
And now for something different ...
And finally ....
– make sure that he / she has an opportunity to rehearse, as with the other students.

• Include other items too, according to the interests of the students. Feed in useful language yourself, as necessary.

• Before recording the programme, give students plenty of opportunity to rehearse what they are going to say. They are bound to be more nervous when recording 'formally'.

• Either record the whole programme in front of the class, or send students (including the presenter) to a different room to record their sections in private. Alternatively, if you have the facilities, you could video the programme.

• Use the finished programme for correction / further language input. The first time students listen, they may be preoccupied – it may be more appropriate to listen a second time for correction work.

module 6

Optional writing

Note: it may be useful to do the Task link on page 66 before setting the writing task.

Make it clear that students can write a review about something different if they wish.

> **Optional writing: structuring a review**
>
> Suggest the following way of structuring a written review:
>
> *Paragraph 1*: start with an interesting lead-in (*... is probably the most terrifying film I have ever seen ...*) followed by factual information (the subject / setting of the film / the stars / director, etc.)
>
> *Paragraph 2*: give more information about the content (details about the story / background, etc.) Emphasise that students do not need to recount the whole story, and point out that stories are often told in the present tense in this kind of review.
>
> *Paragraph 3*: students give their own opinion with reasons (particularly good / bad performances, storyline, scenery, etc.) They could finish by commenting on how successful the film has been / is likely to be, and whether or not they think this is deserved.

Task link (PAGE 66)

'Extreme' adjectives

1 Focus students' attention on the poster, and ask what the film's name is, what they think it is about and who Brad Pick and Jordan Jones are. Check the meaning of: *pirates, screenplay, script, performance*. Discuss answers with the whole class (*the reviews are mixed*).

2 Students work individually or in pairs before checking answers with the whole class.

> **ANSWERS**
> a appalling   b hilarious   c terrific   d ridiculous

3 Look at the example together and check students understand 'extreme' and 'ordinary'. Students do the rest of the exercise individually or in pairs. Check the pronunciation and stress of the 'extreme' adjectives.

> **ANSWERS**
> tragic – sad; furious – angry; fascinated – interested; astonished – surprised; boiling – hot; terrified – frightened; freezing – cold; terrible – very bad

4 Ask students about the type of language used in headlines in their own country. Point out that 'extreme' adjectives are often used in headlines in English newspapers. Check the meaning of: *temperature,* *standards, slugs, interference*. Students work in pairs before checking answers with the whole class.

> **ANSWERS**
> a brilliant   b freezing   c astonished
> d ridiculous   e appalling   f fascinated*
> g furious   h tragic
>
> * note that the preposition changes to *by* here

5 Students work in pairs before discussing / checking answers with the whole class.

> **ANSWERS**
> very / really interested; absolutely / really furious; very / really surprised; absolutely / really fascinated
>
> *Notes:* very cannot be used in front of 'extreme' adjectives; absolutely can only be used in front of 'extreme' adjectives; really can be used with both ordinary and 'extreme' adjectives

ADDITIONAL PRACTICE

RB Resource bank: 6C *Adjective snap* ('extreme' adjectives), page 137, Instructions page 100

Do you remember?

> **ANSWERS**
> 1 children's programmes, cartoons, game shows, soap operas, sports programmes, murder mysteries, thrillers, chat shows, documentaries
>
> 2 a embarrassing
>   b disappointed / depressed / upset
>   c annoying / irritating
>   d excited / surprised / pleased
>   e depressed / upset
>
> 3 built, caused, discovered, elected, found, given, held, hurt, invented, produced, sold, taken
>
> 4 1 has been stolen   2 is believed   3 happened
>   4 were attending   5 were seen
>   6 has been arrested   7 are asking
>   8 has been offered / is being offered
>
> 5 a *to be surprised* (all the others describe negative feelings)
>   b *to be attacked* (all the others are positive actions)
>   c *to be arrested by* (all the others are associated with films / plays)
>   d *to be destroyed by* (all the others are positive actions)
>
> 6 good – fantastic / brilliant; bad – terrible / awful; surprised – astonished; cold – freezing; angry – furious

module 7

Part A Language

Speaking and reading (PAGES 68–69)

See *Teacher's tips: making the most of the Mini-dictionary* on page 14.

1 Check that everyone understands what is meant by *to go out*. Before doing the questionnaire ask students to describe to a partner an occasion when they went out recently and had a very good or a very bad time. Introduce the questionnaire and ask students to predict the type of questions it will ask. Students scan the questionnaire quickly to see if they were right.

2 Check the pronunciation of: *attitude* /ˈætɪtjuːd/, *punctuality* /ˌpʌŋktʃuˈælɪti/, *popular* /ˈpɒpjələ/, *share* /ʃeə/.

3 Circulate, supplying any vocabulary students need. Discuss the questions with the whole class to find out if there were any differences of opinion. With mono-nationality groups, the focus of the discussion should mainly be on regional variations and differences between generations; with multi-nationality groups the focus is more likely to be on international differences.

4 Before reading the results of the questionnaire (if you have not already discussed this), ask students what they know about these customs in other countries. Students read the article and compare answers in pairs or groups, before discussing them with the whole class.

Going out around the world: additional comprehension questions

If you feel students need additional comprehension work, write the following *True / False* questions up:

a Social life around the world is becoming more similar. (*T*)
b American culture does not have much influence in Russia and Japan. (*F*)
c Most young people believe that the man should pay if a couple go out on a date. (*F*)
d Most parents these days treat their sons and daughters equally. (*F*)
e Parents in big cities are normally stricter than those outside. (*F*)
f An evening out tends to start at about the same time all over the world. (*F*)
g Parents in Argentina are particularly worried about the amount of alcohol that their teenage children drink. (*F*)

---

5 Students discuss the questions in groups or with the whole class. Circulate, supplying vocabulary they need.

Vocabulary (PAGE 70)

Social occasions

1 Check students understand the meaning of the social occasions in box A, adding others that are important in the students' culture. Point out that *go round to someone's house* is more common than *visit someone*.

From box B check the pronunciation of the following: *acquaintance* /əˈkweɪntəns/, *bow* /baʊ/, *refuse* /rɪˈfjuːz/, *shake* /ʃeɪk/.

Check they understand the difference between *hold hands*, *shake hands* and *wave*. Students work in pairs before discussing the answers with the whole class. Feed in any phrases needed to describe customs not mentioned in the box, but avoid comparing customs in different countries at this point, as this may pre-empt the task in Part B.

2 Students discuss this in groups or with the whole class.

Language focus 1 (PAGES 70–71)

Polite requests

See *Teacher's tips: using a discovery approach in the teaching of grammar* on page 15.

Mini-task

Make sure that everyone understands what a request *is, and write up a few examples. Students work in pairs answering the questions. Give them a few minutes to do this.*

Feed in any useful language (for example: give me a light / tell me the time), but do not focus explicitly on the request forms themselves, as this will be dealt with later. Instead, pay attention to how well students are already able to use request forms, which should give you a good idea of how much time you need to allow for the Language focus *which follows.*

- *Are students able to use polite forms at all? (If not, you might cut down the number of alternatives in the* Language focus.*)*
- *Do they use just* Can you ...? *and* Could you ...? *or are they already using a wide range of other forms?*

Make a note of any useful errors for correction after the Analysis.

1 Ask students to imagine that they have just arrived in an English-speaking country, and ask them what kind of situations they would find most difficult from a language point of view. If students have experience of this, ask them

55

module 7

what situations they found most difficult. Focus their attention on the pictures and make sure they understand that the white man is the foreign visitor. Students work in pairs predicting what the people are saying in each case.

2 a) [7.1] Before listening, warn students that the questions they hear will be fast, so they need to listen very carefully. Pause the cassette after each question for students to decide who is speaking. If they do not hear the first time, re-play the question rather than repeating it yourself. Discuss possible answers to each question.

ANSWERS
a a – the woman on the right in picture 3; b – the woman standing up in picture 4; c – the man on the left in picture 3; d – the man standing up in picture 5; e – the woman at the television in picture 1; f – the woman at the bar in picture 2; g – the woman at the table on the left in picture 1; h – the man holding the glass in picture 2
b (a number of different answers are possible)

b) [7.2] Play the answers and compare them to the possible answers students thought of.

ANSWERS
See tapescript for recording 2 on page 160.

Analysis

1 Check that students understand the diagram, making sure that they see the difference between asking if you can do something (*a request for permission*) and asking someone else to do something (*a request*). Get students to copy a larger version of the diagram in the *Analysis* into their notebooks. Play recording 7.2 again, while students write what they hear in the correct section of the diagram. As you go over the answers with the whole class, ask students if they can think of any other phrases.

2 It is probably better to do this exercise and the pronunciation as you are checking the answers to Exercise 1, to avoid playing the cassette too many times.

ANSWERS AND LANGUAGE NOTES
1 a *asking if you can do something*: Is it okay if ...?; Do you mind if ...?; Is it alright if ...?; Can I ...?;
answering 'yes': Sure, go ahead!; Sure – here you are!; Yes, of course.
answering 'no': Sorry, but ...; I'm afraid ...;
asking someone else to do something: Can you ...?; Would you mind ... -ing?; Could you possibly ...?; Do you think you could ...?
answering 'yes': Certainly; Of course not; Sure – here you are; Yes, of course.
answering 'no': Sorry, but ...; I'm afraid ...

Point out that:
- *will* / *would* are only used to ask other people to do things; *can* / *could* can be used with both types of request.
- the modal verbs here are followed by an infinitive without *to*, but *Do you mind* / *Would you mind* are followed by either a gerund or an *if* clause.
- strictly speaking with *Do you mind* / *Would you mind* ...?, the answer if you want to say *Yes* is *No* or *Of course not*.

b Common phrases to add to the lists are:
Will you ...?, Would you...?, Could / Can I possibly ...?
Other more polite phrases are:
Do you think you could possibly ...?, Would you be so kind as to ...?
These are not used very commonly, however, and students may sound sarcastic or ridiculous to native speakers if they use them inappropriately.

c *quite casual*: Is it okay if ...?; Is it alright if ...?; Can I ...?; Can you ...?; Sure – go ahead!; Sure – here you are; Sorry, but ...
more polite: Do you mind if ...?; Would you mind ... -ing?; Could you possibly ... ?; Do you think you could ...?; Certainly; Yes, of course; I'm afraid ... ; Of course not.

Pronunciation

1 [7.3] Point out that how you say these polite requests, is just as important as the words you choose. Point out the intonation patterns in the book and get students to copy them. Exaggerate or hum the pattern to help them hear it better if necessary.

2 Students copy the other requests and responses.

PRACTICE

1 Write the example up without the handwritten additions and ask students what is wrong with it. Ask for their suggestions about how to make it more polite, and compare what they say with the corrections in the book. Check the meaning of: *to pass someone something, to bring something, to give someone a light, to give someone a lift, to tell someone the way, to pick something up from somewhere, to lend someone something*.

Students work in pairs or individually, before checking answers. Focus on appropriate levels of formality and remind them that an overly-polite phrase for a simple request can sound sarcastic. Get students to practise the dialogues in pairs, paying attention to intonation.

ANSWERS
a A: <u>Is it okay if</u> I use your scissors?
   B: Yes, <u>sure</u>.
b A: <u>Could you</u> pass me my coat?

56

module 7

B: <u>Of course</u>, here you are.
c A: <u>Could you possibly</u>* lend me £5 until tomorrow?
B: <u>I'm really sorry, but</u>* I haven't got any money with me.

*this is potentially quite embarrassing even between friends, so this very polite language is appropriate

d A: <u>Would you mind bringing</u> the bill, <u>please</u>?
B: Yes, <u>certainly (madam / sir)</u>.
e A: <u>Could you</u> give me a light?
B: <u>I'm afraid</u> my lighter isn't working ... <u>sorry</u>.
f A: If you're going into town, <u>could you possibly</u> give me a lift to the bus stop?*
B: Yes, <u>no problem</u>.

* this depends on who is talking to whom – this polite phrase might be appropriate between colleagues, but unnecessary between family members

g A: <u>Can you</u> tell me the way to the National Gallery?
B: <u>Sorry, I'm afraid</u> I don't know this area very well myself.
h A: <u>Would you mind picking</u> my suit up from the dry-cleaner's while you're at the shops?
B: <u>Sorry, but</u> I don't think I'll be able to carry it – I'll have a lot of other things.

Practice Exercise 1: alternative suggestion

- Copy the lines of the dialogues onto pieces of card (ideally the A parts should be one colour and the B parts another). If you have more than sixteen students you will need to duplicate some dialogues – if you have fewer, omit some of the dialogues.
- Give each student one line of dialogue and ask them whether or not it sounds polite. Tell them to think of a way of making it sound more polite, then to spend a few moments repeating the polite version to themselves to memorise it.
- Students mingle, repeating their line until they find the other half of the dialogue. When they have found their partner, get them to practise their dialogues, making sure they sound polite.
- At this point students can either sit down and work through the other dialogues using the book, or keep swapping cards with each other until they have done all the dialogues. Circulate, correcting intonation. They can act out the dialogues to the rest of the class at the end.

2 Give students a few minutes to think of the requests, circulating to supply any vocabulary they need. Students can either circulate making the requests, or ask each other across the class. This exercise will be more fun if you get students to actually do what they are asked. Insist that if students say 'No', they give a reason why not.

ADDITIONAL ACTIVITY / PRACTICE

RB **Resource bank:** 7A *Vocabulary extension* (informal words and phrases), page 138, Instructions page 101

Workbook: Polite requests, page 44; Ways of making offers, page 45

Language focus 2 (PAGE 72)

will (instant decisions and responses)

See *Teacher's tips: using a discovery approach in the teaching of grammar* on page 15.

Language focus 2: language notes

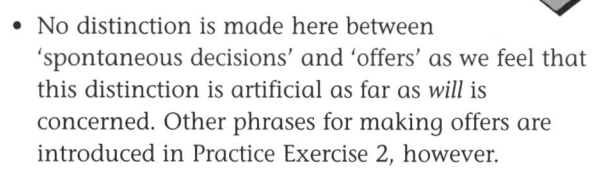

- No distinction is made here between 'spontaneous decisions' and 'offers' as we feel that this distinction is artificial as far as *will* is concerned. Other phrases for making offers are introduced in Practice Exercise 2, however.
- Students are not asked to discriminate between *will* and *going to* as we feel it is more useful to practise common phrases used for 'responding on the spot'. The distinction between *will* and *going to* is mentioned in the *Language summary* on page 146 of the *Students Book*.

1 Focus students' attention on the pictures, and get them to guess what the people are saying. Keep this stage very brief. Check the meaning of: *to be in a meeting, to drive someone mad, to miss a bus*.

2 Students match the dialogues with the pictures and then complete the dialogues in pairs. Before they start, focus briefly on the following conversational phrases: *actually* (for emphasis *not* meaning now), *hang on, never mind, it's no trouble*. After checking answers, get students to practise the dialogues in pairs.

ANSWERS
a 2 b 3 c 1
(possible answers)
a I'll phone him later / I'll be in early tomorrow morning / I'll speak to him tomorrow, etc.
b come and help you / help you / have a look / do it for you, etc.
c walk / call a taxi / phone my father, etc.

Analysis

Students answer the questions individually or in pairs before checking answers in the *Language summary*. As you read the notes in the *Language summary*, emphasise that if we have decided beforehand, *going to* is used.

57

module 7

> **ANSWERS**
> They decide at the moment of speaking in response to what the other person has just said.
> *Will* (almost always contracted to *'ll*) is used.

PRACTICE

1 Check the meaning of: *to chat, to complain, to share, to be stuck with your homework, to pop out*. Students work in pairs before checking answers with the whole class. Correct the pronunciation of *I'll* where necessary.

2 Check the meaning of: *elderly, chaos, to scream, to pour with rain*. Point out that they are all situations in which someone needs help. Draw their attention to the alternative phrases in the speech balloons. Elicit a possible response to situation a) (*Shall I carry your bags?*), and drill the three phrases using this as an example. Note that intonation is very important here in order to sound polite.

> **POSSIBLE ANSWERS**
> (In all cases, the three options *I'll ... / Shall I ...? / Would you like me to ...?* are possible.)
> a I'll carry those bags for you if you like. / I'll help you with those bags.
> b Would you like me to do something to help? Shall I feed the baby? / I'll make lunch for us if you like.
> c I'll go with you if you like. / I'll phone you afterwards to see how it went.
> d I'll have a look at it if you like. / Shall I try and mend it for you? / Would you like me to phone an electrician for you?

3 Tell students to choose three situations from Exercises 1 and 2 and invent a dialogue of their own including at least one offer or response with *I'll*. Remind them of the conversational phrases like *actually*, etc. They can either write the dialogues or work orally. Circulate, supplying any useful language. Get some pairs to act out their dialogues, noting down any useful errors for correction later.

> **Additional activity: making a wall poster**
>
> Amongst the language studied in this module are many 'fixed' or 'semi-fixed' polite phrases which will be useful in a wide range of social situations. It might be useful to make a wall poster or a series of posters to remind students of these phrases. Possible sections are:
>
> **in a restaurant**: *Could you bring me the bill? / Could I have a light? / Could you bring me the menu?*, etc.
> **at someone's house**: *Could you pass me the salt? / Is it alright if I smoke? / Would you like me to open the wine? / Could I use your phone? / I'll do the washing-up.*
> **in the street / on the train, etc.**: *Can you tell me the time? / Could you tell me the way to ...? / Could I get past, please? / Is it alright if I open the window?*
> **helping people**: *I'll do that for you if you like. / I'll lend you ... if you like. / I'll help you with that. / I'll have a look at it for you if you want. / I'll give you a lift.*

ADDITIONAL PRACTICE

Workbook: *will* (instant decisions and responses), page 46

Wordspot (PAGE 73)

go

See *Teacher's tips: working with lexis* on pages 12–13.

1 Students work individually or in pairs before checking answers with the whole class.

> **ANSWERS**
> a go back / go up / go down / go on / go away
> b anything you plan or organise in advance can *go wrong* – a journey / a meal you cook, etc.
> food such as cheese, meat, fruit *goes bad*
> a man *goes bald*
> a person as they get older *goes grey* or *white*
> a person or animal *goes mad* (to become insane or very angry)
> c *Go away!*: if someone is annoying you
> *Go to sleep!*: to a child who won't sleep or to someone who wakes up in the night
> *Go on!*: if someone is hesitating about whether or not to do something, or to tell someone to continue speaking if they've been interrupted

2 Get students to suggest other possibilities to *go* in the gaps rather than just copying the phrases in the diagram. As you check answers, highlight the use / non-use of the article and prepositions in these phrases. Add *go home* to the list, which does not even have a preposition.

> **POSSIBLE ANSWERS**
> go swimming, jogging, riding, walking, climbing, sailing, skiing, skating, cycling, dancing
> go for a swim, a drink, a walk, a run
> go to church, to hospital, to college, to university, to prison

3 Remind students to form the questions correctly, and emphasise they need only find *one* person for each sentence. Do this exercise as a mingling activity.

4 Prepare this in advance by copying the diagram onto a poster-sized sheet of paper. The additional phrases that students think of in Exercise 2 can be copied directly on to the poster as you go through them.

58

Part B Task

Preparation for task (PAGE 75)

See *Teacher's tips: making tasks work* on pages 8–9 and *Responding to learners' individual language needs* on pages 10–11.

1 Focus students' attention on the map and pictures of Thailand and ask what they know about it. If necessary, ask questions to prompt students:

Which part of the world is it in?, What's the capital city?, What sort of climate does it have?, What is the religion?, What kind of buildings / scenery would you expect to see there? What kind of food would you expect to find?, Is it a popular tourist destination?

If students have no idea about social customs, move straight on to the extract from the travel guide.

2 Focus students' attention on the extract, explaining that it is about social behaviour and customs in Thailand. Check the meaning of: *hospitality, to address someone, to say a prayer, to be respectful, chopsticks*. Get students to scan the extract quickly to see which social customs are mentioned, then read it again more slowly to answer question b) individually or in pairs. If students cannot guess, move quickly on to the listening.

ANSWERS
a meeting people, couples going out in public, being invited to someone's home, eating a meal

3 [7.4] Focus students' attention on the photo of Nikam Nipotam. Check that students understand who he is and who he is talking to before playing the cassette.

ANSWERS
1 their first name 2 both men and women
3 older people 4 kissing in public
5 not respectful 6 always take off your shoes
7 a spoon and fork

4 Students compare answers in pairs before checking with the whole class.

Task (PAGE 75)

1 Ask students to imagine that someone from a very different culture is coming to their country. They are going to advise this person about social behaviour in their country in the same way as Nikam Nipotam. Check the list of topics and put students into groups to brainstorm ideas. Circulate, supplying useful language they need and noting down useful language points to look at later.

2 This stage will need to be conducted differently depending on whether you have a mono-nationality or multi-nationality class.

If you have a mono-nationality class:

- Put up a list of students' ideas on the board or an OHT (*kissing on both cheeks / staying out very late*, etc.) Focus students' attention on the phrases in the *Useful language* box, briefly explaining any language problems, specifically: the meaning of *should, expect, polite*, the use of the plural after *people* and the singular after *everyone*, the use of the impersonal pronoun *it* + infinitive.

- Explain to students that they are going to have a conversation like Nikam Nipotam's, explaining dos and don'ts in your culture to a foreign visitor. Point out the role play options and give students the role of the foreign visitor (A) or the person giving tips (B).

- Give students a few minutes to plan what they will say. Ask Student A to think of other questions to ask.

- Put students into pairs to act out the dialogues. Circulate, making notes of errors for analysis / correction later on.

If you have a multi-nationality class:

- Explain that students are going to present their tips, but go over the phrases in the *Useful language* box first.

- Give students a few more minutes to think about how to express what they want to say, checking with you about anything that other students might find difficult to understand. If necessary, rehearse these difficult parts with them individually.

- Get students to present their tips in groups or to the whole class, and to ask each other questions about anything they do not understand or are surprised by.

Optional writing

Note: it may be useful to work through the Task link *on page 76 before setting this writing task.*

Refer students to the *Tips for foreign visitors to Thailand* text again, suggesting that they use it as a model. Point out any useful language in the text (*is famous for ... / it is polite to ...*, etc.) Point out that the style of many of the phrases in the *Useful language* box, although informal, is acceptable for this kind of travel guide.

Task: alternative suggestions

a *If you do not have enough time to cover the whole task in one lesson*: do the *Preparation for task* and get students to make a list of tips in one class (Task, Exercise 1) and present them in the next (Task, Exercise 2).

b *If you think students may not be interested in Thailand*: provide your own model for the task by:

- giving a talk about social customs in an interesting or exotic place that you have visited.
- giving a talk on Britain / the USA / Australia, etc.

module 7

or invite a guest speaker in to do this.
- making a cassette of your own in which you interview a fluent English-speaker about social customs in an English-speaking country or another interesting place he / she has visited. Base your interview on the one with Nikam Nipotam, making sure that the speed / level, etc. is appropriate for your class.

You will need to set some comprehension questions for all of these options.

c *If you have a young, mono-nationality class who have difficulty in seeing their own culture from an outside perspective:* in this case it might be useful to:
- get students to think of a specific culture or person to focus their advice on. It could be a Thai person, such as Nikam Nipotam or a famous British / American person they identify with (a film star, footballer, etc.)
- get them to think about British and American films and any differences in social behaviour they have noticed before imagining what these people would find strange in their culture.
- tell them about some of the things you found strange when you first arrived in their country.

If you are not confident that any of these will work, a more radical option is to get them to invent a country / culture or alien species and to present their strange social customs to the rest of the class. To help them to imagine these, provide a name for the culture or species, and some pictures or illustrations if possible.

d *If you have well-travelled students in your class:* get students to work separately on tips about a country they have visited to present to the whole class.

Task link (PAGE 76)

Making generalisations

1 Focus students' attention on the photos. Explain that all the texts are about cultural groups in the USA, but that the facts described in one of them are no longer true. Check the meaning of: *a clan, a crèche, a nomad, to hunt.*

> **ANSWER**
> All of them used to be true, but the Inuits (Eskimos) no longer follow this lifestyle.

2 Point out the phrases that have already been underlined in the first extract. Students work individually or in pairs and do the same with the others. As you check answers, highlight:
- the position of the adverb of frequency in the sentence (between the subject and the verb / after the verb *to be*).
- the impersonal construction *it is ... for ... someone ... to ... do something.*

- the use of the verb *tend* for making generalisations.

> **ANSWERS**
> b it is quite normal / young couples tend / Many schools
> c generally live / It is usual for / most new husbands

3 Students work individually, before comparing answers in groups. There will obviously be differences in multi-nationality groups, but even in mono-nationality groups there may be differences of opinion for students to discuss / explain. As you compare answers highlight:
- the use of the singular verb after *nobody / everybody*
- the plural verb after *people*
- Also write up and drill: *quite a lot of people, not many people, the majority of people, some people, most people, almost everybody, it's quite common to, it's quite normal to, it's unusual to*

4 Elicit a few examples to check that students understand how the diagram works. Students work in pairs or groups making sentences – this is probably best done as a spoken exercise initially. Students can write their sentences for further consolidation if necessary.

ADDITIONAL PRACTICE

RB **Resource bank:** 7B *Doonbogs!* (making generalisations), page 139, Instructions page 101

Real life (PAGE 77)

Making a social arrangement

1 [7.5] Explain that this extract is only part of the conversation. Students scan the text quickly for the answers to the questions. Play the cassette before checking answers with the whole class.

> **ANSWERS**
> a Laurence and Roger are probably old friends; Roger and Millie are probably a couple.

2 Emphasise that students only need complete columns 1 and 2. Students can search for the phrases individually or in pairs. Check answers with the whole class, drilling the phrases. Point out that on the phone we say *It's Laurence* or *It's Laurence speaking* (not *I am Laurence*).

> **ANSWERS**
> **on the phone:** Listen, I won't keep you.; I was just phoning to ask if ...; I'll let you get back to ...; Give me a ring in a week or so ... .
> **inviting and arranging:** ... would you like to come for a meal?; How about the following Saturday instead?; We'll look forward to seeing you.

module 7

3 a) Read through the phrases in columns 3 and 4 together. Either play the cassette straight through or stop after the appropriate phrases, depending on how well you think students will be able to remember them.

b) Ask students if they remember any other general phrases we use on the telephone, before playing the cassette again if necessary.

ANSWERS
a **accepting an invitation:** I think that should be fine. That'd be great! I'll call you back if there's any problem.
refusing an invitation: We can't, I'm afraid. What a shame!
b I haven't heard from you for ages!; How are things with ...?; I can hear you're busy ...; I won't keep you ...; Thanks for calling.

4 a) Re-play the cassette or model the phrases yourself for students to drill, encouraging them to copy intonation.

POSSIBLE ANSWERS
1 **useful phrases for talking on the phone:** *Could I speak to ..., please?; I'll just get him / her; Can you give him / her a message?; Can you ask him / her to call me?,* etc.
2 **Inviting and arranging:** *What about ...?; Do you fancy coming round for a meal?,* etc.
3 **accepting an invitation:** *That sounds great!; We'd / I'd love to come!*
4 **refusing an invitation:** *Thanks for asking, but ...; What a pity!; I'm really sorry, but ...*

b) Put students in pairs and go through the role play. Explain that they can act out several conversations, but they must have some where they accept and some where they refuse the invitation. Remind them that if they refuse, they need to give a reason. If this is because they already have another arrangement, they will probably need to use the Present Continuous (Roger: *My friend's getting married and we're going to the wedding*.) Circulate, making a note of errors / language for analysis and correction later on.

ADDITIONAL PRACTICE

[RB] **Resource bank:** 7C *What time shall we meet?* (making a social arrangement), pages 140–141, Instructions page 101

Do you remember?

ANSWERS
1 a Various answers are possible using the phrases: Sure ...; Yes, of course; Certainly; Sorry, but ...; I'm afraid ... .
b *Would you mind giving* – Do you think you could (possibly) give; Could you possibly give
Do you mind if I use – Could I (possibly) use; Is it alright / okay if I use (*though not as polite*)
I'll carry – Shall I; Would you like me to carry
Would you like to play – Shall we
Shall I – I'll; Would you like me to

2 a <u>It is</u> very common for Brazilians to have big families.
b After work I'm going to <u>go</u> shopping.
c It's very hard for young people <u>to</u> find a job at the moment.
d Go <u>away</u>! I don't want to talk to you!
e Shall we go for <u>a</u> drink after class?
f If you're tired, why don't you go <u>to bed</u>?
g Hello, Jack. <u>This</u> is Fiona.

3 a if you *lend* something, you give it to someone else to use for a limited time; if you *borrow* something, you ask someone else to give it to you for you to use for a limited time
b if you *go out for the night*, you go to a restaurant / cinema, etc. and then come home; if you *go away for the night*, you spend the night in a hotel / at a friend's house, etc. and do not come home
c these two have the same meaning
d you *shake hands* with someone when you meet them for the first time, or to say 'hello'; you *hold hands* with your girlfriend / boyfriend, etc., for example as you walk in the street
e if you *wave* to someone, you hold your arm up in the air and move your hand, to greet someone or to say 'goodbye'; if you *bow* to someone, you bend your top body forward in greeting or to show respect
f you *pay* the bill when you have finished your meal and are ready to leave; you *leave a tip* (often ten per cent) for the waiter / waitress if the service has been good
g if prices *decrease*, they go down; this is the opposite of prices *going up*
h if you *pass* something to someone, you hand it to them; if you *go past* someone, you walk in front of him / her

4 a loves b live c tend d believes
5 a respectful b behaviour c invite
  d acceptable

61

module 8

Part A Language

Language focus 1 (PAGE 79)
Defining relative clauses

See *Teacher's tips: using a discovery approach in the teaching of grammar* on page 15.

Create interest by asking students how much they know about computers. Tell them they are going to do a quiz to find out what they know. Check the meaning of: *a piece of equipment, to meet someone in person, telephone wires, to store (information)*. Students do the quiz in pairs or groups. (If possible, mix students who know a lot about computers with those who don't know anything.) Check answers with the whole class. (Note the pronunciation of *technophobe* /ˈteknəfəʊb/, *cyberbuddy* /ˈsaɪbəˌbʌdi/, and *nerd* /nɜːd/. These are low-frequency words and do not need to be practised.)

> **ANSWERS**
> a technophobe b the Internet c a modem
> d a cyberbuddy* e a mouse f a disk
> g cyberspace h a computer nerd **
>
> *buddy is common American slang for 'a friend'; in modern usage, the prefix *cyber-* is added onto anything relating to the Internet
> **nerd is a common slang expression in both American and British English

Analysis

1 Do the first example together before getting students to work individually. Check answers with the whole class. (It would be useful to have a copy of the sentences either on the board or an OHT, for reference and analysis later.)

> **ANSWERS**
> a who doesn't like modern machines
> b which allows millions of computer users
> c that allows information to be sent
> d who you only ever communicate with
> e which you move with your hands
> f plastic you use for storing
> g where electronic messages
> h whose life is dominated by computers

2 Students work individually or in pairs before checking answers with the whole class.

> **ANSWERS**
> a *who* (*that* is less usual for people – it's rather informal)

b *which / that* (students may want to use *what* here – emphasise that this is considered bad English)
c *whose* (this might be difficult for students to understand – the best way to explain is by changing the relative clause back into a normal sentence (*his life is dominated by computers*) and point out that *whose* always replaces *his / her / its / their*, etc.)
d *where* (point out that no preposition is used with the relative pronoun *where*; if you use a preposition, *where* is replaced by *which*: *an imaginary place in which electronic messages exist*)

3 Students work individually – encourage them to guess the answers if they don't know.

> **ANSWERS AND LANGUAGE NOTES**
> The relative pronouns can be omitted in sentences d) and f) because they are the **objects** rather than the **subjects** of the relative clauses. If students have difficulty in understanding this, write sentences d) and a) on the board and ask students to break them into two simpler sentences. Write these underneath the originals:
> *A cyberbuddy is a friend* (who) *you only ever communicate with through computers.*
> *A cyberbuddy is a friend. You only ever communicate with* (him / her) *through computers.* (*who* = *him / her* = OBJECT)
>
> *A technophobe is a person* (who) *doesn't like computers.*
> *A technophobe is a person.* (He / She) *doesn't like computers.* (*who* = *He / She* = SUBJECT)
>
> Ask students which word in the second sentence *who* refers to. Point out that *who* is the object of the verb underlined and that we can leave it out. Emphasise that we cannot omit the other relative pronouns because they are the subjects of the sentence. Point out that *whose* and *where* cannot be omitted.

PRACTICE

1 Students work individually or in pairs before checking answers with the whole class. Do not pre-teach any of the words, but offer help if students need it. When discussing the answers, check whether or not the pronoun can be omitted.

> **ANSWERS**
> a *a vegetarian*: who / that (cannot be omitted)
> b *a thermometer*: which / that (cannot be omitted)
> c *a widow* whose; who / that (neither can be omitted)
> d *a theatre*: where / on which (cannot be omitted)

module 8

e *a scarf*: which / that (can be omitted)
f *an opponent*: who / that (can be omitted)

2 Direct students to the appropriate page and do one example together. Point out that all the words come from earlier in the book, but that they can use their mini-dictionaries to remind them of the meanings if necessary. Insist, however, that they close their mini-dictionaries before writing their definitions. Emphasise that they should <u>not</u> use the relative pronoun if it is not needed. Stronger students may be able to do the activity without writing their definitions first.

ADDITIONAL PRACTICE

RB **Resource bank:** *Relative clauses crossword* (defining relative clauses), page 142

Workbook: Defining relative clauses, pages 51–52; Prepositions with defining relative clauses, page 52

Reading (PAGES 80–81)

1 Focus students' attention on the title and check the meaning of *inventor* and *successful*. Elicit / teach related words: *invent* / *invention* and *succeed* / *successful*. Ask students to predict what kind of advice / suggestions there will be in the text. Make sure students know what the people / objects in the photos are before guessing the connection. Do not tell them the answers at this stage.

2 Tell students to scan the text quickly to find out the answers. Set a time limit of two minutes if necessary.

ANSWERS
paper machine – wasp's nest; Velcro – seed pods; fax machine – Giovanni Caselli; telephone – Alexander Graham Bell

3 Check the meaning of: *a light bulb, to be patient, purpose, to understand the potential of something, a dot, a screen, a button, a knob, a net*. Students work individually or in pairs before checking answers with the whole class.

ANSWERS
a yes b Denis Papin c George Stevenson
d Because it took eighty years to develop.
e Elisha Gray f Both of them were the result of observing nature. g To observe the work the scientists had been doing. h no

4 Students discuss the quesions in groups or with the whole class.

ADDITIONAL ACTIVITY

RB **Resource bank:** *How to be a successful inventor* vocabulary extension (word building), page 143

Vocabulary (PAGE 81)

Machines

1 [8.1] Before listening, emphasise that students only have to identify which machine is being discussed.

ANSWERS
a answerphone   b vacuum cleaner
c fax machine   d video recorder

2 Do an example together before getting students to work in pairs. Circulate and explain any unknown vocabulary. Play the cassette, stopping after each phrase is used to check answers. Students discuss the answer to b) in pairs.

ANSWERS
a press that button, hold the button down, a red light flashes
plug it in, unplug it, switch it on
pick up the handset, dial the number, wait for the tone
put a tape in, the tape gets stuck, get the tape out
b *(depending on the individual machine)*
cassette recorder: press the button, hold the button down, plug it in, switch it on, unplug it, get the tape out, put the tape in, the tape gets stuck
a telephone: press the button, hold the button down, a red light flashes, plug it in, unplug it, switch it on, pick up the handset, wait for the tone, dial the number
a camera: press this button, hold the button down, a red light flashes

3 Give students a few moments to think of a machine, preferably one their partner may not be familiar with (either because they do not normally use it, or because this kind of machine tends to be different in individual cases). Students can draw or show the machine as they explain, but be careful of pre-empting the task on page 85. Circulate, supplying any words / phrases students need.

Pronunciation

1 Explain what a compound noun is (a noun consisting of two parts, noun + noun / gerund or noun + adjective), and give an example. Go through the two rules, writing the examples on the board and marking the stress. Repeat the examples yourself several times to make sure that students can hear the difference (exaggerating the stress, or mumbling the rhythm pattern should help). Give students a minute to try and work out where the stress should be in each case, without giving the answers at this stage.

ANSWERS
mobile phone; dark glasses; electric guitar

63

module 8

washing machine*; swimming pool; video recorder; electric cooker; dishwasher; dining room; car radio

Note that gerunds (-ing forms) function as nouns here. Other examples include: shopping bag, running shoes, etc.

2 [8.2] Play the cassette, stopping after each compound noun to allow students time to check / correct their answers. Drill the nouns (again exaggerating / mumbling will be useful to aid correction).

Language focus 2 (PAGES 82–83)

Quantifiers (*a few, a lot of*, etc.)

See *Teacher's tips: using a discovery approach in the teaching of grammar* on page 15.

Mini-task

Give an example yourself by guessing what one of the students keeps in his / her school bag. Students work in pairs. Circulate, supplying vocabulary such as handkerchiefs *or* plasters *as necessary. (It is probably better to leave it up to students whether or not they actually show the contents of their pockets, bags, etc. as some might find this embarrassing.) Note how well students are able to use quantifiers, in particular:*

– *are they able to use* some *and* any *appropriately?*

– *are they using quantifiers like* plenty *and* several *and are they using them correctly?*

– *do they seem aware of the difference between countable and uncountable nouns?*

Do not focus on this language explicitly, but keep a note of any errors for correction after the Analysis. Feedback briefly with the whole class, focusing on whose guesses were best, and any amusing discoveries that anyone has made.

1 Focus students' attention on the picture and briefly discuss the questions. Put the following questions up for students to discuss in groups:
Have you ever thought about owning a shop yourself?
What kind would you like to own? Why?
What do you think the main advantages and disadvantages of owning such a shop would be?

2 [8.3] Check any remaining items of vocabulary from the box and the pronunciation of: *bowl* /bəʊl/, *brooch* /brəʊtʃ/, *necklace* /ˈnekləs/, *dressing gown* /ˈdresɪŋgaʊn/, *mirror* /ˈmɪrə/. Play the cassette. Students compare answers in pairs / groups before checking with the whole class.

ANSWERS
a Denise sells plates, bowls, ashtrays, earrings, brooches, dressing gowns, cards, candles, picture frames.
b The good points are that the location is very good – there are plenty of other shops and cafés nearby and lots of students and young people living nearby; she has several friends living in the area. The bad points are that there is not enough space for all the things in the shop (people keep knocking things over).

3 Emphasise that students should ask you to stop the cassette when they hear one of the sentences. Give them time to write before playing the cassette again. Check answers with the whole class.

ANSWERS
a a couple b A lot of c some d lots of
e a few f plenty of g loads of h several
i enough j too many k enough

Analysis

1 Check that students know the difference between a countable and uncountable noun by asking for / giving a few clear examples (for example, *window* and *fresh air*). Do the first couple of examples together, then students do the rest individually or in pairs. Suggest that they look at the sentences in Exercise 3 as well as thinking logically about the meanings of the words. They can also use their mini-dictionaries (which would be useful dictionary training). As you check answers with the whole class, elicit examples of nouns that can follow each quantifier.

ANSWERS
countable: a few*, too many, several*, one or two, a couple of, not many
uncountable: too much, not much, a little
both: a lot of / lots of, some, (not) enough, plenty of, no, loads of**, (not) any

* *a few* emphasises that there are not many; *several* does not carry this meaning
** *loads of* is colloquial (but very common)

2 Students discuss the questions in pairs before checking answers with the whole class.

ANSWERS / LANGUAGE NOTES
a *Too much / too many* mean that it is a bad thing – here it means more than you can afford to pay / more than it should cost (this will need particular attention if this distinction does not exist in the students' own language); *a lot of* does not imply this.
b *Enough* means that you have as much time as

64

you need; *plenty* means 'more than enough' (perhaps in this example you have time to do something else as well). Again this distinction may not exist in the students' own language.
c Remind students that *any* is only negative when accompanied by a negative verb (a common mistake: ~~I've got any money~~ instead of *I've got no money*; on the other hand *I didn't have no money* is wrong because it is a double negative).

PRACTICE

1 Do the first example together, eliciting several possibilities, and making it clear that students should make the sentences true in their opinion. This is best done by asking them to explain their answers (*Why isn't there enough space for everyone to work?*, etc.) Do this as a spoken exercise initially, but get students to write their sentences after for further consolidation if necessary.

2 Do this as a spoken exercise in pairs or groups. Group students from different areas in the town together so they have more to talk about. Multi-nationality groups can either discuss the town where they are staying, or tell each other about their home towns. Students can write sentences afterwards for further consolidation if necessary.

ADDITIONAL PRACTICE

RB Resource bank: 8C *Camping holiday* (quantifiers – *a few, a lot of*, etc.), pages 144–145, Instructions page 101
Workbook: Quantifiers (*a few, a lot of*, etc.), page 53

Wordspot (PAGE 83)

something

See *Teacher's tips: working with lexis* on pages 12–13.

1 Students work individually or in pairs. As you check answers with the whole class, drill the phrases.
Point out with the adjectives, infinitives and ages that there are many more variations:
- *something new / something unusual / something nice / something awful*, etc.
- *something to read / something to think about / something to help*, etc.
- *twenty-something / forty-something*, etc.

> **ANSWERS**
> **for being imprecise:** *something like* (= approximately); *something to do with; something to tell (someone); thirty-something; do something (about); say something*
> **something + adjective:** *something else; something wrong (with it); something strange*

something + infinitive: *something to do; something to drink*

2 Put students in pairs and refer them to the appropriate page at the back of the book. Do the first example on each card together as a class, making sure they understand they need to reply using a phrase with *something*. Check answers with the whole class.

3 Prepare this in advance by copying the diagram onto a poster-sized sheet of paper.

Part B Task

See *Teacher's tips: making tasks work* on pages 8–9 and *Responding to learners' individual language needs* on pages 10–11.

Preparation for task (PAGE 85)

1 Check that students know the words for the objects, and ask them to guess which person is associated with each one. Pre-teach the following phrases used in the listening: *powerful, a moped, a grand piano, a baby grand, a bust, to get in touch with someone, to be useful, to be practical, antique, nostalgic*.

2 [8.4] Explain that each person is talking either about something they own that is important to them or something that they would like to own. Play the cassette and get students to complete column 1. Check answers with the whole class, before playing the cassette a second time whilst students complete the other two columns.

> **ANSWERS**
> 1 **Emma:** a motorbike; huge, powerful, black, with two seats (one raised at the back); she would pack her bags, grab her passport and go off to Spain, France (ride off without a care in the world)
> 2 **Rodney:** a mobile phone; useful, practical, a little bit heavy; his son can get in touch if he is in trouble, he's living in a flat without a phone
> 3 **David:** a baby grand piano; it must be black; it would help him to relax and get rid of depression
> 4 **Daphné:** a ring; it has a heart on the front, antique silver; it was her engagement ring when she was eighteen, it reminds her of her teenage years

Task (PAGE 85)

1 Give students time to think of an object, emphasising that it can be something that they already own, or something that they would like to own. Tell them that it can

module 8

be large or small, expensive or cheap, and give a few more suggestions – a watch, a wallet, a car, a piece of furniture, a special picture or photo, a type of house, etc. Suggest that they either show the object if they have it with them, or draw a picture of it. Give students a few minutes to make notes in the table. Circulate, supplying vocabulary.

2 Before starting the talks, refer students to the appropriate sections of the *Useful language* box, briefly checking any constructions / features of form likely to cause problems, in particular:

- *to be made of, to remind you of, to belong to someone*
- the use of *what / something* at the beginning of sentences in: *What I'd really like is ..., Something I'd love to own is a ...* .
- the use of *would / wouldn't* for talking hypothetically / imagining an object you would like to own (do not give a full presentation of the 'second conditional' as this will be covered in Module 9 – students should be able to manage here with just *would / wouldn't* taught as phrases).

Students work in groups of about four, if possible arranged round tables, so they can show their objects and pictures more easily. Circulate, making notes about useful language / errors for analysis and correction later on (it may be more useful to do this before the optional writing stage).

Optional writing

Note: this writing can be left until students have done the Task link on describing objects on page 86.

This can be done in class or for homework. Remind students not to write their names on the piece of paper. Read out the descriptions whilst students try to guess who wrote each one. Alternatively put the work up on the wall (perhaps numbering each piece) and give students a few minutes to read them and note down who they think wrote each one.

> **Task: alternative suggestions**
>
> a *Give your own mini-talk*: instead of playing the cassette, talk about something you own that is special to you or that you would really like to have. The following tips may help:
> - If possible bring in the object or a picture of it.
> - It will be more intimate / less daunting if you gather the class into a tight group around you so that they can see the object more easily.
> - Plan briefly what you will say but do not fully script it as it will be rather unnatural. Try to incorporate any small personal anecdotes, relating to the object.
> - Tell students that they must all think of at least one question to ask you while you are speaking.
>
> b *If you are short of time*: use just two of the models on the cassette, selecting those you think your students would be most interested in. You can also split the task over two lessons, setting the *Preparation for the task* as homework. Remind students to bring in their object if possible.
>
> c *Ensuring that students have enough questions to ask each other*: after checking the *Useful language*, devise a list of questions to ask for each type of object. Put the following questions up and ask students to think of four or five questions to add:
> **things you already own:** *How long have you had it? Where did you buy it? Why ...? When ...? Who ...?*
> **things you'd like to own:** *Why would you like a ...? How much would it cost?*
>
> d *A more creative writing option*: get students to write the description as if they were the object (*I've got a big handle on my head*, etc.). They could describe the advantages and disadvantages of life from the point of view of the object, or its likes and dislikes / a typical day / an adventure it had, etc.

Task link (PAGE 86)

Describing objects

1 Check that students know the words (and pronunciation) for the objects in the pictures. Emphasise that students only need to choose one object and make sure they work on this individually without saying what they have chosen. Check the meaning of the following words / phrases in the table:
to be made of (a material), to make a noise, to fit into (your pocket, etc.), to be found in (the kitchen, etc.) to be useful for + -ing form.
Check the pronunciation of: *square* /skweə/, *rectangular* /rek'tæŋgjələ/, *handle* /'hændl/, *battery* /'bætəri/.

2 Students work in pairs guessing each other's objects. If you feel they need more practice, get them to repeat the exercise with a different object.

3 Emphasise that students can choose any object and ask any questions they want (not just the ones in the table). Circulate, supplying any vocabulary they need and making a note of language / errors for analysis and correction later on.

> **Exercise 3: alternative suggestion**
>
> - Bring in a selection of everyday objects (sellotape, string, a paper clip, a drawing pin, etc.) If you cannot bring objects, simply write a list on the board. Pre-teach any unknown words and check pronunciation.
>
> - Choose two objects at random and ask students for any ideas of things they have in common (*both of them are made of plastic / neither of them fit into your pocket*, etc.) Remind students of the phrases

module 8

- _both of them_ and _neither of them._
- Put students into two teams and explain that you will give them other pairs of objects to do the same with. The teams take turns to say one thing that the objects have in common. The last team to think of something wins the point, and starts the next round.
- Select the pairs of objects quite randomly – the team game should ensure that students are imaginative in their suggestions. Keep playing until the game gets repetitive or students lose interest.

Real life (PAGE 87)

Writing 'thank you' letters

1 Elicit students' ideas about what a polite 'thank you' letter should include, before going through the list in the _Students' Book_. Students read the letter and check answers in pairs, then with the whole class.

> **ANSWER**
> He didn't write promptly or mention what the present was. He did all the other things listed.

2 Students work individually or in pairs before checking answers with the class. Before they start, check the meaning of: _hospitality, to make a contribution, an invitation._

> **ANSWERS**
> a 6   b 2   c 4   d 1   e 5   f 3

3 It might be useful to expand one of the letters yourself to show students what is required, for example:

> Julie,
>
> Thanks a lot for lending me your leather jacket. It was really sweet of you – just what I needed to go with my new jeans. I hope I can do the same for you some time.
>
> Fran XXX

Refer students to pages 14–15 and 56 to remind them of the format of formal and informal letters and useful phrases to include. Students select one of the other letters to write. (Note that 1 and 6 are quite specific business letters – unless your students have these kind of needs it would be better for them to choose one of the other options which they should find easier to write.)

Consolidation modules 5–8

> **ANSWERS**
> A 1 to get   2 when   3 will not give   4 until / unless   5 to marry   6 will present   7 will start   8 when   9 returns   10 will feature   11 to do   12 to recognise   13 to buy   14 to build   15 converting   16 until   17 to have   18 is holding   19 to invite   20 arrive   21 when / if   22 will find
>
> B a arrange a night out / take a message / book a holiday
>   b a vaccum cleaner / a freezer / a dishwasher
>   c kiss each other / shake hands / wave
>   d schoolwork / homework / housework
>   e stay in / go on a date / go round to a friend's
>   f a cartoon / a soap opera / a documentary
>   g challenging / well-paid / stressful
>   h annoyed / depressed / terrified
>
> C a grew up in New York and Jamaica; made his first album in 1955; third album 'Calypso' released in 1959; became politically active in the 1960s; has made several films
>   b be given a perfect score of ten in an Olympic gymnastic competition; was voted Heroine of the Year by the Press Association; escaped from Romania; has lived in the United States since 1989
>   c in space; Sputnik 2 was launched in November 1957; could not be brought back to Earth; died in space a week after the launch; one of Russia's most important research institutes, it was named after her
>
> D 3 a two friends; on the phone; Jane wants to borrow a tent; they're going camping at the weekend; Fran's sister has got the tent; Fran will phone her sister and try to sort something out
>   b father and daughter; at home; the daughter wants a lift to the station; the rucksacks will be heavy and there won't be any buses; the father agrees to think about it (but has probably really agreed)

Students can now do _Test two (modules 5–8)_ on pages 164–166 of the _Teacher's Book_.

module 9

Part A Language

Reading (PAGES 90–91)

1 Check the meaning of: *to predict / a prediction* and *life expectancy*. Prompt ideas with a few questions in each case, for example: *Will we find life on other planets?*, *Will people work for longer or for less time?*, *Will we still use the same kind of money that we do now?* Point out the useful phrases in the speech balloons and that we use *don't think* if we think something is negative. Drill the phrases before getting students to work in pairs or groups. Afterwards, discuss suggestions with the whole class. Collect a list of predictions on the board or an OHT for comparison later on.

2 Stress that students only need to identify the correct paragraph – they do not need to understand every word. Set a time limit of two minutes for this.

ANSWERS
(paragraph numbers in brackets)
space travel (3), robots and computers (4), work (5), education (6), life expectancy (7), the media (2), money (3), family life (7)

3 Before reading the text again, check the meaning of: *to be lucky, an alien, a currency, weight control, to take a pill, to share a job, genetic engineering, to vanish, a decade, to be old-fashioned, a serious relationship*. Students work individually or in pairs before discussing with the whole class. Discuss b) with the whole class.

ANSWERS
b a people have robots to do housework; there are shopping channels
   b most people work at home; people share jobs
   c children study mostly at home; they only go to school to play with other children; they will probably live to be 130

4 Discuss this in groups or with the whole class. The discussion can be brief or lengthy depending on interest level.

Language focus 1 (PAGE 92)

Making predictions (modal verbs and other phrases)

See *Teacher's tips: using a discovery approach in the teaching of grammar* on page 15.

Check the meaning of: *a vaccine, tooth decay, healthcare, to disappear, to make life difficult, a world power*. Students work individually at this stage – there will be an opportunity to compare opinions in Practice Exercise 1.

Language focus 1: alternative suggestion (without doing *The Lucky Generation* reading text first)

Either: set the text as homework before the lesson, briefly checking the comprehension questions before moving on to the *Language focus*.

or: use the pictures to get students to speculate about life in 2050. Give them the list of topics in Exercise 1 on page 90 to discuss in groups to prompt ideas. Write their predictions on the board, before focusing on those in the *Language focus*, then proceed as below (students' own predictions can easily be incorporated into Practice Exercise 1). Set the text for homework if students are interested.

Analysis

Point out that all the predictions in the preceding exercise are with *will / won't* and express a definite prediction. Focus on the other phrases and explain how the diagram works. Without explaining the phrases, get students to try and work out where they should go. Discuss answers with the whole class. As you do, contextualise the phrases in an example sentence (for example, *All housework will be done by robots*), drawing their attention to the following problems of form and pronunciation:

- adverbs like *probably, definitely* and *certainly* go after *will* but before *won't*
- the construction *to be likely / not to be likely to do something*
- *may* and *might* can be used in the negative here, but *could* cannot
- we can say *may well, might well* and *could well* if we want to show that something will probably happen.

Drill the phrases both in isolation and in the context of a short sentence (*Crime almost certainly won't disappear*).

ANSWERS AND LANGUAGE NOTES

| will almost certainly | is / are likely to | may (not) might aren't | isn't / (not) likely to | almost certainly won't |

will definitely | will probably | could / may well | probably won't | definitely won't

- *may not / might not*: students may ask which of these is most probable. Grammar books disagree on this – if there is any distinction, it is not significant. Intonation is more important in ascertaining how certain the person is.

68

_____ module 9

> There are a large number of other ways of expressing degrees of possibility / certainty – *it is possible that / perhaps / maybe*, etc. Do not deal with these unless students specifically ask.

PRACTICE

1. Go over the example together and point out that students can change other parts of the sentences as well to reflect their opinions accurately. This should be done as a spoken exercise initially, but the sentences can be written for further consolidation. When checking answers, draw students' attention to the following points:
   - all the phrases from the *Analysis* can be used in front of *be able to* and the passive (*isn't likely to be able to ..., may well be done ...*)
   - in sentence c) if the negative phrases are used *no* will have to be changed to *any* (*there may not be any dentists*).

2. Check the meaning of: *to sneeze, a thunderstorm*. This can be done as a spoken or written exercise, but emphasise that students should try to make the sentences true.

3. Give a few personalised examples of your own – stress that these can be either long or short term predictions.

ADDITIONAL PRACTICE

Workbook: Futures for prediction (*will, might, may*, etc.), page 57

Vocabulary and speaking (PAGE 93)

Society and change

1. Check the meaning of the words / phrases in the 'Topic' column. Students work individually to decide which they think is happening in each case.

2. Students discuss their opinions in pairs or groups. Emphasise that they should give reasons and remind them we use the Present Continuous to describe changing states.

3. This can be done as a race / competition to make it more fun. Write the phrases on the board, drilling them for stress / pronunciation in particular: *increase* /ɪnˈkriːs/, *decrease* /dɪˈkriːs/, *rise* /raɪz/, *fall* /fɔːl/, *improve* /ɪmˈpruːv/, *deteriorate* /dɪˈtɪərɪəreɪt/. Highlight the following:
   - noun forms: *an increase* /ˈɪnkriːs/, *a decrease* /ˈdiːkriːs/, *an improvement* /ɪmˈpruːvmənt/, *a deterioration* /dɪˌtɪərɪəˈreɪʃən/
   - irregular past forms: *rise / rose / risen, fall / fell / fallen*
   - that we can use *become* + comparative form with many adjectives (*becoming more popular / expensive*, etc.)

Language focus 2 (PAGES 93–94)

Real and hypothetical possibilities with *if*

See *Teacher's tips: using a discovery approach in the teaching of grammar* on page 15.

Mini-task

Check students understand the questions in Never say never, *and the following phrases:* under what circumstances, to lie to someone, to walk out of your job, to give someone a lift, to drop out of college, to hit someone, for ever.

Explain that students should think of all the possible circumstances in which anyone might do these things, not just their own answers. Do not highlight 'second conditional' forms explicitly, but make a note of any useful errors for correction after the Analysis.

1. [9.1] Before playing the cassette, check the meaning of: *an operation (medical), a friendship, hypothetical, borrow / lend, personal safety, to be violent, to lose your temper, to hurt someone, to defend yourself, a burglar.* Play the cassette straight through or stop after each section to check answers.

> **ANSWERS**
> a **Part 1:** lending money to a friend, **Part 2:** leaving your country forever, **Part 3:** hitting someone
> b **Part 1:** a – if a friend needed it urgently; b – she would never do it; c – if a friend needed it badly and he was sure they could pay it back
> **Part 2:** a – if there was a war or a dangerous political situation; b – if something terrible happened; c – if he was going to have to go to prison
> **Part 3:** a – if he got really angry; b – if she needed to defend herself; c – if someone tried to hurt his family

2. Students can try to guess the answers first, but tell them not to write in their books until they listen to the cassette. Stop the cassette regularly to give students time to write. It would be useful to write up the complete sentences yourself at this stage for reference in the *Analysis*.

> **ANSWERS**
> a was; had; needed;
> b 'd; would;
> c 'd; thought; needed; was; could;

69

module 9

Analysis

1 Check the meaning of *imaginary* (*hypothetical* may be a better cognate). Give students a moment to think about the answer before checking with the whole class.

> **ANSWERS AND LANGUAGE NOTES**
> a real possibility in the future: *I'll never lend her any money again.*
> b imaginary situation: *I'd never lend a friend a lot of money.*
> *will* is used in the first case, *would* in the second. Students should be familiar with both *will* and *would* but it is worth contrasting them briefly. Highlight:
> - the negative and question forms (*Will he? / he won't; would he? / he wouldn't*)
> - the affirmative and negative (*I'll, I'd, I won't, I wouldn't*) contractions of both forms (*I'll, I'd, I won't, I wouldn't*)
>
> Note: do not at this stage go into the full 'second conditional' structure. Point out that *would* is very often used in sentences on its own. Particularly in speech, full conditional sentences are relatively uncommon – one 'half' of the conditional sentence tends to be assumed.

2 Students work individually or in pairs before checking with the whole class.

> **ANSWERS AND LANGUAGE NOTES**
> Examples of hypothetical clauses using *if*: *if it was a very good friend / if he or she needed an urgent operation / if I knew they really needed it / if I was sure they could pay it back.*
> - These are all past forms, but they don't refer to past time (they refer to present / future / general / imaginary time).
> - This is the subjunctive in English – if students have a subjunctive in their own language / are already familiar with this grammatical term, point this out to them. Stress that the subjunctive is not very widely used in English – this use after *if* is the most important one.
> - Because it is subjunctive, strictly-speaking *were* should be used rather than *was* in the first / third person. These days many native speakers use *was* (for example, *If it was a very good friend ...*) so do not insist that students use *were*.
> - Again point out that this *if* clause is very often used on its own, not necessarily in a full 'second conditional' sentence.

3 Students work individually before checking answers with the whole class.

> **ANSWERS AND LANGUAGE NOTES**
> The first and third sentences are correct.
> The incorrect sentence focuses on a common mistake – the use of *would* after *if*. The correct sentences illustrate the following points:
> - the fact that either clause can begin the sentence
> - the fact that *might* can be used instead of *would* if you are not sure what you would do (we cannot use *may* here)

PRACTICE

1 Look at the examples together, emphasising that students do not need to use full conditional sentences. Circulate, supplying vocabulary. Make a note of errors for analysis and correction later on.

2 Go through the sentences with the whole class and discuss whether they refer to real or imaginary situations. Students work individually making the questions before checking answers with the whole class. Point out that not all the sentences include an *if* clause.

> **ANSWERS**
> a (*imaginary*) If you could live anywhere in the world, where would you live? What kind of house would you choose?
> b (*real*) What will you do if you have some free time this evening?*
> c (*imaginary*) If you could become a famous person for a day, who would you be? Why would you choose this person?
> d (*real*) If you go shopping next weekend, what will you buy?
> e (*real*) Where will you go if you have a holiday next year? Who will you go with?*
> f (*imaginary*) How would your life be different if you were a member of the opposite sex? What would be the best and worst things about it?
>
> Note: in theory, all the sentences in this exercise could be either real or imaginary, but in most cases it is much more likely to be one than the other. For those sentences marked * students may be able to make a good case for using the hypothetical form (if, for example, they work every evening and so never have any free time). Do not go into this, however, unless students ask.

3 Focus on the sample answers, pointing out the use of *probably* with *would* as well as *will* (*definitely* and *certainly* can be used in the same way). Remind students of the correct word order *I'd probably ...*, but *I probably wouldn't ...* . Circulate and make a note of errors for analysis and correction later on.

_____ module 9

Pronunciation

1 🔲 [9.2] Play the cassette as many times as necessary.

ANSWERS
a won't   b I'd   c I'll   d I'll   e I'd / it'd

2 Get students to repeat the sentences individually / chorally. If they are having problems with the pronunciation of *I'll*, suggest they insert a small /j/ sound: I-y-l /aɪ-j-l/.

ADDITIONAL PRACTICE

RB Resource bank: 9A *Election night special* (hypothetical possibilities with *if* – 'second conditional'), page 146; 9B *How would your life be different?*, page 147, Instructions pages 101–102

Workbook: Hypothetical possibilities with *if*, page 58; Real and hypothetical possibilities, page 58; *If* sentences in social situations, page 59

Wordspot (PAGE 95)

make

See *Teacher's tips: working with lexis* on pages 12–13.

Wordspot (*make*): language notes

Students may ask about the difference in meaning between *make* and *do*. The usual explanation is that *make* relates to 'creating' something (*make a cake*) and that *do* relates to completing tasks or duties (*do your homework*). This explanation is basically true, but does not account for many common fixed phrases. We have not brought the two verbs together here as we believe this could make it more difficult to remember phrases with both. However, it may be helpful to give the simple explanation above to convey some basic idea of the difference, especially for students who have only one such verb in their first language.

Note also that *make* meaning 'to force' (*She made them eat all their dinner*) is not included here as we do not believe it is helpful to view it in terms of fixed phrases. This is dealt with in the *Workbook* on page 71 with *let*. If you make a poster of the uses of *make* you could include a separate section for this.

1 Check the meaning of *to lock a door* and *a hole*. Students work individually or in pairs.

2 🔲 [9.3] Play the cassette straight through and check answers with the whole class. Drill the following phrases: *to make up your mind, it makes me laugh, to make it worse, to make the dinner, to make a noise, to make sure*. Put students into pairs to practise the dialogues.

ANSWERS
a 3   b 7   c 5   d 8   e 4   f 6   g 1   h 2

3 Check the meaning of the section headings in the diagram. Highlight the two ways in which *make* is used to mean 'cause' and that with a verb the infinitive is without *to*.

ANSWERS
(section in brackets)
make a suggestion (a);   make a noise (b);   make dinner (b);   make sure (e);   make me laugh (d – *make* + verb);   made of cotton (b);   make up your mind (e);   make something worse (d – *make* + adjective)

4 Make sure students understand that each square represents a letter, and that they need clues (as in a crossword) to complete it. Put students into pairs and refer them to the appropriate page at the back of the book. Get one pair to each read out the first clue, and work out the answers as a class as an example. Circulate and prompt with extra clues if students are having difficulties.

ANSWERS
a make a sandwich   b made of leather   c make a mess   d made in Japan   e make a mistake
f make a noise   g make a profit   h make you cry
i make it clear   j make an appointment
k make a cup of coffee   l make you angry
The hidden message is: *What makes you laugh?*

Part B Task

See *Teacher's tips: making tasks work* on pages 8–9 and *Responding to learners' individual language needs* on pages 10–11.

Preparation for task (PAGES 96–97)

1 Discuss the questions in pairs / groups or with the whole class.

2 Focus students' attention on the map (St Ambrosia is an imaginary island in case students are in any doubt!). Read through the information together, as this is important background information for the task. Students read about the St Ambrosia state lottery before going through the answers to the questions with the whole class.

ANSWERS
a yes – very   b 10 million St Ambrosian dollars
c on 'improving the lives of St Ambrosians'

71

module 9

3 [9.4] **a)** Focus students' attention on the table and explain what they are going to hear. Check they understand what each of the organisations are and that there are no problems with vocabulary. Play the cassette, emphasising that they only have to complete the first column.

> **ANSWERS**
> 1 **St Ambrosian Hotel and Tourist Association:** need SA$4 million to build luxury hotel and golf course.
> 2 **St Ambrosian Sports Association:** need SA$6 million to build a National Sports Centre.
> 3 **University of St Ambrosia:** need SA$4.5 million for equipment in Computer Science and Technology department.
> 4 **St Ambrosian Children's Hospital:** need SA$3.5 million to stay open for another year.
> 5 **International Petroleum Incorporated:** need SA$8 million to look for oil deposits.

b) Students compare answers in pairs, before listening again to complete the second column (emphasise that they should not write anything in the third column yet).

> **ANSWERS**
> 1 **St Ambrosian Hotel and Tourist Association:** will bring 50,000 tourists a year to the island; will improve island's economy and create hundreds of jobs
> 2 **St Ambrosian Sports Association:** will provide social centre for the island; help realise dream of sending a team to the Olympics
> 3 **University of St Ambrosia:** to stop young people (engineers, doctors, lawyers, teachers of the future) from leaving the island
> 4 **St Ambrosian Children's Hospital:** will be able to stay open for another year and help sick children of the island
> 5 **International Petroleum Incorporated:** if they find oil, St Ambrosia will become one of the richest islands in the world

Task (PAGE 97)

1 Check the meaning of *budget* and emphasise that the money can be divided between the different organisations. Give students 5–10 minutes to think about how they want to spend the money, plan what to say and to think about any words or phrases they need.

2 Put students into groups to agree together on a budget. Check through the phrases in the *Useful language* box together. Highlight the following points at this stage, or wait until the correction stage after the task:

- negative opinions are expressed with *I don't think ...*
- *agree* is an ordinary Present Simple verb (not ~~I am agree~~)

3 This presentation stage can be 'formal', with representatives of each group standing up to present their budget to the rest of the class. Make it clear that if students have not reached a final solution, they should explain why and what they agreed / disagreed about. Write up the following phrases: *We all think ... , None of us think ... , We couldn't agree about ...* . If students are still interested once everyone has presented their budgets, try to agree on a budget together as a class.

Task: alternative suggestions

a *If you are short of time or have a class with weak listening skills*: miss out the listening stage and give all the information about the different organisations yourself. If possible, spend time creating interest in St Ambrosia and its lottery.

b *If you cannot finish the task in one lesson*: get students to do Task, Exercise 1 as homework, before moving onto the group / class discussion in the following lesson.

c *If you don't think your students will be very motivated by discussing an imaginary island*: create a 'parallel' task, using the students' own country or region. Either invent the organisations bidding for lottery money yourself, or get students to invent them. The following tips may help:

- Make sure you have a good range of organisations to appeal to different interests (education, arts, sport, business, etc.) Include a mixture of business interests to create more wealth, and social concerns to appeal to students' humanitarian instincts.

- Include a high risk / high returns option (such as the oil option), which could be a complete waste of money, or make the area really rich.

- If there is a national lottery in the students' own country, include some controversial 'real life' organisations which receive lottery funding.

- If possible, introduce some organisations which will spark discussion about current controversies in your country, (an AIDS foundation, etc.)

d *If you prefer to do the task as a role play / simulation*: instead of playing the cassette, get some students to take on the roles of the representatives of the various organisations, while others take on the role of the Lottery Commission members. The following tips may help:

- Prepare role cards in advance for the representatives, based on the information in the tapescripts on pages 163–164 of the Students' Book.

- Make sure that everyone has enough time to prepare what they are going to say. While representatives are preparing their speeches, Lottery Commission members should prepare questions, for example: *How much money do you*

module 9

need?, How exactly would you spend it?, etc. Circulate, supplying vocabulary.
- Representatives take turns to present their case to the Lottery Commission members, answering any questions they have.
- After the representatives have made their speeches, they can join in the discussion, continuing to argue their own case. The commission members must then vote on who should receive the funding.

Task link (PAGE 98)

Ways of saying numbers

1 [9.5] Get students to guess how the numbers are said in pairs before playing the cassette. Pause after each number for students to repeat.

2 [9.6] Check the meaning of: *an estimate / estimated, speed, to vote in an election*. Students try to guess in pairs before checking against the cassette. Pause if necessary to allow students time to write. When checking answers, make sure students read out the full numbers correctly.

> **ANSWERS**
> a 5.7 billion b −89°C c 71% d 55,680,000 km
> e 199,859 f 300,000 km / sec g 86,000,000
> h 483,080 m² i 99.9999% j 26,000

3 Put students into pairs and refer them to the appropriate page at the back of the book. Check that students understand the categories for the numbers given. Do the first example on each card together and check that students can form the questions correctly.

ADDITIONAL ACTIVITIES

RB **Resource bank:** 9C *Hear ... Say!* (ways of saying numbers), page 148; 9D *Vocabulary extension* (talking about numbers, amounts and ages without being exact), page 149, Instructions page 102

Real life (PAGES 98–99)

Dealing with money

1 Focus students' attention on the photos and discuss the questions with the whole class. Check the meaning of: *a receipt* /rɪˈsiːt/, *a market stall, to bargain*.

> **ANSWERS**
> 1 They are in the street – a taxi driver and passenger.
> 2 They are in a street market – they are customers and the marketstall holder.
> 3 They are in the ticket office of a museum – they are a mother, father and children and the ticket seller.
> 4 They are in a clothes shop – they are a customer and shop assistant.

2 Check the meaning and pronunciation of: *reduction* /rɪˈdʌkʃən/, *roughly* /ˈrʌfli/, *owe* /əʊ/, *the change* /tʃeɪndʒ/, *sign* /saɪn/ *your name*. Students work individually or in pairs before checking answers with the whole class.

3 [9.7] Play the cassette and see if students hear the phrases the first time round. If necessary, play the cassette again, pausing to check and practise the phrases.

> **ANSWERS**
> b picture 4, shop assistant, customer
> c picture 2, customer, marketstall holder
> d picture 1, passenger, taxi driver
> e picture 2, marketstall holder, customer
> f picture 3, ticket seller, customer
> g picture 1, passenger, taxi driver
> h picture 4, customer, shop assistant
> i picture 1, passenger, taxi driver
> j picture 2, customer, marketstall holder
> k picture 4, shop assistant, customer

4 Put students into pairs and ask them to choose a situation (try to make sure that all the situations are covered). Make sure they understand the instructions and give them a few minutes to plan what to say. Students act out their role plays whilst you circulate and make a note of any errors for analysis / correction later on. Get one pair to act out each situation for the whole class.

Do you remember?

> **ANSWERS**
> 1 a inflation; unemployment; technology (• /ə/ • /ə/ • /ə/);
> facilities; per cent; pollution; government (/ə/• /ə/ • /ə/ /ə/ •);
> definitely; certainly; probably; perhaps (• /ə/ • /ə/ • /ə/ /ə/ •)
>
> 3 a to get worse (the other verbs mean 'to go up')
>   b to go up (the other verbs mean 'to go down')
>   c to deteriorate (this means 'to get worse', the opposite of *to improve / to get better*)
>
> 4 a I probably wouldn't know what to say.
>   b I decide to go out tonight.
>   c I didn't have anything to eat.
>   d I might retire. / I'd retire.
>
> 6 ninety-eight point five per cent; forty-eight point five square metres; seventy-six point four million; six thousand million; four hundred and fifty-five thousand; a (one) hundred thousand square kilometres; minus five degrees Celsius / Centigrade; twenty-nine degrees Celsius / Centigrade.

module 10

Part A Language

Language focus 1 (PAGE 101)

Past Perfect and Past Simple

See *Teacher's tips: using a discovery approach in the teaching of grammar* on page 15.

Focus students' attention on the cartoons and check the meaning of *caption*. Students work in pairs or groups before checking answers with the whole class. Go through their ideas for the missing caption, but do not spend too long on this.

> **ANSWERS**
> a 3   b 4   c 2   d 1
> Cartoon 5 does not have a caption; the original caption was: *Suddenly Melissa remembered she had never learnt how to swim.*

Analysis

1 Give students a few moments to underline the verbs, then check the form of the Past Perfect on the board, highlighting:
   - the form (*had* + past participle for all persons).
   - the question and negative forms.
   - the contractions '*d* and *hadn't*.

   > **ANSWERS**
   > a had already made   b had bought
   > c had finished   d had been

2 Students discuss the questions in pairs before checking answers with the whole class.

   > **ANSWERS AND LANGUAGE NOTES**
   > The third rule is correct. For many students the concept of the Past Perfect will cause few problems since it will be very similar in their own language (get mono-lingual groups to translate the captions to ensure that they have made this connection).

   The two incorrect rules highlight common misconceptions about the Past Perfect:

   a This is a common misconception about the Past Perfect. Point out that the Past Perfect is only used in reaction to a Past Simple action to show that it came first. If you are talking about a simple action in the past, however long ago, you use the Past Simple (*Dinosaurs <u>died</u> out millions of years ago*). Point out that, because of this relationship between two past events, the Past Perfect is commonly found in the following constructions:
   - after verbs like *knew* (see caption b) and *thought* (*He thought I'd told everyone*) and *remember* (*He remembered he hadn't locked the door*).
   - with time words like *when* (caption a) *after* (caption c) and *before* (caption d).

   b students confuse the Past Perfect with the Present Perfect. Present Perfect always relates a past action to the present (it describes 'the time before now'); Past Perfect relates a past action to one further in the past (it describes 'the time before the past'). Draw their attention to the time lines on page 148 of the *Language summary* to make this clear.

Make sure that students are clear about the difference between the way the Present Perfect and Past Perfect are formed. Point out that many of the same time words are used with both (*already* in caption a).

PRACTICE

1 Put students into pairs and refer them to the appropriate page at the back of the book. Focus on the two columns headed 'situation' and 'explanation'. Choose a pair of good students and do an example together, with A reading out the situation and B looking for an explanation. Write the complete explanation up, and then get B to read out a situation with A providing the explanation. Point out that in the second set of situations, they have to think of explanations themselves.

2 **a)** Get students to draw a picture of the scene or get them to close their books while you dictate the scene to them. Alternatively, draw the picture on the board yourself. Check the meaning of: *a phone box, to lie dead, the receiver (of a phone)*.

b) Look at the example question and make sure students understand they can only ask you *Yes / No* questions, and that you will only answer them if they use the Past Perfect correctly (they should not, however, 'over use' the Past Perfect in inappropriate cases). Students work individually or in pairs making a list of questions. Students call out their questions to you – give them clues if necessary to help them (for example, *Find out why the sea is important in the story*).

c) [10.1] When time runs out or if students start getting bored, play the answer on the cassette or read it out yourself to check.

> **ANSWER**
> The man had been fishing and had caught a very big fish. He was ringing up his wife to tell her about

74

it. As he was describing the fish he flung out his hands to show how big the fish was, breaking the glass on both sides of the phone box, cutting his wrists and killing himself.

ADDITIONAL PRACTICE

RB **Resource bank:** 10A *Ralph and the guitar case* (Past Perfect, Past Simple, Past Continuous), page 150, Instruction page 102

Workbook: Past Perfect or Past Simple, page 63; Present Perfect or Past Perfect, page 63

Language focus 2 (PAGES 102–103)
Reported speech and reported questions

See *Teacher's tips: using a discovery approach in the teaching of grammar* on page 15.

Mini-task

Put students into groups of three or four so that it does not matter if some students do not have a story to tell. If necessary, prompt students with questions about types of 'difficult' phone calls (When was the last time you made a complaint about something? / Did you have to give someone some difficult news? / Were you telling a lie for some reason?).

Do not focus explicitly on the Past Perfect at this stage, but make a note of any useful errors for correction after the Analysis.

In particular, notice whether:
- *students show any awareness of the tense shifts.*
- *they use correct word order to report questions.*
- *they use* say *and* tell *correctly.*

1 Create interest in the story and check the meaning of: *to be separated, a tattoo, an owl, phone in sick, urgent, dial a number*. Students work individually or in pairs before checking answers with the whole group. Make sure that students are clear about the names of the two brothers, and which one is which to avoid confusion later on.

ANSWERS
a They were brothers who were separated during the Second World War.
b He was sixteen years older than his brother, and he had a tattoo of an owl on the back of his hand.
c Because she was off sick, and he wanted to know what appointments he had. He found a number with the name 'Bell' and 'urgent' written next to it.

2 Students work individually or in pairs, before checking answers with the whole class. As you check answers copy the story in the correct order onto the board, leaving space between each sentence to write in the direct speech version later on.

ANSWERS
2 The woman said she was sorry, but …
3 She asked him to ring back later …
4 Michael said he would ring back later, …
5 The woman said that it was.
6 Becoming excited now, …
7 She told him that she had …
8 When Michael's secretary came back …
9 The secretary told him …
10 Thanks to this amazing coincidence, …

3 [10.2] Write in the direct speech version of the first part of the conversation, under the reported version, in a different colour if possible. Students can do the rest in pairs or groups. Check the answers, pausing the cassette after each line of the dialogue or break it into sections if necessary. Write up the rest of the direct speech version under the reported version on the board as above.

ANSWERS
See tapescript, Module 10, recording 2 on page 164 of the Students' Book.

Analysis

1 Give students a few minutes to compare the texts individually before checking answers with the whole class. (Only a few tenses are covered here – others are covered in the *Language summary*, so you may wish to refer to this at this stage to give students a fuller picture of tense shift patterns.)

ANSWERS AND LANGUAGE NOTES
Present Simple > Past Simple; Present Perfect > Past Perfect; Past Simple > Past Perfect; *will* > *would*

Time words in reported speech: these have to reflect the past time frame (*the next day* rather than *tomorrow* in direct speech). This is perfectly logical, and should not cause too many problems if they are using reported speech in a natural context.

2 Get students to underline the reported questions in the text before checking with the whole class.

ANSWERS AND LANGUAGE NOTES
a *ask* (*to wonder* is also quite common); *if* / *whether* are used with *yes* / *no* questions (*Michael asked if he could speak to Mr Bell*).
There is no difference in meaning between *if* and *whether* and they are not needed in *wh-* questions where the question word acts as a conjunction (*He asked her who had given her his brother's number.*)
b There is no inversion of subject and verb in reported questions. Again, this is perfectly logical, because reported questions are not true questions.

module 10

3 Copy the dialogue and its reported version onto the board and give students a few minutes to read it. Ask if they notice anything about the reported version (if necessary underline the relevant verbs to make this clearer). Ask them why they think the verbs do not change into the past form (if the same is true in their own language, translate to make this clear). Discuss the answers to the questions with the whole class.

ANSWERS AND LANGUAGE NOTES
a The verbs are not changed into the past because the situation is still true. Again this is logical, since, unlike the reported speech in the story, they do not refer to a past time frame. In modern English it is increasingly common to use present tenses here – indeed there are many cases where a tense shift sounds strange in these circumstances.
b It is possible to shift tenses here, but to many native speakers it would probably sound very formal or old-fashioned.

PRACTICE

1 Go over again with students who Harry and Michael Findlater were and what happened to each of them. If necessary, summarise this information on the board: *Harry – 16 years older than Michael, tattoo; Michael – younger brother, spent 30 years looking for his brother, finally phoned him by mistake because his secretary was off sick.*
Students write sentences individually or in pairs before checking answers with the whole class.

ANSWERS
a Michael told Harry that he couldn't believe that he had finally found him.
b Harry asked Michael how he had got his phone number.
c Michael asked Harry if he would show him his tattoo.
d Harry told Michael that he was certainly taller than when he had last seen him.
e Michael told Harry that he had spent nearly thirty years looking for him.
f Michael asked Harry if he had ever tried to look for him.
g Harry said that it was lucky that Michael's secretary was / had been off sick that day.
h Michael said that he thought he would give her a pay rise.

Note that the tense shift is used throughout, because this forms part of a story which happened within a past time frame.

2 Check the meaning of any unknown words before getting students to think about the questions for a few minutes. Students walk around the class asking their questions. Point out that they only need to ask each person one question. They can repeat this several times to increase the amount of practice, but be careful that this does not become too repetitive. Unless your class is very strong, get students to write out the reported speech versions before feeding back to the class. Alternatively, get them to feedback orally, then write up the results of their questionnaire for homework in reported speech.

ADDITIONAL PRACTICE

RB **Resource bank:** 10B *Jungle survivors* (reported speech), page 151; 10C *Vocabulary extension* (verbs to use instead of *say*), page 152, Instructions page 102

Workbook: Reported statements, page 64; Reported questions, page 64; *say* and *tell* page 65

Reading and listening
(PAGES 104–105)

1 Students discuss the questions in groups before reporting back to the whole class. If necessary, give students the names of famous robberies and ask if they know what happened, or extend the discussion to other types of crimes (famous murders, etc.)

2 Check the pronunciation of: *deposit* /dɪˈpɒzɪt/, *owe* /əʊ/, *fingerprint* /ˈfɪŋɡəprɪnt/, *pretend* /prɪˈtend/, *insurance* /ɪnˈʃʊərəns/. (See *Teacher's tips: making the most of the Mini-dictionary* on page 14.)

3 Emphasise that students should only read the first part of the text at this stage. (Get them to cover the second text with a piece of paper.)

ANSWERS
a To keep money and jewels in – often they were people who didn't want to put their money in a bank account (perhaps because they didn't want the police, for example, to be able to find it).
b Parvez Latif was one of the owners of 'Security Deposits' – he had a lot of debts and no way of repaying them. Valerio Viccei was an Italian bankrobber who had escaped to London, where he still robbed banks. He was a customer of 'Security Deposits'.
c They became friendly and realised that, if they worked together, they could solve both of their problems.

4 a) Get students to close their books while they think of a plan. Discuss some of the plans with the whole class before reading the second part of the text.

b) Students discuss answers in pairs before checking as a whole class.

module 10

> **Part two of the story: additional comprehension questions**
>
> If students have clearly understood the story, move straight on to the cassette. If you want to check their comprehension further, put up some / all of the following questions.
>
> a How did each of the two men prepare for the robbery?
> b What kind of day was it when the robbery happened?
> c When Viccei phoned up, who did he pretend to be?
> d How did Latif respond?
> e What did Viccei do when Latif was showing him round?
> f What did Latif do?
> g What happened to Viccei while he was stealing the money?
> h How much money did the robbers take?

5 [10.3] Get students to close their books again and plan their escape. Discuss their ideas and predictions for what the police will do. If necessary, ask questions to prompt these: *What kind of clues will they look for? Who will they interview?*, etc. Play the cassette and get students to read the tapescript as well if you think they will find it difficult to understand without reading.

> **ANSWERS**
> *The importance of the pictures is:*
> a *the fingerprint*: the police found a fingerprint on the broken security boxes, which turned out to belong to Viccei.
> b *Whites Hotel / the Ferrari*: a black Ferrari was often parked in front of this hotel, where people who knew Viccei often met.
> c *car window*: a policeman reached in to grab the keys from Viccei's Ferrari as it stopped at some traffic lights.
> d *phone bill*: the police found a phone call to Latif in Viccei's phone bill.
> e *Judge*: the judge sentences Viccei to twenty-two years in prison, Latif to eighteen.

> **Additional suggestion: role play and writing activity**
>
> Get students to role play one of the following interviews:
> • Latif and the police just after the robbery happened.
> • One of the security guards and the police at the same time.
> • Viccei and the police after he was arrested.

Give students a few minutes to imagine how they are feeling (if they are the suspect) and decide what they are going to ask / say. Afterwards get students to write a report of the interview as if they are the policeman (remind them that reported speech would be appropriate here).

Wordspot (PAGE 105)

say and *tell*

See *Teacher's tips: working with lexis* on pages 12–13.

1 Check the meaning of: *the truth, a lie, a prayer, a joke*. Students work in pairs before checking answers with the whole class.

> **ANSWERS**
> *say*: 'hello' / ' goodbye', 'thank you', 'yes' / 'no', you're sorry, a prayer
> *tell*: someone off, the truth / lies, someone to do something, someone about something, the difference between two things, a story / joke, someone what to do

2 Do the first example together, then get students to complete the gaps individually. Check answers with the whole class before getting students to ask and answer the questions in groups.

> **ANSWERS**
> a say   b tell   c telling / tell   d tell   e say
> f tell   g tell   h told

3 Prepare this in advance by copying the blank diagrams onto a poster-sized piece of paper. Copy the answers to Exercise 1 directly onto the poster as you go through them.

Part B Task

See *Teacher's tips: making tasks work* on pages 8–9 and *Responding to learners' individual language needs* on pages 10–11.

Preparation for task (PAGE 107)

Focus students' attention on the pictures and emphasise that they all relate to a true story called *The Waratah Omen* which students will listen to later. Students check the meaning of the words in groups with the whole class. Check the pronunciation of: *knight* /naɪt/, *gale* /geɪl/, *to scream* /skriːm/, *a sword* /sɔːd/.

module 10

Task (PAGE 107)

1 Put students into groups of three or four and tell them they have to invent a story using all the pictures. Read through the questions and give them a few minutes to think before discussing the answers in groups. Tell them they can make notes if they want, but that they should not write out the whole story at this stage.

2 Students work individually or in pairs. Emphasise that they may have to tell the story to the whole class so it needs to be clear and comprehensible. Focus on the *Useful language* box, drilling the phrases and checking any problems. Help weak students with their pronunciation, so that the story sounds clear enough for the rest of the class to understand (individual correction is probably more appropriate with this task than whole class correction at the end).

3 It could be repetitive if all the groups tell their stories, so start with one story and invite students in other groups to say how their story differs from it. If theirs is completely different, they can tell it in full.

4 [10.4] Play the cassette and, if necessary, get students to read the tapescript at the same time. Discuss how close their stories were to what actually happened.

> **Task, Exercise 4: additional suggestion**
>
> If you think your students might have problems understanding / following the story on the cassette, put up some comprehension questions for them to answer, as follows:
>
> a Who was Claude Sawyer?
> b What was the *Waratah*?
> c What dream did Sawyer have while he was on the ship?
> d What did he decide to do as a result?
> e What dream did he have after he left the ship?
> f What did he do this time?
> g What happened to the *Waratah* after it left Durban?
> h What did the investigation find?

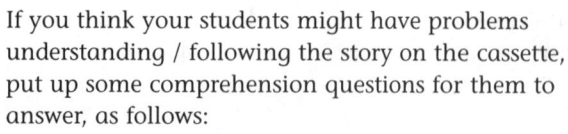

Optional writing

Read through the list of options and give students a few minutes to choose one. This can be set for homework, although it would be useful to start it off in class. Refer students to the *Useful language* box for phrases to include.

> **Task: alternative suggestions**
>
> *If you have an active, creative group:* they may prefer to tell their own frightening stories, right from the beginning. However it would still be useful to provide a model. You could do this in a number of ways:
>
> a *Using the cassette:*
> - Do the vocabulary work in the *Preparation for task*, then play the cassette straightaway (if their listening skills are not strong, you may prefer them to listen and read).
> - Either in pairs or as a whole class, get them to reconstruct the story using the pictures, and discuss their reactions to it briefly.
>
> b *Providing a model yourself:*
> - Tell a story of your own about a mysterious / frightening event (it could either be something that happened to you, or one of your friends, or a story you have read or heard elsewhere).
> - As a task you could write a list of key words from the story onto the board, then tell students to listen and order them or explain their significance in the story.
>
> c *Making a cassette of your own:*
> If you know any English speakers (preferably teachers who know how to 'grade their language') who have had any strange or frightening experiences, you could interview them and get them to tell the story on cassette for you. In class:
> - Make sure you introduce the story clearly, pre-teaching any key vocabulary, so that students understand the story as well as possible.
> - Set a task, writing up a list of key words as in b) above.
> - After listening it would again be useful to get them to re-construct the story, to make sure that they understood it properly.
>
> The next stage is to get students to tell their own stories. It is simplest if each student works individually. The following framework should help:
>
> - Give them a few moments to think of a story, suggesting various possible sources (films, novels, personal experiences, friends' experiences, stories people have told them, nightmares, etc.) The story does not have to have a supernatural element – it could be frightening, for example because they were in terrible danger.
> - Give students 15–20 minutes to plan their stories, asking you about any words / phrases they need and referring them to the *Useful language box* on page 106 as necessary.
> - If you think they need additional practice, get them to tell their stories in pairs before telling the whole class.

module 10

> • If you have a large class, instead of listening to everyone's story as a class, get students to tell their stories in larger groups. (Alternatively, you could spread the story-telling out over the next few lessons, with perhaps a couple of people telling their stories at the beginning, and a couple at the end.)

Task link (PAGE 108)

Adverbs for telling stories

1 Students work individually / in pairs or as a whole class. As you check the answers, drill stress and pronunciation as necessary.

ANSWERS
eventually /ɪˈventʃuəli/ – immediately /ɪˈmiːdiətli/
surprisingly /səˈpraɪzɪŋli/ – naturally /ˈnætʃərəli/, obviously /ˈɒbviəsli/
strangely /ˈstreɪndʒli/ – naturally, obviously
gradually /ˈɡrædʒuəli/ – suddenly /ˈsʌdnli/
sadly /ˈsædli/ – /ˈfɔːtʃənətli/

2 Focus students' attention on the picture and get students to match the two sentences which go with it. Students match the other sentences individually or in pairs before checking answers as a whole class.

ANSWERS
a 3 b 6 c 1 d 10 e 7 f 9 g 5 h 2
i 8 j 4

3 Do the first example together, making it clear that students must continue the sentences logically, according to the meaning of the adverbs.

Do you remember?

ANSWERS
1 a George left the company when James started.
  b Jill finished her work at ten o'clock.
  c My boss is in hospital because he's broken his leg.
2 a INTERVIEWER: At what age does a woman stop being interested in men?
     WOMAN: I don't know. Ask me again when I'm older.
     MAN: I think I am a dog.
     PSYCHIATRIST: This is a very unusual problem. Can you sit down on the sofa?
     MAN: I can't – I'm not allowed on the sofa.
  b A patient asked his doctor if he could promise him that he would live longer if he gave up smoking, drinking and women. The doctor said he couldn't promise he would, but that it would feel like longer.
  A schoolboy asked his teacher if he could be punished for something he hadn't done. The teacher said of course he couldn't. The schoolboy said 'good', because he hadn't done his homework.
3 *say:* 'hello', 'goodbye', 'thank you', 'yes' / 'no', you're sorry, a prayer
  tell: the truth, lies, a story, a joke, the difference (between two things)
4 a *security guards* (the others are all criminals / types of criminals)
  b *a gale* (the others are connected with *knight*)
  c *naturally* (the others describe something you did not expect)
  d *a ghost* (the others are connected with ships)
  e *a prayer* (the others all go with *tell*)
5 a gradually; immediately; eventually; fortunately; obviously

module 11

Part A Language

Language focus 1 (PAGES 110–111)
Obligation and permission

See *Teacher's tips: using a discovery approach in the teaching of grammar* on page 15.

Mini-task

Check that students understand what *rules* and *regulations* are and elicit an example. Students make lists in pairs – stress that they only have to make notes. Do not focus explicitly on modals, etc. of obligation and permission at this stage.

Circulate, making notes of how well they are using them, in particular:

- are they only using *must* or are they using *have to* and *have got to*?
- do they seem to understand the difference between *must* and *should*?
- are there any problems with *mustn't* and *don't have to*?

Make a note of useful errors for correction after the *Analysis*.

1 a) Check the meaning of *sign* and *notice* and discuss the questions with the whole class.

b) Check the meaning of *transit lounge* and focus students' attention on the picture. Check the meaning of: *a duty free shop, staff, luggage, to leave something unattended, a boarding card / boarding gate, wet paint*. Students discuss the questions in pairs before checking answers with the whole class.

2 Look at the first example together before getting students to do the rest individually or in pairs. Check answers with the whole class, dealing with any problems students have with the verbs. (The *Analysis* may therefore just be a summary of points you have already discussed.)

ANSWERS AND LANGUAGE NOTES
The following mean the same as the signs in the picture, the others do not:

b *have to* and *have got to* (the meaning is the same, though *have got to* is more informal)

c *are allowed to** (means basically the same as *can*)

d *mustn't* and *aren't allowed to* (again the meaning is basically the same)

e *mustn't* (because you can't smoke here: *don't have to* means 'it is not necessary, but you can if you want to')

f *should* is better – it means 'it is a good idea to / it is the right thing to do' (*must* is too strong, since the notice says 'please')

g both are acceptable, but *mustn't* is better, since the sign is strongly worded

h *should / ought to* **(the meaning is basically the same 'it is a good idea to be careful')

* *(not) be allowed to* has a narrower meaning than *can* since it is only used to refer to rules / things that are officially authorised in some way (this point may be too complex for students unless there is a precise translation in their own language).

** grammar books disagree about whether or not there is a difference between these two. At this level where *ought to* is only likely to be for passive recognition, there is no need to worry about this.

Analysis

1 If you have already dealt with the language points above, most students should be able to complete the table individually or in pairs. Check answers with the whole class, highlighting the problems of form below. The phrases can be drilled, although pronunciation is dealt with later on in the module.

Highlight the following if you think they might present problems:

- the use of the bare infinitive after *can*, *must* and *should*
- the use of *to* after the other verbs
- the fact that *be allowed to* is a passive form and therefore needs the verb *to be*
- the formation of the negatives and their contractions: *can't / mustn't / shouldn't / oughtn't to*/ don't have to / haven't got to*

  *this form is not very commonly used

- question forms: *Can I ...? / Must you ...? / Should we ...? / Ought we to ...?* / Do you have to ...? / Have we got to ...? / Are they allowed to ...?*

  *again, this form is not very commonly used

- the fact that *can, must, should* and *ought to* do not change forms in the third person singular, but we say *does he have to .... ?* and *has he got to ...?*

ANSWERS
it is necessary: have to / have got to / must
it is okay / permitted: can / are allowed to
it is a good idea / the correct thing: should / ought to
it is not necessary: don't have to
it is not okay / it is prohibited: can't / mustn't / aren't allowed to
it is not a good idea / not the correct thing: shouldn't

80

module 11

2 Students work individually or in pairs before checking answers with the whole class.

ANSWERS AND LANGUAGE NOTES:
a With *must* the obligation comes from the speaker (it is probably the doctor speaking here), with *have to* the obligation comes from someone other than the speaker (the speaker is explaining what the doctor said). This may be hard for students to understand, but they will still be understood perfectly well if they use either form.
b The difference here is much more clearly defined: *mustn't* means *can't* (there is an obligation not to do something, there is no choice), *don't have to* means *it is not necessary to do this* (but there is a choice, you can if you want to).

PRACTICE

1 Emphasise that students have to complete the sentences to make them true. Before starting, check the meaning of: *to cross the road, a seat belt, a motorway, to reserve a ticket, a first / second class ticket, a compartment*.
This can be done as a spoken or written exercise, with students working in pairs or groups. As you check answers, encourage students to give alternative suggestions as there is not necessarily one correct answer. For example, students might want to say any of the following:
Lorries are allowed to drive through the city centre. (there's no law against this)
Lorries shouldn't drive through the city centre. (it's not a good thing – it causes pollution)
Lorries don't have to drive through the city centre. (there is a ring road round the outside of town)
The important thing is that the students know why they are using the form they have chosen. Get them to explain their sentence where there is any doubt.

2 a) Get students to attempt this in pairs without pre-teaching vocabulary, as this will give the answer away.

ANSWER
a swimming pool

b) Put students into pairs and refer them to the appropriate page at the back of the book. Give them a few minutes to think of rules for each place, and circulate to help them with vocabulary. Check the answers with the whole class, eliciting the rules that students gave each other, and correcting any mistakes with the verbs for obligation and permission.

Pronunciation

1 [11.1] Play the cassette or read out the sentences yourself at natural speed. Pause after each sentence to give students time to write. Re-play / repeat if necessary until students hear all the words. Discuss which place the rules apply to.

ANSWERS
a a library   b a plane   c a school / office
d a train   e a restaurant   f a hotel   g a hotel
h a library   i a library   j a plane

2 Re-play the cassette, pausing after each sentence to highlight the pronunciation of the forms. Pay particular attention to the following:
- *can* is weak and unstressed, whereas *can't* is stressed
- the weak form of *to* in all cases where it is used before the infinitive
- the linking in *you're allowed to*
- the 'v' in *have to* (and the 's' in *has to*) are pronounced /f/ and /s/ (in contrast to when *have* is used as a verb on its own)
- the silent letters in *mustn't, should,* etc. (you could also mention the pronunciation of *ought to* /ɔːt/ here)

Drill the verbs in isolation, then get students to repeat the complete sentences, paying attention to stress and incorporating weak forms and linking where appropriate.

ADDITIONAL PRACTICE

Workbook: Obligation and permission, page 69; *Must* and *have to*, page 70.

Language focus 2 (PAGES 112–113)
Obligation and permission in the past

See *Teacher's tips: using a discovery approach in the teaching of grammar* on page 15.

1 Check that students understand the difference between *a rule* and *a law* and the meaning of:
a beard, a nobleman, to pay tax, male, female, to resign from your job, a vehicle, a flag, to solve a problem.
Students work individually or in pairs before checking answers with the whole class.

ANSWERS
a 5   b 4   c 3   d 1   e 2

2 At this stage students will need to use past forms of verbs of obligation. Either correct them as necessary and use the *Analysis* simply as a summary of the forms, or leave mistakes uncorrected until you get to the *Analysis*. Discuss answers with the whole class.

81

module 11

ANSWERS
a Noblemen were not allowed to wear beards.
b People had to pay a tax on the number of windows they had.
c Female teachers were not allowed to get married or go out with a man.
d If you were driving a car, someone had to walk in front of you waving a red flag.
e People were not allowed to eat ice-cream sodas on Sunday.

Analysis

1 Students work individually, working out the forms before checking answers with the whole class. Check the pronunciation of: *could* /kəd/, *couldn't* /kədənt/, *were allowed to* /əlaʊdtə/.

ANSWERS AND LANGUAGE NOTES
could, couldn't, had to, didn't have to, (hadn't got to*), (had to**), was / were allowed to, wasn't / weren't allowed to

* *must* has no negative form of its own so *had to* is used. In the negative form we use *couldn't* or *weren't allowed to*.
** *had / hadn't got to* is not standard English, *had to / didn't have to* are used in the past form
The past form of *should* is dealt with in Module 12.

PRACTICE

[11.2] Check the meaning of: *to cause crime, to vote, a servant, his master, to be strict*. Students work in pairs before playing the cassette to check answers.

ANSWERS
a couldn't / weren't allowed to; had to
b weren't allowed to / couldn't; had to
c weren't allowed to / couldn't
d weren't allowed to / couldn't; were allowed to / could
e weren't allowed to / couldn't; weren't allowed to / couldn't; had to; had to

ADDITIONAL PRACTICE

Workbook: Obligation and permission in the past, page 70.

Vocabulary and speaking (PAGE 114)

Rules and behaviour

See *Teacher's tips: making the most of the Mini-dictionary* on page 14.

1 Write the questions up on the board (adjusting the tenses if necessary to suit the age group of your students) and check the meaning of *a household chore* and *jewellery*. Students discuss the questions in groups. Circulate, supplying any vocabulary they need to tell their anecdotes, etc. The discussion can be brief or lengthy depending on time and interest level.

2 At this stage deal with basic form, meaning and pronunciation of the words in bold – extension work on the vocabulary is better left until after the discussion. Highlight the following:

- the meaning of *sensible* (not stupid, practical) if it is a 'false friend'
- the pronunciation of: *well-behaved* /ˌwelbɪˈheɪvd/, *sensible* /ˈsensəbəl/, *punishment* /ˈpʌnɪʃmənt/, *treat* /triːt/, *shout* /ʃaʊt/.

Check the meaning of *strict* and *liberal* before putting students in groups to discuss the questions.

3 Remind students that if they are talking hypothetically about being a parent, they should use *I would ..., I wouldn't ... / I would never ...* . Discuss the questions either in groups / with the whole class.

Listening (PAGE 114)

School rules

1 Before starting, do some vocabulary work on different types of schools by presenting / eliciting the following:

- *primary school* (*elementary school* in US English)
- *secondary school* (*high school* in US English)
- *a comprehensive school* (the normal type of secondary school in Britain – all pupils can go there, they are not selected on their ability)
- *mixed schools / single sex schools*
- *private schools* (*public school* in US English; in British English a *public school* is a high status private school, such as Eton College)
- *state* (or *state-run*) *schools*
- *convent schools*
- *boarding schools*

Get students to read the paragraph and tell you what they found out about Joan and Gareth's education.

2 Put students in pairs to guess who mentions which topic. Check the pronunciation of: *prayer* /preə/, *lonely* /ˈləʊnli/, *trainer* /ˈtreɪnə/, *chemistry* /ˈkeməstri/.

3 [11.3] **a)** Emphasise that the first time students listen, they only have to identify who mentions which topic. Play the cassette straight through before getting them to check answers in pairs.

b) Ask them if they can remember what the exact rules were in each case before playing the cassette again to check.

82

module 11

ANSWERS
going to church (J), staying at school after class (G), snobbery (J), mealtimes (J), school uniform (G), good manners (J), speaking French (J), the chemistry lab (G), wearing trainers (G), being lonely (J); *saying prayers* is not mentioned at all

4 Students discuss the questions in groups. Circulate, supplying any vocabulary they need. The discussion can be brief or lengthy depending on interest level.

Wordspot (PAGE 115)

do

See *Teacher's tips: working with lexis* on pages 12–13.

1 Focus on the diagram and check that students understand the section headings. Students work individually or in pairs / groups before checking answers with the whole class. Drill the phrases as you check them.

ANSWERS AND LANGUAGE NOTES
(section in brackets)
do badly (e); do a course (a); do Economics at university (a); do your homework (a); do the ironing (d); do nothing (e); do overtime (b); do a test (a); do the washing (d); do some work (a / b); do yoga (c)
It is more common to say *do French at university* than *study French at university*.
We have not at this stage contrasted *do* with *make*, but they are contrasted in the *Consolidation* at the end of Module 12.

2 [11.4] **a)** Get students to draw their own larger box in their notebooks if necessary. Emphasise that they can write their answers wherever they like and that they should only write single words or phrases. Pause the cassette after each question, explaining if necessary, and allowing students time to write.

b) When they have finished, get students to swap books and ask each other questions (demonstrate this if necessary by 'borrowing' one of the student's notebooks and asking questions like the example given).

....

Part B Task

See *Teacher's tips: making tasks work* on pages 8–9 and *Responding to learners' individual language needs* on pages 10–11.

Preparation for task (PAGE 117)

1 Create interest by focusing attention on the photos and discussing briefly what issues they deal with. Explain that students are going to read about some controversial issues. Check the meaning of:
arms, military service, a duty, to have a right to do something, legal / illegal / to legalise, to be prosecuted, to be convicted (of an offence), a life sentence, guidelines, to control, to give birth, mentally fit, physically fit, terminally ill, soft / hard drugs, licensed to sell.
Check that students understand the headlines and do the first example together. Make it clear that students do not have to understand every word in the text, before putting them in pairs or groups to match the headings. Check answers with the whole class.

ANSWERS
2 a 3 e 4 d 5 c 6 f (*three strikes and you're out* is a phrase used by politicians and newspapers to describe this law – it means 'you only have three chances and then you'll be sent to prison')

2 Check that students understand the True / False statements before getting them to do the exercise in pairs / groups. Remind them to correct the false statements.

ANSWERS
a T
b F (*but this used to be true*)
c T
d F (*anyone can carry a small amount; only special cafés can sell it*)
e F (*they both have to do it, but for men it is three years, for women two*)
f F (*this is only true if it is your third offence*)

Task (PAGE 117)

1 It may simplify the task to write up statements for each law (see *Task: alternative suggestion*, option a). Give students ten minutes to think about their opinions and how to justify them. Circulate, supplying any vocabulary they need.

2 Put students into groups of three to five (try to include a mix of quieter / more opinionated students in each group). Make it clear that if they agree quickly or do not have very strong opinions about any of the laws, they should move on (there will probably be other issues about which they have a lot more to say). Focus their attention briefly on the *Useful language* box. Drill and practise these phrases in short sentences, for example:
Personally I don't think military service is a good idea.
Everyone should be free to choose.
I think it's wrong for ordinary people to have guns.
(It may be more appropriate to wait until after the task, rather than interrupt the flow of students' thought too much at this stage.) If some groups finish before others, ask them to prepare how they will summarise their group's opinion.

83

module 11

3 and 4 The summarising stage can either be formal, taking everyone's opinion into account, or an opportunity for more free discussion now that students have formulated and rehearsed their views. If students are still very keen to discuss the issues, do not structure the discussion too much. If students have less to say, put the emphasis on describing different points of view and reasons for them and look at useful language points that have come out of the task.

Optional writing

Note that you may decide to do the Task link *on page 118 before setting the writing activity.*

Get students to do a rough draft first and help them to correct it before doing a final draft for homework. Encourage students to express their ideas as simply as possible, using language they already know – many of the phrases in the *Useful language* box can be used here too. Remind students of simple sentences for listing arguments: *firstly, secondly, finally,* etc.

> **Task: alternative suggestions**
>
> a *If you are short of time or feel that the reading text is too 'heavy'*: adapt the task in one of the following ways:
>
> - Set the reading / comprehension activities for homework the previous lesson, and start by checking the answers, before moving on to the discussion.
>
> - Do the *Preparation for task* in one lesson, then get students to prepare their own opinions for homework, thinking about any vocabulary they need to express what they feel. In the next lesson circulate and supply vocabulary they need, before moving on to the discussion stage.
>
> - Omit the reading and replace it with the following simplified statements.
>   *Everyone should have the right to euthanasia if that is what they want.*
>   *Women of any age should be allowed to have children if they are mentally and physically fit.*
>   *Everyone should have the right to carry a gun for their personal protection.*
>   *The use and sale of cannabis should be legalised.*
>   *Both men and women should do a period of military service.*
>   *Anyone who commits three or more crimes, however small, should go to prison for life.*
>
> Then proceed with the task as normal. The reading could then be done after the task, or set as homework.
>
> b *If you think your students will find this kind of discussion difficult for any reason*: adapt the task in one of the following ways:
>
> - Replace some / all of the issues with ones you know are topical for your students. Present these in the form of 'extreme' sentences for students to agree / disagree with, for example:
>   *People who smoke should not have the right to free healthcare.*
>
>   The reading text can be used either as a more general preparation for the theme of controversial issues, or as a means of introducing useful vocabulary and practising reading skills after the discussion.
>
> - Some students (particularly younger ones) may respond better to these issues if they are re-formulated in more personal terms, for example:
>   *If I had incurable cancer, I would want to be able to choose whether or not to die.*
>   *It would not worry me to have a mother who was sixty or seventy years old.*
>   *I think that I should be able to carry a gun to protect myself if I feel that it is necessary.*
>   *I am / would be happy to do military service for a year or two.*
>   *I should be able to smoke cannabis if I want to.*
>   *If someone committed a crime against me or one of my family, I would want them to go to prison for a very long time.*
>
>   Introduce the theme and move straight on to the discussion, following the stages of the task in the *Students' Book*. Set the reading text for homework.
>
> - Some students may have cultural problems with the possible conflict of ideas that this kind of discussion may provoke. In this case change the focus of the task by asking students to think about all the possible arguments for and against each law (or each group can do this for one or two of the laws). Do the first example together, making a list on the board of points, for example:
>   **for:** *your life may be completely miserable if you are in terrible pain*
>   *no one has the right to end a human life*
>   **against:** *it is a waste of money to keep people alive who will never get better and who don't want to live*
>   *relatives or the state may try to persuade people to die for financial reasons*
>
>   Extend these lists in the group discussion and present them to the whole class. If students want to discuss their own opinions, they can still do this as part of the class discussion at the end of the task.
>
> c *If you think your students will enjoy a formal debate*: re-format the task as follows:
>
> - Divide the class into pairs, and give each pair one issue, saying whether they are to argue for or against it. (Make sure you have one pair arguing for and another pair arguing against!) Reduce the issues to simple statements (see option a).
>
> - Circulate, supplying students with vocabulary and

module 11

helping them to think of arguments if necessary.
- Tell students that one of each pair will be the 'proposer' (who will speak first) and another the 'seconder' (who will support the proposer). Between the proposer and the seconder the other side will speak, so the seconder should be ready to answer any further arguments that he / she comes up with which have not been mentioned before. (You will probably need to re-explain all of this as the first debate goes on.) Feed in some language for debating and listing arguments: *Ladies and gentlemen ..., Firstly ..., Secondly ..., Thirdly ..., What is more ..., Finally ...,* etc.
- Set out five chairs at the front of the class, the middle one for the chairperson (either you or a student), and two on either side for the teams for and against. For the first debate, choose an issue which both sides have prepared well. Start by reading out the motion, and asking students in the audience to vote: 'for', 'against' or 'undecided'. Then start the debate.

(Note that if you appoint a student as the chairperson, teach him / her a few useful phrases: *Let him / her finish what he is saying, Please don't interrupt, Order, please, One person at a time please, Any questions?, Does anyone else want to speak?,* etc.)

- After the two sides have spoken, the chairperson gives the audience the opportunity to ask questions or express their own opinions. Then take another vote to see if opinion has been changed by the debate. Move on to the next issue, changing speakers and repeating the process. If you are not acting as chairperson, make notes about errors in the usual way.

ADDITIONAL ACTIVITY

RB Resource bank: 11A *Freedom of choice?* vocabulary extension, page 153, Instructions page 102

Task link (PAGE 118)

Linking words

1 Do a couple of examples together before getting students to do the rest individually or in pairs. If necessary, give examples from the *Language summary* as they do the exercise rather than waiting until the end. Read through the *Language summary* together as a class while checking answers, particularly the information on word order and punctuation.

> **ANSWERS**
> similar meaning to *and*: also, besides, what is more
> similar meaning to *but*: although, however, despite this
> similar meaning to *so*: for this reason, as a result, therefore

2 Check the meaning of: *to prevent, to control your weight, unhealthy, to be depressed, a cure, a disease, heart disease*.
Do an example together, showing students how they can start with *and*, *but* or *so* to help them choose the right word, and highlighting the punctuation. Elicit different possibilities for b), highlighting the punctuation again.

> **ANSWERS**
> a • What is more, Also, Besides,
>   • However, Despite this, although,
> b • For this reason, Therefore,
>   • What is more, Also, Besides,
> c • What is more, Also, Besides,
>   • As a result, For this reason, Therefore,
> d • although, However,
>   • What is more, Also, Besides,
> e • As a result, For this reason, Therefore,
>   • although, However, Despite this,
>
> Note that if we use *although*, we do not need a new sentence as it is a conjunction not an adverb.

Real life (PAGE 118)

Agreeing and disagreeing

1 Do the first example together, before students do the rest in pairs. Check answers with the whole class, before playing the cassette and getting students to mark where the stress falls. Check answers, playing the cassette again if necessary, and drilling the phrases as you go along.

> **ANSWERS**
> *(There may be variations on the order of phrases in the middle of the line)*
>
> strongly agree — I agree in theory, but, — I suppose so. — I think it depends. — I'm not really sure. — Yes, but — I completely disagree. — strongly disagree
>
> I completely agree. — I agree in some ways. — I don't really agree. — That's absolute rubbish.

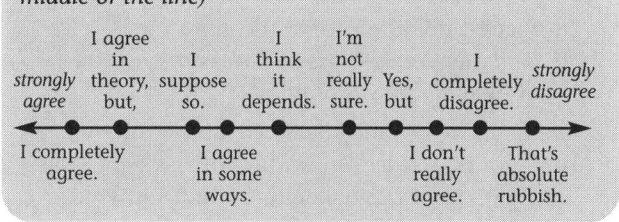

2 [11.6] Check the meaning of: *to gamble / gambling, to be banned*. Pause the cassette after each statement. With stronger classes, elicit a response straight away, with weaker students elicit what was said and explain it first before asking for a response. Encourage students to give a brief reason for their opinion, and drill the stress and intonation of the phrases again if necessary.

3 [11.7] Play the cassette straight through, asking students to write down whether or not the second speaker agreed or disagreed in each case. Check answers, asking students if they understood why the second person agreed or not.

85

module 11

4 Students make their lists in pairs before checking in the tapescript. Highlight and drill the following phrases used to express opinions:
I think ..., I personally believe ..., I really believe ..., If you ask me ..., In my opinion ..., Actually I think ... .
Point out that *actually* is used to add emphasis to the opinion, and does not mean 'at the moment'. Students read the dialogues in pairs.

5 If possible, supply small pieces of paper for students to write their opinion on. Circulate, supplying vocabulary students need. As you read out students' opinions, re-phrase them if necessary so that the English is correct.

ADDITIONAL PRACTICE

RB **Resource bank:** 11B *In my opinion ...* (agreeing and disagreeing), pages 154–156, Instructions page 103

Do you remember?

ANSWERS
1 a *mustn't* = it is prohibited / not allowed; *shouldn't* = it is not a good idea / the right thing
  b *must* = the obligation comes from the person speaking; *have to* = the obligation might (but not necessarily) come from another person
  c *mustn't* = it is prohibited / not allowed; *don't have to* = it is not necessary
  d there is no difference in meaning
  e there is no difference in meaning
  f *must* = it is not necessary now; *had to* = it was necessary in the past
  g there is no difference in meaning
  h *didn't have to* = it was not necessary; *wasn't allowed to* = it was prohibited

2 well-behaved – badly-behaved; housework – homework; a rule – a law; however – despite this; to obey – to disobey; therefore – that's why; to punish – a punishment; to be alone – to be lonely; to be healthy – to be unhealthy; (*disadvantage* has no partner)

3 b cloud c bought d four e stood f so

4 a She's always shouting <u>at</u> her children.
  b The teacher told them <u>off</u> for being late.
  d I'm going to do <u>some</u> shopping. Do you want anything?
  e I think it depends <u>on</u> the situation.
  f They missed the bus so they had <u>to</u> walk home.

5 *possible answers*
  a do the washing up, do some cooking, do some cleaning, do the ironing
  b do some homework, do some work, do some studying, do some exercises, do some yoga
  c do a degree, do a course, do some studying, do an exam, do some homework

6 a Although it was the middle of winter, the weather wasn't cold.
    It was the middle of winter. However, the weather wasn't cold.
  b The train drivers have not had a pay rise this year. As a result / For this reason, they're going on strike.
  c He has been ill recently. What is more, he has had a lot of personal problems.
    He has been ill recently. He has also had a lot of personal problems.
  d Although there was a bomb in the city centre last night, most of the shops are open as normal today.
    There was a bomb in the city centre last night. However, most of the shops are open as normal today.
  e There has been a serious accident. As a result / For this reason there are a lot of traffic jams.
    There has been a serious accident, therefore there are a lot of traffic jams.

86

module 12

Part A Language

Language focus 1 (PAGES 120–121)
could have, should have, would have

See *Teacher's tips: using a discovery approach in the teaching of grammar* on page 15.

1 Tell students not to read the story at this stage, but to try and guess what happened just by looking at the pictures. Check the meaning of: *the desert, a volcano, to slip, to be injured, to be unconscious, to be alive*.

2 After students have read the story, check comprehension with questions such as:
Where was the volcano?
Who were Larsen and Pritchard?
What advice did local people give them?
What did they do when they arrived at the volcano?
What happened when they reached the top?
What did Larsen decide to do?
What happened when Pritchard woke up?
How long did he wait?
How did the story end?

3 Students discuss the questions in pairs / groups. These questions should create a need for the language which follows in the *Analysis*, but do not feed it in at this stage unless students ask you specifically (if you do any whole class feedback after the discussion, the emphasis should be on the content of what students say, rather than the forms that they use to express it). Elicit as many possibilities as you can in each case, as this will help when students do the activities in the *Analysis*. List answers on the board in note form like this: *didn't take guide / enough water*, etc.

Analysis

1 Give students a minute to read the sentences and the meanings (tell them not to worry about writing their own sentences at this point). As you check the answers, give students time to think of two more sentences of their own for each one. Write their suggestions up on the board (whether or not the form is correct). Refer students back to the underlined sentences and point out the constructions used in each case:

should / could / would + *have* + past participle. Remind students of the negative forms *shouldn't / couldn't / wouldn't* and that *would* can be contracted to *'d*. Correct the sentences on the board if necessary, reminding them of the meaning in each case.

SUGGESTED ANSWERS
a This means it was a good idea to take a local guide with them, but they didn't. Other possible sentences: *They shouldn't have gone to the volcano. / They should have listened to local people. / They should have taken more water. / They should have rested when they arrived at the volcano. / Pritchard shouldn't have moved when he came round.*
b This means it was possible for him to stay with his friend, but he didn't. Other possible sentences: *Larsen could have tried to signal to an aeroplane. / Larsen could have taken the water with him. / Pritchard could have stayed inside the volcano.*
c This describes an imaginary situation in the past. Other possible sentences: *I wouldn't have gone on a journey like that. / I would have taken a guide. / I wouldn't have left Pritchard on his own. / I would have taken the water myself*, etc.

2 Omit this if you have already highlighted the form clearly, but it is useful for students who are working through the *Analysis* independently.

ANSWER
should / shouldn't, could / couldn't, would / wouldn't; past participle

3 Discuss this question with the whole class.

ANSWER
past time

Pronunciation

1 [12.1] Pause the cassette after each sentence to give students time to write or read out the sentences yourself at a natural speed. Re-play / re-read the sentences if necessary.

2 Point out the weak pronunciation of *have* and the vowel sound /ʊ/ in the modal verbs (/kʊdəv/, /ʃʊdəv/, /wʊdəv/). Drill the three forms as isolated phrases, before practising the full sentences. Re-play the cassette and practise the sentences, breaking up the longer sentences into shorter word groups where necessary.

PRACTICE

1 Focus students' attention on the three pictures and ask them what they can see. Check the meaning of:

87

module 12

to bang on the glass, to ignore someone, foggy weather, a cliff, to put up a tent, the edge.

Students discuss their answers in pairs or groups. Circulate, supplying vocabulary. (Weaker classes can write their answers before discussing them together.)

> **POSSIBLE ANSWERS**
> a The woman should have asked what he wanted / she shouldn't have ignored him / she shouldn't have been so rude.
> The young man could have grabbed the phone earlier / could have tried to find another phone.
> If I'd been in his position, I would have shouted really loudly / In her position, I would have felt really angry with myself.
> b They should have found a camp site earlier / they shouldn't have been walking around in a forest on a night like that / they should have taken a torch with them.
> They could have fallen over the cliff / they could have died.
> If I'd been in their position, I'd feel horrified / relieved / lucky / I'd never go camping again.
> c The man should have bought a map / he should have noticed what was happening earlier.
> He could have asked for directions.
> In his position, I would have stopped much earlier.

2 Check that students understand the situations and highlight the common phrase *I should never have ...* . Give a few personal examples of things you should / shouldn't have done. Give students about ten minutes to write their sentences, circulating and supplying any vocabulary they need. Put students into groups to discuss what they have written. Encourage them to ask questions and make suggestions, as in the example.

ADDITIONAL PRACTICE

Workbook: *could have / should have / would have*, page 75

Language focus 2 (PAGES 123–124)

Past sentences with *if*

See *Teacher's tips: using a discovery approach in the teaching of grammar* on page 15.

Mini-task

Do the first stage as a whole class or put students in pairs. Elicit one or two examples (choosing a university course, deciding to get married, etc.) Put students in pairs for the second stage – if you feel they are too young to have made many big decisions, or may find the topic too personal, suggest they talk about other people's big decisions (family, friends, etc.) The last two questions should prompt students to use 'third conditionals',

but do not do any input at this stage. Make a note of errors to analyse / correct after the Analysis.

1 [12.2] Focus students' attention on the photos and ask students to describe where Luke and Sandra are, how old they are, guess what jobs they might do, etc. Check the meaning of:
to regret something, a Business Studies course, a director of a company, a successful career, a pressurised job, a glamorous job, drama school, to make up your mind, to panic, to give something up.
Before playing the cassette, emphasise that students only have to listen for answers to the three questions listed. Compare answers before playing the cassette again if necessary. Discuss the questions in c) with the whole class.

> **ANSWERS**
> **Luke:** a He decided to leave his business studies course and become an actor. He panicked and felt very depressed, then he decided to try acting to see if he was good enough to do it professionally.
> b No, he doesn't regret it now.
> **Sandra:** a She gave up her job as the director of a travel company to look after her two small children full-time. She realised she couldn't do her job well and be a good mother, she didn't want to see her children only at bed-time.   b She doesn't seem to regret it now.

2 [12.3] Elicit a few predictions about Luke and Sandra and write them up in note form, for example: *less money, more time with children*, etc. Do not worry if students do not produce correct 'third conditional' sentences. Play the cassette and check answers.

3 Students should be able to attempt this – it does not matter if their guesses are wrong (tell them not to write in their answers, though, until they hear the cassette). Play the cassette straight through once, and then again if necessary, pausing after each clause to give students time to check and write in their answers.

> **ANSWERS**
> **Luke:** a 'd done / would have made / wouldn't have met   b 'd have stayed / hadn't decided
> **Sandra:** c 'd stayed / would have suffered   d was / wouldn't be / would really miss   e 'd be / hadn't left

Analysis: language notes

Most classes will find this *Analysis* challenging so it is advisable to work through it step-by-step as a class, rather than leaving them to work it out for themselves. We have dealt with 'mixed conditionals' as well as 'third conditionals',

88

module 12

because in most real-life communicative situations these are found together. However, if you think your class will find this *Analysis* section too hard, omit the 'mixed conditionals' and only analyse Luke's responses and c) of Sandra's responses (question 1 of the *Analysis*). Students can still do the practice activities which follow.

Analysis

1 Check the meaning of *hypothetical*. Write the sentences up on the board, and ask students if the verb refers to a past or present situation. Ask what form is used after *if* (Past Perfect), and what form is used for describing the hypothetical possibilities that follow (remind students that this is the same form they looked at in the last *Language focus*). Write up the following formula to summarise:

ANSWERS

past condition (imaginary) → past result (imaginary)
if + Past Perfect   +   would / wouldn't + have
                                    + past participle
If I had done business studies, I would have made more money.

Emphasise that we don't use *would have* after *if* and that *had* and *would* can be contracted to *'d*. Leave this summary on the board for comparison with the ones that follow.

2 Write up d) on the board, and again ask if each verb refers to the past or a general / present situation. Ask what form is used after *if* and what form is used to describe the hypothetical situations which follow (point out that you have already looked at this in Module 9). Write up the following formula to summarise:

ANSWERS

present / general condition (imaginary) →
present / general result (imaginary)
if + Past Simple   +   would / wouldn't
                                    + verb
If I was at work all day, I wouldn't be there at all the important moments of my children's lives.

Point out the parallels with the formula in 1 above, showing there is a tense shift after *if* in both cases because they are describing an imaginary situation. (You could point out that this is subjunctive if students have a subjunctive like this in their own language.) Leave this formula on the board for comparison with the others.

3 Write up the full sentence on the board, and again ask students if each verb refers to the past or the present. Point out that in this sentence you are talking about the present / generally in one part of the sentence and about

the past in the other, so we need to mix the forms we have looked at above. Write up the following formula to summarise:

ANSWERS

past condition (imaginary) → present / general result
                                                      (imaginary)
if + Past Perfect   +   would / wouldn't + verb
We would be a lot richer now if I hadn't left my old job.

Emphasise that the use of verbs here is entirely logical. It may be useful to translate the 'mixed conditional' sentence to make this clear. Students may ask you if they can mix the conditional the other way round (a present / general condition with a past result). This is also possible, for example:
If I didn't enjoy being with children so much, I wouldn't have left my job.
Do not go into this unless students ask specifically.

PRACTICE

1 a) Check the meaning of: *to conquer, to be shot, to be united*. Students work in pairs, or with the whole class if their knowledge of history is limited. Check answers with the whole class.

ANSWERS

Napoleon didn't conquer Russia. > He didn't become Emperor of all Europe.
Karl Marx wrote *Das Kapital*. > Many countries became communist.
The USA became the most powerful country in the world. > English became a world language.
Kennedy went to Dallas. > He was assassinated.
The Berlin Wall came down. > East and West Germany were united.
Nelson Mandela was released from prison. > Apartheid ended peacefully.
Germany lost World War One > Hitler came to power.

b) Write up the first historical fact and its result:
Napoleon didn't conquer Russia. He didn't become Emperor of all Europe. Compare this with the example before getting students to work individually or in pairs writing sentences for the others. If their knowledge of history is good, they can write other sentences about other events.

ANSWERS

Pehaps if Karl Marx hadn't written *Das Kapital*, many countries would not / might not have become communist.
If the USA had not become so powerful, English might not have become a world language.
If Kennedy hadn't gone to Dallas, perhaps he wouldn't have been assassinated.

89

module 12

If the Berlin Wall hadn't come down, East and West Germany wouldn't have been united.
If Nelson Mandela hadn't been released from prison, apartheid might not have ended so peacefully.
If Germany hadn't lost World War One, perhaps Hitler wouldn't have come to power.

2 Give one or two personal examples of your own, before getting students to work in pairs / groups. This exercise can be either spoken or written – weaker students can write sentences first before telling other students. Circulate, monitoring and supplying vocabulary.

ADDITIONAL PRACTICE

RB **Resource bank:** 12A *Suzie's story* (past sentences with *if* and *should(n't) have* – 'third conditional'), page 157, Instructions page 103

Workbook: Past sentences with *if*, page 76

Vocabulary (PAGE 124)

Problems and solutions

See *Teacher's tips: making the most of the Mini-dictionary* on page 14.

1 Focus students' attention on the pictures and ask them what they think they show. Elicit / Explain that the pictures show the history of a problem. Point out that the sentences tell the same story, but they are in the wrong order. Students order the sentences in pairs, working out the meaning of the words / phrases in bold at the same time. Check answers with the whole class, going over language points relating to phrasal verbs. Drill the phrases both as isolated phrases and as longer sentences.

> **ANSWERS AND LANGUAGE NOTES**
> *(Note that logically there are various ways of ordering the sentences.)*
> 1 Frank had a carefree life until one day a problem came up.
> 2 At first, Frank tried to ignore the problem, hoping it would just go away.
> 3 But the problem gradually became more serious, and eventually Frank decided he would have to do something about it.
> 4 He thought it over for a long time.
> 5 He talked it over with some of his friends.
> 6 But he didn't know what to do.
> 7 He kept changing his mind about the right thing to do.
> 8 But in the end he made up his mind.
> 9 His idea seemed to work; he thought he had sorted the problem out.
>
> **Notes on phrasal verbs:**
> • *come up* is inseparable; *talk something over, think something over, sort something out, make up your*

mind are separable. With a noun they can either be separated or not separated (*to talk over your plans* is also possible) but with a pronoun they must be separated (not ~~to talk over it~~).

> **Exercise 1: alternative suggestion**
> Do this as a 'disappearing story' in the following way:
> • As you check the order of the story, write it out on the board.
> • Tell students to close their books and get a student to read the story aloud from the board, correcting pronunciation as necessary.
> • Rub out one or two of the phrases in bold in Exercise 1, replacing them with gaps.
> • Get another student to read the story aloud, filling in the gaps as necessary.
> • Repeat the process, removing one or two phrases each time, until all the target phrases are replaced by gaps. (As the reading aloud stage gets more difficult, it may be necessary to ask other students to help to keep up the pace.)
> • Finally, get students to write out the story from the remaining prompts. Alternatively, they could write a more complete story, explaining what the problem was either in class or for homework.

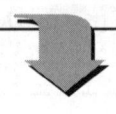

2 Give students a few minutes to memorise the phrases and get them to close their books. Elicit / Give a few suggestions of what the problem could have been, and put students into pairs or groups to think of the whole story. Circulate, prompting ideas and supplying vocabulary. Get some students to re-tell the whole story to the rest of the class or to summarise the problem and solution they came up with. If your students have problems coming up with ideas, put up the following prompts:

He had a very good, secure and well-paid job, but he was bored to death of it. / His debts were getting worse and worse but he couldn't stop spending money. / He was terribly in love with his boss, a married woman ten years older than himself. / He was terribly jealous of his wife / girlfriend although he had no evidence that she was being unfaithful to him.

Wordspot (PAGE 125)

think

See *Teacher's tips: working with lexis* on pages 12–13.

1 Do the first one as an example before getting students to work individually or in pairs.

> **ANSWERS**
> a 2 b 8 c 4 d 9 e 7/1 f 3 g 1/7 h 5
> i 6

module 12

2 Focus on the diagram and explain the meaning of the category headings. Students work individually or in pairs before checking answers with the whole class. As you go through the answers, you may find it useful to translate some of the phrases into the students' first language to show that *think* can be used for a number of different verbs.

> **ANSWERS**
> (*sections in brackets*)
> What do you think of …? (a); I'm thinking of changing … (b); Just think! (d); think of a solution (c); I think so. / I don't think so. (d); think it over (b); Do you think you could …? (d); I don't think … (a)

3 Do an example of a) and b) with the class to check that students understand what to do.

> **Exercises 2 and 3: additional suggestions**
>
> a *Make a poster to display on the classroom wall*: prepare this in advance by copying the diagram onto a poster-sized piece of paper. As you go through the answers to Exercise 2, write the phrases in 'the correct' section.
> b *Intonation work*: in a) if students want to show that they really aren't sure, they can emphasise this with the following intonation pattern:
>
> I think so. I don't think so.
> Drill this before they do the exercise.
> c *Additional practice of other phrases*: students can write mini-dialogues of their own using the following phrases: *Do you think you could …? / I'll think about it … / I'm thinking it over … / I'm thinking of … / What do you think of …? / Just think!*
> Put up the following example:
>
> A: Is this Doctor Martin's office? I've got an appointment at 10.00.
> B: Yes it is, do you think you could wait over there, please?

Part B Task

Preparation for task (PAGES 126–127)

See *Teacher's tips: making tasks work* on pages 8–9 and *Responding to learners' individual language needs* on pages 10–11.

1 Introduce the topic and discuss the questions either in groups or with the whole class.

2 Read out the three summaries then give students two minutes to read the letter again and select an answer (*sentence c*).

3 Explain that in this newspaper readers send in their opinions on someone's problem, rather than a journalist or 'agony aunt' answering it. Check the meaning of: *a sense of responsibility, to be mature, to be innocent / innocence, to cope with a situation, to have an adventure, to risk something, to miss an opportunity*. Students read silently before discussing answers in pairs. Check answers briefly with the whole class.

> **ANSWERS**
> **Letter 1**: she thinks he should let her go; she is a mother of a grown-up daughter, but seems to have quite liberal views.
> **Letter 2**: he thinks he should let his daughter go; he is a 21-year-old who has spent a lot of time travelling the world – he seems quite an adventurous person.
> **Letter 3**: he doesn't think the man should let his daughter go – he is very worried about the safety of young people (perhaps a little old-fashioned).

4 Check the meaning of: *to be retired, to be elderly, an old people's home, to suspect someone, evidence, to humiliate, a compulsive gambler, a debt, to support a child*. Emphasise that students only have to read to find out what the problem is. As you check answers, make sure that they understand any other important circumstances, as this will affect how well they do the task.

> **ANSWERS**
> a He suspects his boss is stealing money from the owners of the restaurant where he works, but he doesn't have any evidence. He likes both his boss and the owners and doesn't know what to do.
> b His fiancée broke off their engagement a year ago, humiliating him in front of his friends and family. She has suddenly re-appeared and wants to start the relationship again. He still loves her, but doesn't know if he should go back with her.
> c Her husband has a very bad gambling problem and she wanted to divorce him, only now she has found out that she is pregnant. Her husband says he will stop gambling and support the baby, but he has promised to stop many times before.
> d She is a middle-aged woman with a husband, two teenage sons and an old mother, who she looks after. Her husband has been offered a job in the USA and he and the children all want to go. She knows the mother won't come, and that there is no one else to look after her if she goes.

Task (PAGE 127)

1 Allocate students a problem each or give them a few moments to choose one. Give them a few minutes to think silently about the problem before putting them in groups of about four with other students who are thinking about the same problem. Tell students to make a list of all

91

module 12

possible solutions, deciding which they think is the best / the worst. Encourage students to persuade each other of their point of view if there are differences of opinion, but do not insist that they reach a common solution if this is not possible. Circulate, supplying vocabulary.

2 Re-group the students with others who have been discussing a different problem. Refer them to the *Useful language* box, and highlight the following points (you may prefer to do this after the task):

- the use of *I don't think (she should)* for negative opinion.
- the use of the *-ing* form after *He could try (telling)* ...

Tell them to explain their problem and list the possible solutions, before saying what they think the person should do. Emphasise that they should discuss the problems with their new group to see if they agree. At this stage collect errors / useful language for analysis and correction later on.

> **Task: alternative suggestions**
>
> a *If you want to make the task shorter or split it over two lessons:* do one of the following:
>
> - Give students a list of difficult vocabulary from the texts to check in their mini-dictionary before the lesson.
> - Read the first problem and solutions for homework before the lesson. Check comprehension before going on to the other four problems and the task. (This homework could be combined with the vocabulary work above.)
> - Do the *Preparation for task* in one lesson and the task itself in the next lesson. This would give students plenty of time to think about solutions and how to express them in English. Start the second lesson with a brief opportunity to ask you about vocabulary, etc.
> - Reduce the number of problems you look at in the *Preparation for task*. These problems have been designed to appeal to a range of ages, but you could omit those that you think your students will have problems relating to.
>
> b *Role play:* as a follow up to the task, get students to act out a conversation between the writer of the letter and a friend who is advising him / her what to do. Feed in some phrases for asking for / giving advice, for example:
> *I've got a (bit of a / terrible) problem ...*
> *I just don't know what to do ...*
> *What do you think I should do?*
> *Do you think I should ...?*
> *Perhaps you should ...*
> *Have you thought about ...?*
> *You should definitely ...*
> *Try not to worry too much ...*
> If students role play different problems, they act out their conversations for the whole class.

ADDITIONAL ACTIVITY

RB Resource bank: 12B *What should I do?* (giving advice), page 158, Instructions page 103

Task link (PAGE 128)

Verbs to describe behaviour and reactions

1 Check that everyone knows what 'a soap' is (short for *soap opera*). Ask students to read the two descriptions and tell you the kind of story each has. Check the meaning of: *corruption, scandal, heartbreak*. Before students look through the extracts, check the meaning of: *a share of a business, to give someone a bribe, to sign a contract*. Students work individually or in pairs / groups before checking answers with the whole class.

> **ANSWERS**
> a G b G c O d G e O f G g O h O
> i G j O

2 Emphasise that students should use their mini-dictionaries to look up any meanings they do not know, but help when necessary. Check answers and drill the pronunciation of the verbs: *deny* /dɪˈnaɪ/, *threaten* /ˈθretn/, *insist* /ɪnˈsɪst/, *persuade* /pəˈsweɪd/, *agree* /əˈgriː/, *suggest* /səˈdʒest/, *promise* /ˈprɒməs/, *insist* /ɪnˈsɪst/, *suspect* /səˈspekt/.

> **ANSWERS**
> threaten – d; admit – j; persuade – i; refuse – a; agree – b; suggest – h; promise – g; suspect – e; insist – c

3 Students work individually or in pairs before checking answers with the whole class.

> **ANSWERS**
> **verbs followed by the infinitive**: threaten to do something / refuse to do something / agree to do something / promise to do something
> **verbs followed by the *-ing* form**: deny doing something / admit doing something / suggest doing something
> **verbs followed by an object + infinitive**: persuade someone to do something
> **verbs followed by a preposition + the *-ing* form**: suspect someone of doing something / insist on doing something
>
> The following verbs can also be followed by a *that* clause: deny, threaten, admit, agree, suggest, promise, insist, suspect

4 Look at the example together and do the next one with the students if necessary. Students do the rest in pairs before checking answers with the whole class.

module 12

> **ANSWERS**
> b He / She agreed to do business with him / her.
> c She insisted on wearing the dress.
> d He threatened to kill him if he ever told the newspapers.
> e She suspected Carl of seeing someone else.
> f He denied offering bribes to politicians.
> g He promised never to leave Darlene.
> h She suggested having a beach party.
> i He persuaded him to sign it.
> j He admitted being in love with Patsy for nearly two weeks.
>
> Note that many of the sentences can also be re-written using *that* + clause.

Creative writing (PAGE 129)

Give students a few minutes to read through the options and decide which one they would like to do. Once they have decided, go through the detailed instructions for each one either with the whole class, or on an individual basis with each pair or group. For the 'script' option point out the following features of a script:

- the list / description of the characters at the beginning
- the description of the location
- the punctuation used for a script (*Name:*)
- the stage directions given in brackets

Give students plenty of time to do their piece of writing. Circulate, supplying vocabulary they need and correcting where necessary. When they have finished get some / all of the groups to read out their letters and stories, or act out their scenes. If there is time, follow this up with a correction slot. Students could write a more 'polished' version for homework, incorporating the corrections you have gone over in class.

Consolidation modules 9–12

> **ANSWERS**
> A1 1 flew 2 made 3 had arrived 4 got out
>   5 spent 6 noticed 7 had destroyed 8 was
>   9 spoke 10 spoke / could speak 11 asked
>   12 managed 13 was born / had been born
>   14 replied 15 had spent 16 decided
>   17 tried 18 wasn't 19 refused 20 was
>   21 employed / had employed 22 didn't speak
>   23 was being driven 24 knew 25 drove
>
> 2 ... who tried to explain that he wasn't in Rome but New York. > '... you are not in Rome, you are in New York ...'
>
> *Mr Scotti refused to believe him, and said he was very surprised the Rome police employed an officer who didn't speak Italian.* > 'I don't believe you, and I'm very surprised the police here employ an officer who doesn't speak Italian!'
>
> *... Mr Scotti told his interpreter that now he knew he was in Italy because that was how they always drove.* > 'Now I know that I'm in Italy because this is how they always drive!'
>
> B 1 a ought to / should
>   b have to / must; don't have to
>   c should have
>   d aren't allowed to / aren't supposed to
>   e didn't have to speak
>   f may well / are unlikely to
>
> 2 there is a difference in meaning in a) and f): *aren't allowed to* = it is prohibited, *aren't supposed to* = they should not do it; *may well* = it is very possible, *are unlikely to* = it is not probable
>
> C 1 a speaker 3 b speaker 1 c speaker 3
>
> D *make*: a noise, your mind up, someone smile, a profit; *do*: some research, the washing up, a test, your best; *say*: you're sorry, 'thank you', a prayer; *tell*: the truth, a child off, someone to go away, a joke;
> *think*: of a brilliant idea, something over, about your boyfriend, of leaving your job
>
> E 1 a the differences between country and city life
>   b smoking in public places
>   c your ideal job
>
> F 1 deny 2 improve 3 gradually 4 over
>   5 illegal 6 refuse 7 rise 8 suddenly
>   9 punish 10 promise 11 threatened
>   12 increase 13 allowed 14 fair 15 suggest
>   16 badly-behaved 17 scream 18 sword
>   19 admit
>   The hidden message is 'You've finished at last.'

Students can now do *Test three (modules 9–12)* on pages 167–170.

ADDITIONAL ACTIVITY

RB Resource bank: *Preposition challenge* (revision of prepositions), pages 159–160

93

Resource bank
Index of activities

Activity	Language point	When to use	Time (minutes)
Learner-training worksheet 1	Being an active learner	near the start of the course	25–35
Learner-training worksheet 2	Working with monolingual dictionaries	near the start of the course	25–35
Learner-training worksheet 3	Dictionary skills race	after Learner-training worksheet 2	20–25
Learner-training worksheet 4	Learning about new words	near the start of the course	25–35
Learner-training worksheet 5	Recording and remembering vocabulary	near the start of the course	25–35
1A Get to know the *Students' Book*		first day of the course	25–30
1B Three person snap	Short answers with *do, have, be*	after Practice Exercise 4, page 7	15–20
1C Vocabulary extension	Phrases for talking about people around you	after Vocabulary Exercise 3, page 8	25–30
1D Something in common	Present Simple and Continuous	after Practice Exercise 3, page 11	25–35
1E Who am I?	Expressions of liking and disliking	after Task link Exercise 4, page 14	20–30
2A Past tense pelmanism/ What about you?	Irregular Past Simple forms	any time in Module 2	15–25
2B Alibi	Past Simple and Continuous	after Practice Exercise 2, page 20	45–55
2C School reunion	*used to, still, not any ... longer / more*	after Practice Exercise 2, page 21	30–40
3A The best place in the world	Superlatives (and Present Perfect)	after Practice Exercise 2, page 27	30–45
3B *Amazing cities!*	Vocabulary extension (word building)	after Reading Exercise 5, page 31	30–40
3C The City Language School	Recommending and advising	after Task link Exercise 3, page 34	25–35
3D How do I get to ...?	Asking for and giving directions	any time in Module 3	25–35
4A *Twin lives*	Vocabulary extension (dependent prepositions)	after Reading Exercise 4, page 37	30–40
4B Find someone who ... lied!	Present Perfect Simple (for experience)	after Practice Exercise 3, page 39	20–25
4C How long have you had it?	Present Perfect Simple and Continuous (for unfinished past)	after Practice Exercise 2, page 41	20–25
5A *How organised are you?*	Vocabulary extension (phrasal verbs)	after Speaking and reading Exercise 4, page 48	25–35
5B The great diamond robbery	Future clauses with *if, when*, etc.	after Practice Exercise 2, page 53	20–35

Resource bank

Activity	Language point	When to use	Time (minutes)
5C Vocabulary extension	Talking about work and training	after Vocabulary Exercise 3, page 52	25–35
6A Passive dominoes	Passive forms	after Practice Exercise 2, page 63	15–25
6B Vocabulary extension	Passive verbs often in the news	after Practice Exercise 2, page 63	30–40
6C Adjective snap	'Extreme' adjectives	after Task link Exercise 5, page 66	25–35
7A Vocabulary extension	Informal words and phrases	any time in Module 7	25–35
7B Doonbogs!	Making generalisations	after Task link Exercise 4, page 76	30–40
7C What time shall we meet?	Making a social arrangement	after Real life Exercise 4, page 77	30–40
8A Relative clauses crossword	Defining relative clauses	after Practice Exercise 2, page 79	15–25
8B *How to be a successful inventor*	Vocabulary extension (word building)	after Reading Exercise 4, page 80	30–40
8C Camping holiday	Quantifiers (*a few, a lot of*, etc.)	after Practice Exercise 2, page 83	30–40
9A Election night special	Hypothetical possibilities with *if* ('second conditional')	after Practice Exercise 3, page 94	30–40
9B How would your life be different?	Hypothetical possibilities with *if* ('second conditional')	after Practice Exercise 3, page 94	15–25
9C Hear … Say!	Ways of saying numbers	after Task link Exercise 3, page 98	15–20
9D Vocabulary extension	Talking about numbers, amounts and ages without being exact	after Task link Exercise 3, page 98	25–30
10A Ralph and the guitar case	Past Perfect, Past Simple (Past Continuous)	after Practice Exercise 2, page 101	20–40
10B Jungle survivors	Reported speech	after Practice Exercise 2, page 103	30–45
10C Vocabulary extension	Verbs to use instead of *say*	after Practice Exercise 2, page 103	25–30
11A *Freedom of choice?*	Vocabulary extension	after Task Exercise 4, page 117	20–30
11B In my opinion …	Agreeing and disagreeing	after Real life Exercise 5, page 118	25–35
12A Suzie's story	Past sentences with *if* ('third conditional') and *should(n't) have*	after Practice Exercise 2, page 124	20–30
12B What should I do?	Giving advice	after Task Exercise 2, page 127	20–30
12C Preposition challenge	Revision of prepositions	at the end of the course	20–30

Test one (modules 1–4) pages 161–163   **Test two** (modules 5–8) pages 164–166   **Test three** (modules 9–12) pages 167–170

Instructions pages 96–103   **Resource bank key** pages 171–175

95

Instructions

The activities in the *Resource bank* are designed to consolidate and extend material covered in the *Students' Book*. It has been indicated in the index the first point at which each activity in the *Resource bank* can be used (this has also been indicated at the appropriate point in the teacher's notes). This is to be taken as a guideline only, however – teachers may choose to do an activity in the same class as the practice activities in the *Students' Book*, in the following class as a 'warmer' or 'filler', or after a longer time-space as a revision exercise.

For those activities involving cards it is a good idea to invest time in preparing class sets which can be re-used again and again. Do this by cutting up the photocopied sheets, sticking each card onto thick paper or cardboard, and then covering them with adhesive film.

Learner–training worksheet 1
(Being an active learner)

You will need: one copy of the worksheet per student

1 Pre-teach difficult phrases and answer any questions on vocabulary students have as they read through the texts. Give students time to absorb the information.
2 Get students to underline first the good habits of each learner, and then the bad habits. Encourage discussion rather than give the 'answers' yourself.
3 Pre-teach any difficult vocabulary before students read the analysis.
4a Handle this discussion sensitively, avoiding any judgmental comments, particularly about individual students. Take a positive attitude to any resolutions they make, encouraging realistic aims students can stick to.
 b Be positive about any suggestions students make. If necessary, bring up important issues yourself (such as homework, and the use of English within the lesson), and suggest that you come to some kind of agreement about them.

Learner–training worksheet 2
(Working with monolingual dictionaries)

You will need: one copy of the worksheet per student

Note: do this worksheet as soon as possible after the beginning of the course. First discuss briefly with students the value of a monolingual dictionary, and find out who has used one before. Strong students can work through the questions in pairs/groups before checking answers with the whole class. With other classes, it may be best to check answers after every question.

1 Check that students understand what a transitive/intransitive verb and a countable/uncountable noun are. Do the first example together.
2 Note that there is no definitive answer for any of these. The aim is simply to illustrate that students do not always need to understand the definition to grasp the meaning of the word – the example can sometimes be more useful.
3 Students do the exercise individually or in pairs, before checking answers with the whole class.
4 Check that students understand what a preposition, an *-ing* form and an infinitive are. Remind them of the list of irregular verbs on page 152 of the *Students' Book*.
5 Explain the different types of information in the box before students do the exercise individually or in pairs.
6a Make sure that students understand what word stress is and how it is marked. Give more examples of your own if necessary before getting students to do the exercise individually or in pairs.
 b These words have been selected because they only contain one sound which is difficult to transcribe. If you need to teach the phonemic script, it is probably best done in short slots at the beginning of the course, covering four to six sounds per session, and incorporating lots of revision. The emphasis should be on students being able to recognise rather than transcribe the symbols.

Learner–training worksheet 3
(Dictionary skills race)

You will need: one copy of the worksheet per student

This can be done in a separate lesson from *Learner–training worksheet 2* as a useful way of consolidating skills. It can be done in pairs, groups or as a team game. If necessary, add more questions of your own.

Learner–training worksheet 4
(Learning about new words)

You will need: one copy of the worksheet per student

1 Explain the meaning only of the words in the box (the point of the exercise is to show that just knowing the meaning is not sufficient to be able to use a word effectively). For discussion point 1, give examples of each type of information, based as far as possible on mistakes students have made forming the sentences.
2a Give a time limit for students to look at the phrases, then ask them to cover them. Provide explanations of the phrases if students ask.
 b Emphasise that students must not look back at the phrases. Students should work individually rather than in pairs, as it is more instructive if they get some of the sentences wrong. The main point of the discussion is that common phrases tend to consist of words that students 'know' individually – they may sometimes have no difficulty in understanding them passively, but producing them correctly is often a different thing.

Instructions

Learner-training worksheet 5
(Recording and remembering vocabulary)

You will need: one copy of the worksheet per student

1. Go over the different methods to make sure that students see the differences, without commenting on how effective they might be. Give students time to think about the advantages and disadvantages of each one before starting the discussion. During the discussion, avoid saying categorically that any method is always right or wrong – they are probably all appropriate for some types of vocabulary and inappropriate for others. This would be a good point at which to suggest/insist that everyone buys a separate vocabulary notebook. Spend some time together writing new words into the notebook during the next lesson. Remind students to use their vocabulary notebooks at regular intervals and check them whenever possible.

2, 3 Again the emphasis should be on trying out different methods and finding the ones that suit students best individually, rather than prescribing the 'right' one. Encourage suggestions from students and emphasise that they must take active steps of their own if they are to improve, particularly if they are not studying in an English-speaking environment.

1A Get to know the *Students' Book*

You will need: one set of cards for each pair of students

- Shuffle each set of cards. Put students into pairs. Place the sets of cards face down in piles at the front of the class and allocate one set to each pair.
- One student from each pair comes up to the front of the class and takes **one** card only from the top of his/her pile before going back to his/her partner. They write the answer to the question on the card.
- When a pair has completed a card they take it to the teacher to check the answer. If it is correct, the student keeps the card and takes the next one from his/her pile. If the answer is not correct, he/she must return to his/her partner and find the correct answer.
- The first pair to find all the correct answers are the winners.

1B Three person snap

You will need: one set of Question cards, *two sets of* Answer cards *for each group of three students*

Students work in groups of three.

- Give Student A a set of *Question cards*, face down in a pile. Give Students B and C a complete set of *Answer cards* **each**, and tell them to spread them out in front of them, face up.
- Student A turns over the first *Question card* and reads the **question only** out loud. Students B and C try to find the correct *Answer card* as quickly as possible and give it to Student A, saying the answer correctly at the same time. The first student to find the correct answer card takes both cards as a 'trick'.
- The student with the most tricks at the end is the winner. Students then do the activity again, with a different student turning over the *Question cards*.

1C Vocabulary extension

You will need: one copy of the worksheet per student

- Exercises 1 and 2: students work individually or in pairs before checking answers with the whole class.
- Exercise 3: make sure that students understand they can make changes to the questions if they want to and give a few examples of possible follow-up questions. Students mingle asking/answering questions before feeding back to the whole class.

1D Something in common

You will need: one set of role cards per twelve students (role cards 1–8 are needed to complete the activity; role cards 9–12 are optional)

- Tell students they are at a party where there are a lot of people they don't know. Elicit the following questions you could ask a stranger at a party: *Do you live near here? / Do you know many people here? / What do you do? / Are you enjoying the party? / What do you do in your spare time?* Pre-teach the expression *Me, too*.
- Give each student a role card and allow time for them to check the information. Students move around the room asking one another the questions above. **The aim of the activity is for the students to find at least four people at the party with whom they have something in common.** As they find them, they write the other students' names on their role card. Encourage students to ask suitable follow-up questions.

1E Who am I?

You will need: one copy of the worksheet per student

- **Before** giving out copies of the worksheet, write a number at the top for each student in the class. (If you have ten students, for example, write the numbers 1 to 10.) Distribute the worksheets in **random** order.
- Students complete the description for themselves, **without** writing their name. Students work individually and must not look at their classmates' papers.
- Collect the worksheets and shuffle them, before sticking them up round the classroom.
- Students work individually or in pairs reading the numbered descriptions and deciding which student in the class wrote each one. The student/pair of students who guessed the most correct answers are the winners.

97

Instructions

2A Past tense pelmanism / What about you?

You will need: one set of cards per three or four students; one copy of the What about you? *worksheet per student*

STAGE 1
- Students work in groups of three or four. Give each group a set of cards and tell them to spread them out in front of them **face down**.
- Each student turns over two cards. If they find a verb and its irregular past tense, they keep the cards as a 'trick' and have another turn. If the cards do not match, they replace them **in exactly the same place**.
- The activity continues until all the cards are matched up. The student with the most tricks is the winner.

STAGE 2
- Give each student a copy of the *What about you?* worksheet. Make sure they write their answers on a **separate** piece of paper **in random order**. They should write single words or short phrases, not complete sentences. Set a time limit of five minutes.
- Students work in pairs or small groups, and swap papers. They ask each other to explain why they have written the items on the paper. Encourage them to find out more information by asking suitable follow-up questions. Students report back to the class on the most interesting things they found out about their partner(s).

2B Alibi

You will need: two Suspect *role cards, two* Police officer *role cards per four students*

- Tell students there was a robbery at the school between 7pm and midnight yesterday, and that all the money was stolen from the school safe. The police suspect the students from your class were responsible!
- Divide the class equally into police officers and suspects. (If there is an odd number of students, have more police officers than suspects.) Put the suspects into pairs. Give each pair *Suspect* worksheet A or B and send them out of the room to prepare their story.
- Put the police in pairs or groups and give them the corresponding *Police officer* worksheet. Allow them time to prepare questions.
- When all the students are ready, bring the suspects back into the room. Separate them, and match them with a corresponding police officer. The police officers interview the suspects and make brief notes of the suspects' answers.
- When the interviews have finished, the police officers return to their original pairs/groups and compare notes to see if there are any discrepancies in the suspects' stories. The suspects return to their partners to discuss the answers they gave to the questions, and see if they made any mistakes.
- The police officers report back to the whole class in turn and say if they think their suspects are guilty or innocent, giving reasons for their decision.

2C School reunion

You will need: one role card, one Find someone who … *worksheet per student (role cards 1–8 are needed to complete the activity; role cards 9–12 are optional)*

- Tell students that they were all in the same class at Springfield High School fifteen years ago, when they were all seventeen or eighteen years old. Now there is going to be a school reunion, and they are going to meet their old classmates again.
- Give a role card to each student, and allow time for them to read and understand the information.
- Give each student a copy of the *Find someone who …* worksheet. Students move around the room talking to their old classmates. **The aim of the activity is for them to find at least one person for each of the items on the worksheet.** When they have found someone, they must write down their name and then ask if they still do the same thing now.
- When they have finished, students check their answers in pairs/groups, using *used to, still,* and *not … any longer/more.*

3A The best place in the world

You will need: one copy of the board per three/four students; one dice, three/four counters per group

- Students work in groups of three or four. Give each group a board, counters and dice. If one student has a watch with a second hand, make him/her the timekeeper.
- Students take it in turns to throw a number. When they land on a superlative square, they have to talk about the topic for thirty seconds without stopping. If you have a quiet class, allow each student fifteen seconds' thinking time before speaking.
- If a student cannot think of anything to say or stops talking before the thirty seconds are up, he/she has to move back to the original square. The student who reaches the *Finish* square first is the winner.

3B *Amazing Cities!* vocabulary extension

You will need: one copy of the worksheet per student; a set of monolingual dictionaries (not the Mini-dictionary)

- Give each student a copy of the worksheet. Students work through the exercises individually or in pairs before checking answers with the whole class.

3C The City Language School

You will need: one copy of the advertisement per student; enough New student *worksheets for half the class, enough* Old student *worksheets A and B for the other half*

- Give each student a copy of the *Learn English for life* advertisement and ask them to decide on the **two** best things about the school.

Instructions

- Divide the class into two groups – old students and new students. (If there is an odd number of students in the class, include an extra old student.) Give each new student a copy of the *New student* worksheet. Divide the old students into two groups. Give one group *Old student A* worksheets, and the other group *Old student B* worksheets. Give students time to read and understand the information on the worksheets.
- Pair one new student with one old student. The new student asks the old student for recommendations/advice and writes brief notes in the first column.
- Rearrange the class so that each new student is talking to an old student who has the other worksheet. The new student again asks for recommendations/advice, and makes notes in the second column.
- When they have finished, allow new students a short time to decide what courses/extra classes, they are going to do, etc. While they do this, old Students A and B tell each other what advice they gave.
- The new students report back to the whole class on their decisions, giving their reasons.

3D How do I get to …?

You will need: one copy of the worksheet per student

- Students do Exercise 1 individually or in pairs, before checking answers with the whole class. Students do Exercises 2 and 3 in pairs, following the instructions on the worksheet.

4A *Twin lives* vocabulary extension

You will need: one Which preposition? *worksheet per student; one copy of Student A or Student B questions per student*

STAGE 1
- Students complete the *Which preposition?* worksheet in pairs without looking at the text.
- Students scan the text to check their answers.

STAGE 2
- Divide the class into two groups. Give one group the list of questions headed Student A and the other the questions headed Student B. Students fill in the correct prepositions to complete the questions.
- Re-group the students so that one Student A is sitting next to one Student B. Students take it in turns to ask and answer their questions. Encourage students to ask at least one follow-up question after each answer.
- Students report back to the class on the most interesting answers.

4B Find someone who … lied!

You will need: one LIAR! *question sheet and four* LIAR! *cards per student*

- Give each student a copy of the question sheet and four *LIAR!* cards. Check through the prompts on the question sheet with the whole class.
- Tell students that they are going to ask one another *Have you ever …?* questions based on the prompts. Emphasise that they can ask the questions in any order they like.
- When a student is asked a question, he/she can either lie or tell the truth. The student asking the question (Student A) is then allowed a maximum of **three** follow-up questions (in the Past Simple) to help them decide if the other student (Student B) is lying or not.
- If Student A thinks the other student is lying, he/she can challenge him by holding up a *LIAR!* card.
  – If Student B **is** lying, he/she has to take the *LIAR!* card from Student A.
  – If Student B is telling the truth, he/she can give one of **his** *LIAR!* cards to Student A.
  – If Student B **is** lying, but Student A **doesn't** challenge him, Student B can give Student A one of his/her *LIAR!* cards.
  – If Student B is telling the truth and isn't challenged, then no cards change hands.
- Students move around the class asking one another *Have you ever …?* questions and try to give away their *LIAR!* cards. The winner is the student who has the **least** *LIAR!* cards at the end of the activity.

4C How long have you had it?

You will need: one copy of one question card per student

- Give each student **one** question card.
- Tell students they have to find out the answers to the questions on their card. Allow time for them to write down the two questions they will need to ask the other students (for example: *Have you got a best friend?/How long have you known him/her?*)
- Students move around the class asking their questions and making brief notes of their classmates' answers on the back of their cards or in a notebook.
- Students work out the answers to the original questions on their cards and report back to the class. (For example: *Ten students have got a best friend. / Ivan has known his best friend since he was two …*, etc.)

99

Instructions

5A *How organised are you?* vocabulary extension

You will need: *one copy of the worksheet per student*

- Give each student a copy of the worksheet. Students work through Exercises 1 and 2 individually or in pairs before checking answers with the whole class.
- For Exercise 3 get students to walk around the class asking other students the questions. Follow this with a brief feedback session at the end.

5B The great diamond robbery

You will need: *one copy of the information sheet and one copy of the map per student*

- Give students the map of the National Museum and the accompanying information sheet. Ask them to read the information and locate the items listed.
- Check that the whole class has understood all the points on the information sheet before dividing students into pairs or groups. Each pair/group has to work out a plan to steal the diamond and escape without getting caught. Encourage students to use some future time clauses from the *Useful language* box.
- When all the pairs/groups have decided on their plans, re-group the students and ask them to explain their plans to each other, again using as many future time clauses as possible. Encourage the other students to ask questions and point out difficulties at this stage.
- At the end of the activity, the students decide which of the plans they have heard is the best. Students can write out their plan for homework.

5C Vocabulary extension

You will need: *one copy of the worksheet per student*

- Exercise 1: students work individually or in pairs before checking answers with the whole class.
- Exercise 2: students read through the advertisement – make sure that they understand what a reporter is and what the job involves. Divide the class into two groups – Student As and Students Bs, and get them to look at the information on the role card. They spend about five minutes preparing what they are going to say in the interview. Supply vocabulary as necessary.
- Put students into A/B pairs (if you have an uneven number of students, put two interviewers together). Students conduct their interviews before feeding back to the class on whether the candidate got the job.

6A Passive dominoes

You will need: *one set of dominoes for each pair of students*

- Students work in pairs. Give one set of dominoes to each pair, and ask them to share them out equally.
- One student places a domino on the desktop between them, and the other student has to make a complete sentence by placing one of his/her dominoes at either end of the first domino. The students then take it in turns to put down their dominoes at either end of the domino chain.
- If one student thinks a sentence is not correct, he/she can challenge the other student. If the students cannot agree, they should ask you to make a final decision.
- If the sentence is incorrect, the student has to take back the domino and miss a turn. If a student cannot make a sentence, the turn passes to his/her partner.
- The game continues until one student has used up all his/her dominoes, or until neither student can make a correct sentence. The student who finishes first, or who has the fewest dominoes left, is the winner.

6B Vocabulary extension

You will need: *one copy of the worksheet per student*

- Students work through Exercises 1, 2 and 3 individually or in pairs/groups before checking answers with the whole class.
- Exercise 4: students work in pairs/groups writing their articles. Go round helping/supplying vocabulary as necessary. When they have finished, the articles can be read out or put up round the classroom.

6C Adjective snap

You will need: *one set of adjective cards and one copy of the* Questionnaire *per student*

STAGE 1

- Students work in groups of three. If there are extra students, have one or two groups of four.
- Give each student a complete set of adjective cards. Student A places her cards **face down in a pile** in front of him/her, while Students B and C lay their cards out **face up** in front of them.
- Student A then turns over the cards one at a time, saying the word on the card as he/she places it down on the desk. Students B and C have to look through their own cards as quickly as possible to find the matching adjective. (For example, if Student A turns over *angry*, Students B and C have to look through their cards for *furious*.)
- The first student to place the matching card on top of the adjective card takes the 'trick'. The winner is the student who gets the most tricks.
- Students then change over so that someone else is Student A, and play the game again.

STAGE 2

- Give each student a copy of the *Questionnaire*. Students work individually and fill in the gaps with a suitable gradable or extreme adjective.
- Students then work in pairs and ask each other the questions. Encourage students to ask suitable follow-up questions where appropriate.

Instructions

- Students report back to the class on the most interesting things they found out about their partners.

7A Vocabulary extension

You will need: one copy of the worksheet per student

- Students work through the exercises individually/in pairs before checking answers with the whole class. Supply vocabulary for Exercise 3 as necessary, before getting students to act out their dialogues.

7B Doonbogs!

You will need: one copy of the worksheet per student

- Students work in pairs or groups. Give each student a copy of the worksheet, and ask them to read the introduction and the letter from the Earth President. Check they understand what kind of information they need to collect. Allow students time to gather ideas for their report from the pictures before they start.
- Students write the report in pairs/groups. Encourage them to use language for making generalisations in each sentence of their report.
- Collect the reports and put them up round the classroom. Students walk around the class reading the reports and deciding which they think is the best.

7C What time shall we meet?

You will need: twice the number of role cards as students in the class (if possible colour-code each set to prevent them getting mixed up)

- Students work in pairs and sit back to back. Give each pair of students matching role cards, and allow them a minute or two to read the information.
- Students act out the role play in their pairs and try to arrange a time and place to meet.
- When they have finished each role play, collect the role cards from them and give them another pair.

8A Relative clauses crossword

You will need: a copy of each crossword for each pair of students

- Divide the class into two groups, A and B. Give a copy of Student A crossword to students in group A, and a copy of Student B crossword to those in group B.
- Students work together in their separate groups to check they know the meaning of the words on their half of the crossword. (All the vocabulary is taken from Modules 1–7 of the *Students' Book*.)
- Put students in pairs, so that one Student A and one Student B are working together. They are not allowed to look at each other's crossword.
- Students take it in turns to describe the words that appear on their half of the crossword to their partner, using defining relative clauses *(It's a place where you …, This is a person who …, etc.)* The partner has to guess the words, and write them in his/her own crossword.
- Students continue until they both have a completed version of the crossword.

8B How to be a successful inventor vocabulary extension

You will need: one copy of the worksheet per student; a set of monolingual dictionaries (not the Mini-dictionary)

- Give each student a copy of the worksheet. Students work through the exercises individually or in pairs before checking answers with the whole class.

8C Camping holiday

You will need: one copy of the Student A worksheet and one copy of Student B worksheet for each pair of students

- Put students into pairs and give one student a copy of Student A worksheet and the other a copy of Student B worksheet. Allow time for students to read and understand the information.
- Students work in pairs, telling each other what they've got in their rucksack and commenting on their partner's choices, using the expressions from the *Useful language* box. **The aim is for students to make a list of what they decide to take with them.**
- When they have finished, students compare their list with other students' lists and comment on them using expressions from the *Useful language* box.

9A Election night special

You will need: one copy of the worksheet for each group of students

- Tell students there is going to be a national election. As well as the main political parties, there are also a number of 'fringe' parties, who are very unlikely to be elected, but are standing nevertheless.
- Put students into groups of three or four. Assign each group a political party from this list (or add your own): *The Animal Lovers' Party, The Sleep Party, The Sports Party, The Television Addicts' Party, The Fit and Healthy Party, The 'I hate English' Party.*
- Give each group a copy of the *Election manifesto* worksheet. Students decide what their party's policies are for each section, and finish the sentences on their manifesto using imaginary conditionals. Remind students to make their policies fit the overall aim of their party. Put the completed manifestos up round the class.
- One representative of each party stands beside their own manifesto, while the other students move round the class to read the other parties' manifestos. As they read, students ask the 'party representative' about aspects of policy they disagree with or don't understand, using imaginary conditionals where possible.
- At the end of the activity, the class vote for the party they think has the best manifesto (students cannot vote for their own party).

Instructions

9B How would your life be different?

You will need: one copy of one question card per student

- Give each student a card and allow them time to complete the question.
- Students move around the class and ask each other their questions. At the end of the activity, students report back to the class on the most interesting or unusual answers to their questions.

9C Hear … Say!

You will need: one copy of each grid per group of three students

- Put students into groups of three and give each student in the group a copy of one of the grids. (If not all students can work in groups of three, put some of them in pairs to work together on one of the number grids.)
- Tell students that they have to listen to the numbers their partners say and find them in the *Hear* column on the grid. They then have to say the corresponding number in the *Say* column for the other students to listen and recognise. Demonstrate this first yourself if necessary.
- When they have finished, get them to change over grids so that they are hearing and saying different numbers.

9D Vocabulary extension

You will need: one copy of the worksheet per student

- Exercise 1: students work individually or in pairs before checking answers with the whole class.
- Exercise 2: put students into pairs. They ask/answer the questions on their cards before feeding back any interesting information to the rest of the class.

10A Ralph and the guitar case

You will need: one set of Skeleton story cards *and one set of* Extra information cards *per group/pair*

- Divide students into pairs or groups, and, if possible, ensure that they have a large area to work in (on the floor for example). Give each pair or group a set of *Skeleton story cards* and ask them to arrange the cards **in alphabetical order** in a column in front of them, card A at the top of the column.
- Give each pair or group a set of *Extra information cards*. These should be placed face down in a pile in front of them, **in number order**, with number 1 at the top.
- Students turn over the cards **one at a time** and try to fit them in a logical place in the story by placing them either side of the column of *Skeleton story cards*. Remind students to focus on the narrative tenses used and the punctuation. If they cannot fit the card into the story, they put it back at the bottom of the pile.

- When students have finished, they can move round the room and compare their stories with other groups.
- Students can write the end of the story for homework.

10B Jungle survivors

You will need: one copy of the newspaper article per student; one set of role cards for each pair of students

- Give each student a copy of the newspaper cutting and check they have understood the main points.
- Divide the class into two groups and give one group *Reporter* role cards and the other *Survivor* role cards. (If there is an odd number of students, include an extra reporter.) Students prepare questions and answers for the role play, following the instructions on the card.
- Rearrange the class so that each reporter can interview a survivor individually. The reporters will need to take brief notes at this stage, in order to report back later.
- At the end of the interviews, rearrange the class so that each reporter is sitting with another reporter who was **not** his/her original partner. Place each survivor with another survivor who was **not** his/her original partner.
- The reporters and survivors tell their new partners what was said in their interviews, using reported questions and statements.
- The reporters write the article for the *Daily Planet*, while the survivors write a letter to a member of their family telling them about the interview.

10C Vocabulary extension

You will need: one copy of the worksheet per student

- Students work through the exercises individually or in pairs, before checking answers with the whole class.

11A *Freedom of choice?* vocabulary extension

You will need: one set of cards for each pair of students; a set of monolingual dictionaries (optional)

PROCEDURE 1

- Shuffle each set of cards. Put students into pairs. Place the sets of cards face down in piles at the front of the class, and allocate one set of cards to each pair.
- One student from each pair comes up to the front of the class and takes **one card only** from the top of their pile. They go back to their partner, read the question, and write the answers **on their card**, referring to the *Freedom of choice* text or an English–English dictionary to find the answers.
- When a pair has completed a card, they take it to the teacher at the front of the class to check the answers. If the answers are correct, the student keeps the card and takes the next card from his/her pile at the front of the class. If the answer is not correct, the student has to return to his/her partner and find the correct answer.
- The first pair of students to finish all the cards are the winners.

Instructions

PROCEDURE 2

If it is not possible for your students to move around the class freely, follow the following procedure:
- Put students into pairs and give each pair a set of cards face down in a pile. Students turn over the cards one by one and write the answers on the cards.
- When a pair has finished, they hand their pile of cards to the teacher for checking. The teacher gives back the cards which are not correct and the students correct their mistakes. The first pair of students to finish all the cards are the winners.

11B In my opinion …

You will need: one copy of the board per three or four students; one set of Opinion cards for each group; one dice, three/four counters per group

- Put students into groups of three or four, and give each group a game board, a set of *Opinion cards*, counters and dice. Tell a student to shuffle the *Opinion cards* before putting them face down in a pile in the centre of the board. If one student has a watch with a second hand, make him/her the timekeeper for the group.
- Explain the code on the *Opinion cards*:
  + means *I strongly agree*
  +/– means *I'm not sure*
  – means *I strongly disagree*
- Students take it in turns to throw a number. When they land on a square with a sentence on it, they pick up an *Opinion card*. They then have to talk for thirty seconds about the sentence they have landed on. They **must** begin with an expression for agreeing and disagreeing which matches their card, and then continue by giving reasons to support this opinion.
- When they have finished talking, they put the *Opinion card* on the bottom of the pile on the board.
- If the student cannot think of anything to say, or stops talking before thirty seconds are up, he/she has to move back to her original square. (If you have a quiet class, allow each student fifteen seconds' thinking time before speaking.) The student who reaches the *Finish* square first is the winner.

NOTE: If you think your class would have difficulty in thinking of ideas to support a point of view that is not their own, the above procedure can be simplified by doing the activity **without** the Opinion cards. When they land on a square they have to give their **own** opinion on the topic, starting with an expression for agreeing or disagreeing and continuing for thirty seconds. Again, allow fifteen seconds thinking time before speaking if necessary.

12A Suzie's story

You will need: one set of cards for each pair of students

- Put students in pairs and give each pair a set of cards. Tell students to put them in the correct order. Check answers with the whole class.

- Students then take it in turns to make a sentence using a past conditional form and/or a sentence with *should have* for each card in the story. For example, for card I: *If Suzie hadn't wanted to be a musician, her father wouldn't have given her a guitar;* for card E: *She shouldn't have spent so much time practising. She should have done her school work too.*
- Students continue making sentences alternately for the rest of the story.

12B What should I do?

You will need: one problem card per student (procedure 1); one set of problem cards for each group (procedure 2)

- Put students in groups and give each group a set of problem cards, which they place face down in a pile in front of them.
- Students take it in turns to turn over a card. They explain their problems to the group, and the other students have to give advice.
- The student with the problem then decides which of his/her classmates has given the best advice, and gives him/her the problem card. The student who collects the most problem cards is the winner.
- Students report back to the class on the best or worst piece of advice they received.

12C Preposition challenge

You will need: one set of preposition cards and one set of sentence cards per three or four students

- Put students into groups of three or four. Give each group a set of *Preposition cards* and ask them to distribute the cards equally among themselves. Tell them to hold them so that nobody else can see them.
- Give each group a set of *Sentence cards* and ask them to place the cards in front of them face down in a pile.
- Student A turns over the top card. If he/she has the correct preposition amongst his/her *Preposition cards*, he/she puts it down next to the sentence.
- If the other students agree that the preposition is correct, the cards are put to one side and removed from the game. If the preposition is not correct, the student has to take back the card and the next person may put down a preposition.
- Students take it in turns to turn over a sentence card and put down a preposition card. If a student does not have the correct preposition card, he/she must pass.
- The winner is the person who gets rid of all his/her preposition cards first, or who is left with the fewest preposition cards at the end of the game.

Cutting Edge Intermediate Resource bank

Learner-training worksheet 1
Being an active learner

1 Read about four different students of English below and number them 1–3 according to how successful you think they will be in learning English (1 = most successful, 3 = least successful).

BERNARD

Bernard takes learning English very seriously. He's particularly keen on English grammar – he spends many hours at home studying grammar books and doing exercises. In class, he always has lots of questions for his teacher – in fact he knows so much about grammar that sometimes his teacher finds it hard to answer! Bernard is also keen to learn vocabulary – he always has his bilingual dictionary next to him in class, and looks up any new words he meets. He prefers this to listening to the teacher's explanations, because he likes to have an exact translation of things. At home, as well as doing his homework and studying his grammar books, he spends twenty minutes every day studying lists of new vocabulary that he has learnt. He quite enjoys his English lessons, but he feels that his teacher wastes too much time on groupwork. He doesn't like speaking to other students – they don't speak English well enough, and he doesn't like making mistakes that the teacher can't correct. So usually during these parts of the lesson, he reads one of his grammar books, or looks through the dictionary – he feels he's learning more this way. ☐

GABRIELA

Gabriela really enjoys her English lessons, though she's very busy in her job and doesn't always have enough time to study. She likes her teacher and her classmates, and enjoys speaking English, both with the teacher and with other students. She always tries to say as much as she can, even if the topic is not something that really interests her – it's still good practice. If there's something she wants to express or doesn't understand, she asks her teacher for the right word. She tries to correct herself and to use new words that she has learnt, but she doesn't worry too much if she makes mistakes. She knows she often gets things wrong, but she believes that you have to make mistakes in order to learn. Gabriela's fairly good at grammar – when she meets new grammar, she tries to work out the rules for herself, but of course she's not always right! Outside her lessons she doesn't always manage to do all her homework, but she does try to do it as carefully as possible, reading it through, and trying to correct the mistakes before she hands it in. Apart from that, she sometimes gets the chance to practise her English at work, when she meets English-speaking colleagues from the international offices of her company. She really enjoys this and makes a special effort to chat to them, even if she sometimes feels a bit shy about the level of her English! ☐

GLORIA

Gloria doesn't really know why she's learning English, but perhaps it'll be useful some day. Anyway, her parents are paying a lot of money for her lessons so, as she sees it, it's her teacher's job to make sure that she learns. She tries to come to most of the lessons, but she's generally a bit late because she's been out dancing the night before, and when she does arrive, she often isn't feeling too good. Her teacher always explains new vocabulary and grammar in English, but Gloria doesn't usually listen very hard to these parts of the lesson – her friend Monica speaks much better English than she does, so she normally asks her to translate what the teacher's said. Sometimes the teacher asks her questions and expects her to answer in English, but the questions often don't interest her much, and anyway she's a bit shy about speaking English, so she usually just answers in one word, or looks at the floor until the teacher asks someone else. They have to do quite a lot of groupwork in her class too, but for Gloria this is a good chance to find out what her friends have been doing, so they usually have a good chat – not in English, obviously! ☐

104 © Addison Wesley Longman Limited 1998 **PHOTOCOPIABLE**

2 Compare answers with other students. Make a list of the habits and attitudes that you think will / won't make each student successful, and discuss the reasons why.

3 Read an analysis below of how successful the three students are likely to be. Were you surprised by anything you read?

What are their chances of success?

Both Bernard and Gabriela have some very positive attitudes. In particular they take an active approach to their studies – they understand that they will only progress if they take responsibility for learning. Their teacher cannot 'wave a magic wand' over them and make them learn English!

Bernard spends a lot of time studying outside the lesson, which is very good, and asks lots of questions, which is also good. Nevertheless, he may not be spending his time in the best possible way – of course, grammar and vocabulary are important, but just as important is to use what you know, whether in the classroom during groupwork, or outside. Perhaps he should take his nose out of his grammar books sometimes and go and see a film in English or, if possible, try to meet some English-speaking people.

In the end Gabriela, may actually be more successful than Bernard for this very reason. Although she feels that she doesn't spend enough time studying at home, she has a very positive attitude during lessons. She takes every opportunity to speak, asking for the words she needs to express what she wants to say, and trying to use the best English she can without worrying too much if she makes mistakes. She should do very well.

As for Gloria – what is there to say? Her English is never going to improve unless she changes her attitude! She may have a busy social life, but at least she could make better use of her time during her lessons! If she tries to answer questions in more than three words, starts listening to her teacher instead of her friend, and makes an effort to speak English rather than her own language, she should soon enjoy her classes more, become a lot more confident and start to make some progress!

4 Discuss the following questions in pairs, or think about them individually.

   a The article mentions the importance of an 'active approach' to learning. Is there anything you could do to take a more active approach? Make three 'resolutions' to help you to become a more successful learner of English – but remember to be realistic about what you can do!

   b Are there any ways in which you would like your teacher to help you?

Cutting Edge Intermediate Resource bank

Learner-training worksheet 2
Working with monolingual dictionaries

> The following exercises are all based on the *Cutting Edge Mini-dictionary*, but other monolingual dictionaries are organised in a similar way (for example, the *Longman Active Study Dictionary* and the *Longman Essential Activator*). The main difference is that our mini-dictionary only contains words and meanings that appear in the *Students' Book*, so it is much shorter than other monolingual dictionaries.

1 ABBREVIATIONS

Match the abbreviations in column A with a grammatical term in column B. Then write the correct abbreviation next to the words below. Use your mini-dictionary to check if necessary.

A	B
adj	uncountable noun
adv	transitive verb
n C	adjective
n U	adverb
v T	intransitive verb
v I	countable noun

a baggage ....   e ideally ....
b commuter ....   f keen ....
c display ....   g matter ....
d housework ....   h wander ....

2 DEFINITIONS AND EXAMPLES

Look up the words below in your mini-dictionary, reading both the definitions and the examples. Then answer the following questions for each word.

- Do you understand from the mini-dictionary definition what it means?
- What helped you most – the definition, the example or both?

a deny *v* T   b invent *v* T   c available *adj*   d hopefully *adv*

3 WHEN A WORD HAS MORE THAN ONE DEFINITION

The words underlined in the following sentences have more than one definition in the mini-dictionary. Look up the words and write the number of the mini-dictionary definition which is being used in this example.

a Ali and Martin are such a friendly couple. ☐
b Jamie's party the other night was brilliant – it's a shame you couldn't come. ☐
c Lily's getting on well in her new job now. ☐
d I had a long chat with your mum the other day – she's really nice. ☐
e Give me a ring when you get home so that I know you're safe. ☐

4 USING THE DICTIONARY TO FIND GRAMMATICAL INFORMATION

> In a monolingual dictionary you can find information about:
> - **irregular verb forms**.
> - the correct **preposition** to use after a word.
> - whether a word is followed by a **gerund** or an **infinitive**.
> - **common mistakes** that foreign learners make when they use the word.

There is a mistake in each of the following sentences. Look up the words underlined in your mini-dictionary, and use the information you find to correct the mistakes.

a Robert <u>awaked</u> to find a stranger standing at the end of his bed.
b Can you get the manager, please? I want to <u>complain of</u> the service!
c I'm really <u>looking forward to go</u> on holiday next month.
d Please can you <u>explain me</u> the homework again?

5 EXTRA INFORMATION YOU CAN FIND IN THE DICTIONARY

> In a monolingual dictionary you can find extra information about:
> - **common phrases** and **word combinations** with a word.
> - important **related words**.
> - important differences between **British** and **American English**.
> - whether a word or phrase is **formal** or **informal**, or only used in **special situations**.

Use the information in your mini-dictionary to answer the following questions.

a If you look up *agency*, which common types of *agency* does the mini-dictionary give you?
b If you look up *colleague*, which common phrase do you find?
c If you look up *boiling*, what related word do you find?
d What is the American word for a *sales assistant*?
e If you look up *guy*, what do you find out about the way people use it?
f If you look up *love-lorn*, what do you notice about the way it is used?

6 USING THE DICTIONARY TO FIND OUT ABOUT PRONUNCIATION

a) Word stress is marked like this in the mini-dictionary:

agree /əˈgriː/ v

Look up the the following words in the mini-dictionary and underline the stressed syllable, as in the example.

For example: a<u>gree</u>

- cathedral
- meanwhile
- per cent
- populated

b) The mini-dictionary also gives you the phonemic spelling of a word. (If you do not know the phonemic symbols, there is a pronunciation table on the inside front cover of the mini-dictionary to help you.) Use the mini-dictionary to find the pronunciation of the following words.

- guilty *adj*
- bow *v* I
- knight *n* C
- fall *v* I

Cutting Edge Intermediate Resource bank

Learner-training worksheet 3

Dictionary skills race

Work in pairs. Answer the following questions using your mini-dictionary as quickly as possible. (You must use your mini-dictionary to check even if you think you know the answer!) The first pair to finish are the winners!

Race: TEST YOUR DICTIONARY SKILLS!

1 Look up the word underlined to find the mistake in this sentence.
- My brother always makes his homework before he has dinner. *(1 mark)*

2 Use your mini-dictionary to find out:
a what a *dealer* is. *(1 mark)*
b three common types of *dealer*. *(1 mark)*

3 Use your mini-dictionary to complete the following common expression with *average*.
- .... average, we sell fifty cars a week. *(1 mark)*

4 Look up the phonemic spelling of *rise* in your mini-dictionary and circle the word below which it rhymes with.
- nice • dies • piece *(2 marks)*

5 What is the American English spelling of *neighbour*? *(1 mark)*

6 Which syllable is stressed in the following words? Underline it.
- increase *v* I, T • increase *n* U *(2 marks)*

7 Use your mini-dictionary to choose the correct form in the following sentence.
- He insisted *to see / on seeing* the hotel manager. *(1 mark)*

8 Use your mini-dictionary to find three words related to *niece*. *(3 marks)*

9 Use your mini-dictionary to complete the gap in the following sentence.
- Well, I'm not really sure – it depends .... the individual situation. *(1 mark)*

10 Use your mini-dictionary to find the Past Simple and past participle of the irregular verb *leap*. *(1 mark)*

TOTAL 15 MARKS

108 © Addison Wesley Longman Limited 1998 **PHOTOCOPIABLE**

Learner-training worksheet 4

Learning about new words

1 WHAT YOU NEED TO KNOW ABOUT NEW WORDS TO USE THEM

If necessary, check the meaning of the following words with your teacher. Then make sentences with the words, using the prompts and completing the gap in d).

> suggest   improve   jealous   assassinate   bring up

a Jack / jealous / his younger brother
b I suggest (you) / take / the fast train / 9.45
c Your schoolwork / show / a big / improve
d Last month a twenty-year-old man / assassinate .... *(write in who)*
e After / his parents / die / Pete's grandparents / bring / him up

Discussion point 1
Read out to your teacher the sentences that you wrote for him / her to correct. In which of the following areas did you need more information before you could use these words properly?
- pronunciation / word stress
- irregular forms
- other forms of the word (for example, the noun / adjective form)
- prepositions that follow the word
- the grammatical construction that follows the word
- when you can / cannot use this word

Where can you get this information?

2 PHRASES AND WORD COMBINATIONS

a) Look quickly at the phrases at the bottom of the page to check that you understand the meanings. If necessary, ask your teacher about any of the phrases that you do not understand.

b) Complete the gaps in the following sentences with one of the phrases in the correct form (do <u>not</u> look back at the phrases). Do this as quickly as possible.

1 If you need to buy some new clothes, you ....
2 If children want to do well at school, they need to ....
3 If you don't want to eat at home, you can ....
4 If you walk round a strange town without a map, you might ....
5 When people grow up / get married, they normally ....
6 If you are rude or unkind to anyone, you should ....
7 If you're tired, it's a good idea to ....

Discussion point 2
- Were you able to use accurately all the phrases that you 'knew' at the beginning or not?
- If not, what kind of mistakes did you make? Why was this?
- How can you remind yourself of these points when you write down phrases and word combinations like this?
- What do you think is the best way to remember phrases like this?

get lost   go shopping   move house   leave school   tell the truth   say you're sorry   do your homework   eat out   make up your mind   have a rest

Cutting Edge Intermediate Resource bank

Learner-training worksheet 5
Recording and remembering vocabulary

1 DIFFERENT WAYS OF RECORDING VOCABULARY

Look at the following ways that students use for recording new vocabulary and discuss the questions in the box below.

a
- divorce rate – percentuale di divorzi
- get married – sposarsi
- average – medio
- career – carriera
- bother with – preoccuparsi di

b
- do the housework
- chat on the phone
- entertain friends

c
- A acquaintance
  aunt
  average
- B best friend
  birthrate
  boss
- C career
  chat
  classmate

d
- social — going out / entertaining friends / chatting on the phone / staying in
- sport — doing exercise / mountain-climbing / playing squash
- work and study — doing a course / studying hard
- domestic — doing the housework / cooking / gardening / looking after the children
- other — relaxing and doing nothing

e

divorce rate –	dɪvɔːsreɪt	number of divorces over a certain time
acquaintance –	əkweɪntəns	someone you know, but not a friend
entertain (friends) –	entəteɪn	invite people to your house and give them food and drink
chat –	tʃæt	have a conversation with a friend

Discussion point 1
- Do you have a special notebook for recording new words and phrases?
- Which of the methods above do *you* use for recording new words and phrases?
- What do you think are the advantages and disadvantages of each one?
- How useful is it to copy out new words and phrases into your vocabulary notebook *after* the lesson?

© Addison Wesley Longman Limited 1998   PHOTOCOPIABLE

2 DIFFERENT WAYS OF REMEMBERING VOCABULARY

a) Here are some different methods language students sometimes use for remembering new words and phrases. Read them, and then answer the questions in the box below.

- repeating the new words over and over again to yourself
- writing new words out three or four times
- inventing sentences / short dialogues in your head, using the new words
- testing yourself by covering up the words and using the definitions / translations to remind you of the word
- using cards with the new word on one side and the meaning on the other to test yourself
- making lists of related new words (for example, 'family vocabulary') and sticking it up on the wall in your house
- reading through your vocabulary notes for ten minutes every day
- selecting the new words that you personally find useful and only trying to learn these

Discussion point 2
- Have you ever tried any of these methods?
- Do you have any other methods for learning vocabulary not included on the list?
- Do you have any suggestions for your teacher about how he / she could help you to remember vocabulary (for example, by giving you vocabulary tests)?

b) Choose one of the methods of study listed above and try it out for the next week or two. Report back to the class on how useful you found it.

3 EXTENDING YOUR VOCABULARY BY YOURSELF

Here are some different ways that you can improve your vocabulary by yourself. Read them, and then answer the questions in the box below.

- reading books in English, including graded readers (such as the *Penguin–Longman Readers*)
- reading an English-language newspaper or magazine
- watching English-language films with subtitles
- finding out the words to English-language songs
- watching an English-language cable TV channel
- listening to the radio in English (the BBC world service or local English-language radio programmes)
- getting an English penfriend

Discussion point 3
- Do you do any of these things already? How useful do you find them for improving your vocabulary?
- Do you have time to start doing any of these things? If so, which appeals to you most?
- If you do these things, how important do you think it is that you understand and study every new word that you meet?
- Can you tell the other students about any places or facilities that might be useful in your area (for example, a cinema that shows subtitled films, or a library that has English-language magazines)?

Cutting Edge Intermediate Resource bank

1A Get to know the *Students' Book*

A
Each module is divided into two halves.
What is in **Part A**? ....
What is in **Part B**? ....

B
On what page is the **Language summary** for Module 5?
....

C
Where is there a list of **irregular verbs**?
....

D
How many **pronunciation boxes** are there in Module 2?
....

E
On what pages are the **tapescripts** for the listening exercises for Module 9?
....

F
What's the title of the **revision page** at the end of Module 1?
....

G
Where can you find a **pronunciation table**?
....

H
What colour is the **Useful language box** in Module 7?
....

I
How many **Consolidation modules** are there in the *Students' Book*?
....

J
There is an **empty box** on each *Task* page of the *Students' Book*. What do you write in it?
....

K
What colour are the **Analysis** boxes in Module 10?
....

L
What word is studied in the **Wordspot** in Module 5?
....

M
On what page is there a **map of Thailand**?
....

N
In which module do you study **past sentences with *if***?
....

O
Which module includes a story called *The Waratah Omen*?
....

P
In which module do you decide how to spend **lottery money**?
....

112 © Addison Wesley Longman Limited 1998 **PHOTOCOPIABLE**

Cutting Edge Intermediate Resource bank

1B Three person snap

Short answers with *do*, *have*, *be*

QUESTION CARDS

Am I late? (**Answer:** *No, you're not.*)	Does your mother cook dinner every night? (**Answer:** *No, she doesn't.*)	Have your parents been to the United States? (**Answer:** *Yes, they have.*)
Are your parents very rich? (**Answer:** *No, they aren't.*)	Did you go abroad last year? (**Answer:** *No, I didn't.*)	Has your father got a new car? (**Answer:** *Yes, he has.*)
Have you got a dog? (**Answer:** *No, I haven't.*)	Is your brother older than you? (**Answer:** *Yes, he is.*)	Do you like getting up early? (**Answer:** *Yes, I do.*)
Has your sister lived in Germany for a long time? (**Answer:** *No, she hasn't.*)	Are we going out tonight? (**Answer:** *Yes, we are.*)	Do your relatives write to you very often? (**Answer:** *Yes, they do.*)
Have we been there before? (**Answer:** *No, we haven't.*)	Was I wrong to say that? (**Answer:** *Yes, you were.*)	Did your sister pass her exam? (**Answer:** *Yes, she did.*)

ANSWER CARDS

No, you're not.	No, she doesn't.	Yes, they have.
No, they aren't.	No, I didn't.	Yes, he has.
No, I haven't.	Yes, he is.	Yes, I do.
No, she hasn't.	Yes, we are.	Yes, they do.
No, we haven't.	Yes, you were.	Yes, she did.

PHOTOCOPIABLE © Addison Wesley Longman Limited 1998

Cutting Edge Intermediate Resource bank

1C Vocabulary extension
Phrases for talking about people around you

1 Read the conversation below and <u>underline</u> the following:

- a phrase which means:
    a colleague   b neighbour   c strangers   d classmates   e flatmate

- a verb which means:
    f to start a conversation with someone you have not met before
    g to have a friendly relationship with someone
    h to develop a friendship with someone you have recently met, by talking and finding out about them

ANGELA: Hi, Mum, I just thought I'd ring and tell you that I've found a flat. It was just luck really – someone at work told me about it. It's got great views, it's on the top floor of a big block of flats.
MUM: Great – and have you met any of your neighbours?
ANGELA: Well, the woman who lives next door's really nice. I went to borrow some milk the other day and we got talking. There are lots of people I don't know, though!
MUM: Oh, I'm sure you'll meet them soon. So how's work going?
ANGELA: It's fine. I really like the job and I get on well with everyone in the office. Oh yes, and I'm taking an evening course – in flamenco dancing!
MUM: That sounds energetic!
ANGELA: Yes, it's great, and the other people on my course are really friendly. There are a couple of girls the same age as me – I'd like to get to know them better. Mike said we should have a party, and invite them.
MUM: Mike? Who's Mike?
ANGELA: Oh, he's just a guy ... Paula introduced me to him a few weeks ago.
MUM: Wait a minute – who's Paula?
ANGELA: Oh Mum, I'm sure I told you – Paula's the girl I share a flat with!

2 Match a question in column A with an answer in column B.

A
a Where did you first meet your best friend?
b How many people on your course are older than you?
c How long did it take you to get to know the people next door?
d Do you ever get talking to someone you don't know on the bus?
e Who do you get on best with in your family?
f What kind of person would you like to share a flat with?
g Do you get on well with the people you work with?

B
1 Someone who cooks well and doesn't forget to wash up!
2 My aunt – she's really similar to me.
3 At school, when we were ten.
4 Most of them – there's only one person I don't really like.
5 Actually, I think I'm the eldest.
6 Sometimes, especially when it's really crowded.
7 Not long at all – their children are the same age as ours so they play together.

3 Choose five of the questions to ask other students. (You can make changes if you want to, for example 'Where did you first meet the girl you share a flat with?') Ask other questions to find out more details.

1D Something in common

Present Simple and Continuous

Role card 1

You live five minutes' walk from here.
You travel around the country selling computers.
You're writing a novel in your spare time.
You hate parties!

Role card 2

You live five minutes' walk from here.
You work for an international bank.
You're studying Chinese in the evenings.
You're really enjoying the party.

Role card 3

You live in a flat round the corner.
You're doing a course in journalism.
You're writing a novel in your spare time.
You know the host of the party very well.

Role card 4

You live in a flat round the corner.
You're working for a television company at the moment.
You're studying Chinese in the evenings.
You only know one person at the party.

Role card 5

You're staying in a hotel for a few days.
You travel around the country selling computers.
You go cycling every weekend.
You only know one person at the party.

Role card 6

You're staying in a hotel for a few days.
You work for an international bank.
You go to the cinema three times a week.
You know the host of the party very well.

Role card 7

You're staying with a friend in the centre of town.
You're doing a course in journalism.
You go cycling every weekend.
You're really enjoying the party.

Role card 8

You're staying with a friend in the centre of town.
You're working for a television company at the moment.
You go to the cinema three times a week.
You hate parties!

Role card 9

You live five minutes' walk from here.
You're doing a course in journalism.
You go to the cinema three times a week.
You only know one person at the party.

Role card 10

You live in a flat round the corner.
You work for an international bank.
You go cycling every weekend.
You hate parties.

Role card 11

You're staying in a hotel for a few days.
You're working for a television company at the moment.
You're writing a novel in your spare time.
You're really enjoying the party.

Role card 12

You're staying with a friend in the centre of town.
You travel around the country selling computers.
You're studying Chinese in the evenings.
You know the host of the party very well.

Cutting Edge Intermediate Resource bank

1E Who am I?

Expressions of liking and disliking

Who am I?

Student number ☐

I absolutely love .... ,

and I really enjoy ....

I'm quite good .... ,

but I'm not very good ....

I don't really like .... ,

and I'm not really interested ....

I spend a lot of time .... ,

and I know quite a lot ....

I spend too much time .... ,

and I don't have enough time ....

I don't know anything .... ,

and I really hate .... !

© Addison Wesley Longman Limited 1998 PHOTOCOPIABLE

2A Past tense pelmanism / What about you?

Irregular Past Simple forms

feel	felt	fall	fell
bring	brought	buy	bought
teach	taught	think	thought
sleep	slept	sing	sang
stand	stood	wear	wore
lose	lost	fly	flew
dream	dreamt	run	ran
spend	spent	read	read

What about you?

On a <u>separate</u> piece of paper, write down <u>short</u> answers to the following points. Write the answers wherever you want on the page, but <u>not</u> in the same order as below.

- something you brought to school today
- how you felt at the beginning of the lesson
- the last time you fell in love
- something you bought last week
- the last time you slept for less than six hours
- something your teacher taught you last lesson
- the last time you sang
- something you thought was frightening when you were a child
- the last time you stood somewhere for over an hour
- something you wore last weekend that you really like
- the last thing you lost
- how much money you spent yesterday
- the last time you flew somewhere
- the last time you ran more than 100 metres
- what you dreamt about last night
- the last book you read

Cutting Edge Intermediate Resource bank

2B Alibi

Past Simple and Continuous

Suspect A

You and your friend went to a **restaurant** yesterday evening.

Before you are interviewed by the police, you must decide what happened yesterday evening. You will be interviewed separately, so you must have exactly the same story – or you will be arrested! Remember, details are important.

Here are some things for you to decide:

- when and where you met
- what you did before the meal
- the name of the restaurant and where you sat
- why you chose that restaurant
- other people in the restaurant
- your waiter / waitress
- what you both ate and drank
- the bill and how you paid
- what you did after the meal
- transport during the evening
- anything else about the evening – you never know what the police might ask you!

Police officer A

You are going to interview a suspect who you think committed last night's robbery. The suspect says that he / she went to a **restaurant** last night with a friend.

With your partner(s), write down some questions to ask him / her. All police officers must write the questions, as you are going to interview the suspects separately, then compare your answers later. Remember – details are important in a police investigation! Make sure that you ask about both the suspects.

You can ask questions about the following:

- when and where the suspects met
- what they did before the meal
- the restaurant and where they sat
- why they chose that restaurant
- other people in the restaurant
- the waiter / waitress
- what they both ate and drank
- the bill and how they paid
- what they did after the meal
- transport during the evening
- any more questions that you can think of.

118 © Addison Wesley Longman Limited 1998 PHOTOCOPIABLE

Suspect B

You and your friend went to the **cinema** yesterday evening.

Before you are interviewed by the police, you must decide what happened yesterday evening. You will be interviewed separately, so you must have exactly the same story – or you will be arrested! Remember, details are important.

Here are some things for you to decide:

- when and where you met
- what you did before the film
- which cinema you went to
- details of the film (actors, story, etc.)
- where you sat in the cinema
- other people in the cinema
- what you both ate and drank
- how much everything cost
- what you did after the film
- transport during the evening
- anything else about the evening – you never know what the police might ask you!

Police officer B

You are going to interview a suspect who you think committed last night's robbery. The suspect says that he / she went to the **cinema** last night with a friend.

With your partner(s), write down some questions to ask him / her. All police officers must write the questions, as you are going to interview the suspects separately, then compare your answers later. Remember – details are important in a police investigation! Make sure that you ask about both the suspects.

You can ask questions about the following:

- when and where the suspects met
- what they did before the film
- which cinema they went to
- details of the film (actors, story, etc.)
- where they sat in the cinema
- other people in the cinema
- what they both ate and drank
- how much everything cost
- what they did after the film
- transport during the evening
- any more questions you can think of.

Cutting Edge Intermediate Resource bank

2C School reunion

used to, still, not … any longer / more

Role card 1

When you were at Springfield High School, you used to play guitar in the school band. Now you are married and work in a bank, so you don't have any time for music. You sold your guitar ten years ago.

Role card 2

When you were at Springfield High School, you used to play tennis every afternoon. You were the best player in the school, and nobody ever beat you. You still play tennis occasionally, perhaps once or twice a month.

Role card 3

When you were at Springfield High School, you used to be brilliant at mathematics. You were always top of the class, and everyone else used to hate you! Now you are a top computer programmer and earn £100,000 a year.

Role card 4

When you were at Springfield High School, you used to get into fights after school. When you left school, you started boxing, and are now a famous boxer. You are fighting for the world title next week in Las Vegas!

Role card 5

When you were at Springfield High School, you used to go out with the English teacher's son / daughter. Your classmates used to make fun of you because of this! You are now married to him / her, and have three beautiful children.

Role card 6

When you were at Springfield High School, you used to be very good at singing. As soon as you left school you made a record, which sold over a million copies. Now you are rich and famous, and have just started recording your fifth album.

Role card 7

When you were at Springfield High School, you used to arrive late for class every day! Your teachers used to punish you, but it didn't make any difference. Now you are an important lawyer, but you are still late for almost every meeting!

Role card 8

When you were at Springfield High School, you used to live next door to the school. Because of this you could stay in bed later than all your classmates! Your family moved away a few years ago, and you now live in New York.

120 © Addison Wesley Longman Limited 1998 **PHOTOCOPIABLE**

Role card 9

When you were at Springfield High School, you used to play the piano in the school band. You are now married with two small children, so you don't have time to play in a band any more. You still play on your own when you have the time.

Role card 10

When you were at Springfield High School, you used to be captain of the school football team. When you left school, you tried to become a professional footballer, but you broke your leg and never played again.

Role card 11

When you were at Springfield High School, you used to be really good at mathematics. However, you haven't done any maths since you left school and have now forgotten everything you learnt. You need a calculator for everything now!

Role card 12

When you were at Springfield High School, you always used to fight with your brother, who was in the same class. Now your brother lives on the other side of the world, and you haven't seen him for years. You miss him a lot, because you have nobody to fight with!

Find someone who ...	**Name(s)**	**Does he / she still do this?**
... used to play a musical instrument		
... used to be good at sport		
... used to fight a lot		
... used to be late all the time		
... used to live close to the school		
... used to be very good at singing		
... used to be good at mathematics		
... used to go out with one of the teacher's children		

Cutting Edge Intermediate Resource bank

3A The best place in the world
Superlatives (and Present Perfect)

GO FORWARD TWO SPACES!

YOUR OLDEST LIVING RELATIVE

THE MOST EMBARRASSING MOMENT OF YOUR LIFE

THE MOST FAMOUS PERSON YOU'VE EVER MET

YOUR MOST VALUABLE POSSESSION

FINISH

MISS A TURN!

THE BEST BOOK YOU'VE EVER READ

THE HAPPIEST DAY OF YOUR LIFE

THE MOST EXPENSIVE ARTICLE OF CLOTHING YOU'VE EVER BOUGHT

THROW AGAIN!

THE BEST PARTY YOU'VE EVER BEEN TO

THE HOTTEST PLACE YOU'VE EVER VISITED

START

THE MOST EXCITING PLACE YOU'VE EVER VISITED

THE MOST EXPENSIVE RESTAURANT YOU'VE EVER BEEN TO

YOUR YOUNGEST RELATIVE

122 © Addison Wesley Longman Limited 1998 **PHOTOCOPIABLE**

Cutting Edge Intermediate Resource bank

- GO BACK TWO SPACES!
- THE FUNNIEST TV PROGRAMME IN YOUR COUNTRY
- THE WORST THING ABOUT LEARNING ENGLISH
- THE LONGEST YOU'VE EVER GONE WITHOUT EATING
- THE BIGGEST CROWD OF PEOPLE YOU'VE EVER SEEN
- THE LONGEST EVER YOU'VE GONE WITHOUT SLEEPING
- THE COLDEST PLACE YOU'VE EVER BEEN TO
- GO BACK TWO SPACES!
- THROW AGAIN!
- THE MOST EXPENSIVE HOTEL YOU'VE EVER STAYED IN
- THE MOST FAMOUS BUILDING IN YOUR COUNTRY
- THE RICHEST PERSON YOU'VE EVER MET
- THE BEST FILM YOU'VE EVER SEEN
- GO BACK THREE SPACES!
- THE THING YOU'RE MOST FRIGHTENED OF
- THE MOST DIFFICULT EXAM YOU'VE EVER TAKEN
- GO FORWARD ONE SPACE!

PHOTOCOPIABLE © Addison Wesley Longman Limited 1998

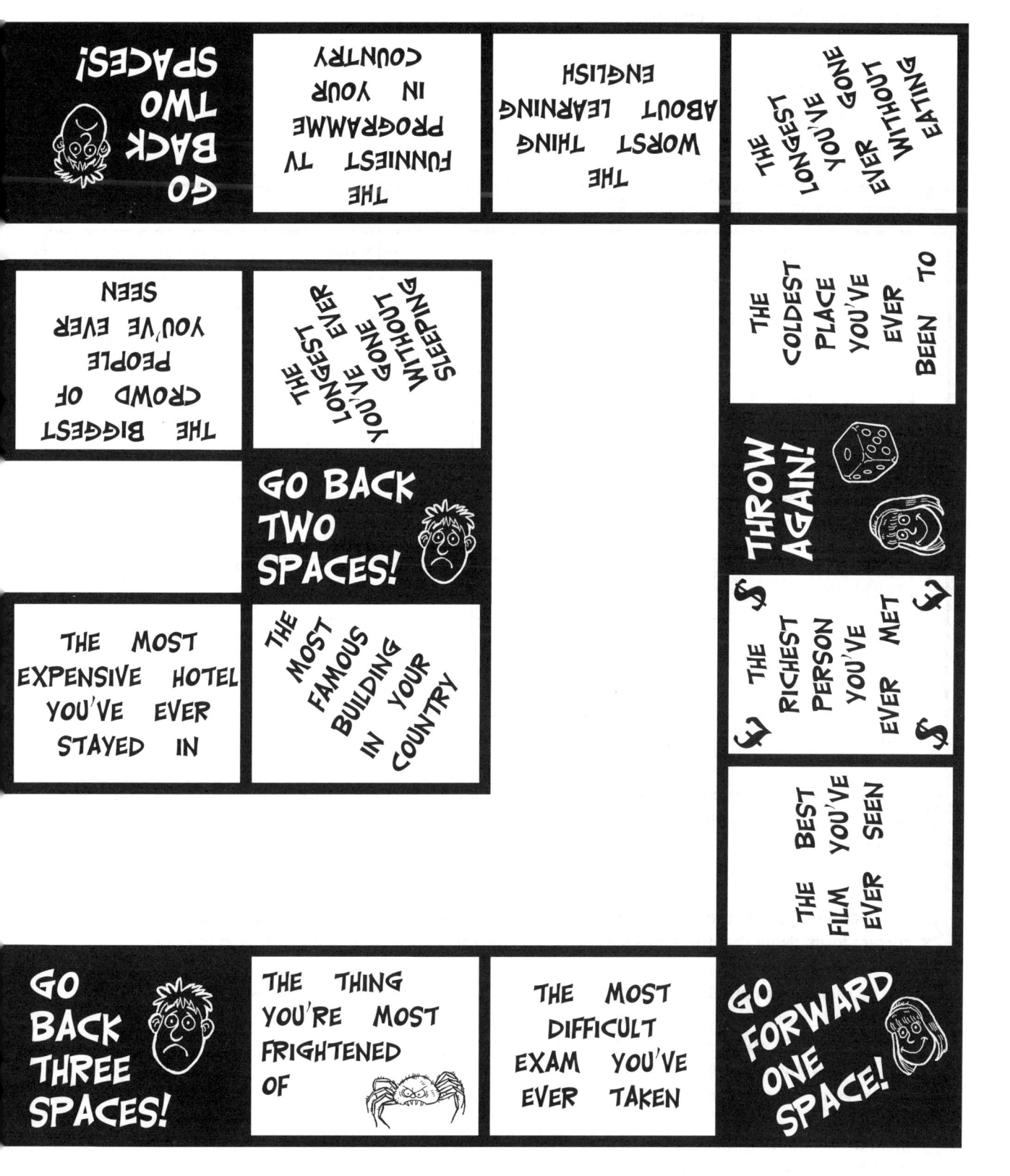

123

Cutting Edge Intermediate Resource bank

3B Amazing cities!

Vocabulary extension (word building)

1 The following words all come from the text *Amazing cities!* on pages 30–31 of the *Students' Book*. Find the words in the text and underline them.

a history *(line 4)*
b disappeared *(line 12)*
c democracy *(line 19)*
d invention *(line 19)*
e decisions *(line 22)*
f leaders *(line 23)*
g crimes *(line 24)*
h imagine *(line 26)*
i developed *(line 45)*

2 Are the words above verbs, nouns or adjectives? Write them in the correct column of the table. (Make sure you keep the words in the same order as above.)

	verb	noun	adjective	opposite adjective
a		history	• histórical • histór ic	
b				
c				
d		• • 👤		
e				
f		• 👤 •		
g		• • 👤		
h			• •	
i				

👤 = the person

3 Complete the rest of the table with the verb / noun / adjective / opposite adjective forms of the words as appropriate. Use an English–English dictionary to help you if necessary. Mark where the stress is on each word, as in the example.

4 Complete the gaps in the following sentences with a word from the table. If it is a verb, put it in the correct form. (Note that the sentences do *not* follow the same order as the words in the table.)

a The island is completely .... – the houses don't even have any water!
b Britain is a .... country, and there is an election every five years.
c If you want to write a novel, you need to have a very good ....
d The fall of the Berlin Wall was a .... moment.
e The police are investigating the .... of a twenty-year-old man, last seen a month ago.
f I'm a very .... person; I can never make up my mind what to do.
g In most countries, selling drugs is a .... offence.
h The car is probably the most important .... this century.
i Tony Blair .... the Labour Party to victory in the 1997 United Kingdom election.

3C The City Language School
Recommending and advising

Learn English for life . . .
. . . at the City Language School!

Here at the *City Language School*, we offer you a wide range of courses:

- classes in the morning, afternoon or evening
- part-time English classes (6 hours a week)
- intensive English courses (15 hours a week)
- extra classes in   - Pronunciation
   - Vocabulary
   - Listening

The *City Language School* also offers you a variety of extra facilities:
- a **self-study centre** equipped with the latest computers
- a **language laboratory**
- a large **library** with over 1,000 books for you to borrow
- a **coffee bar** offering a variety of drinks and snacks

We also offer a **Conversation Club** where you can talk to native English speakers in a relaxed and friendly environment.

So come and join us at the *City Language School* – where students come first!

New student

You have decided to go to the *City Language School* to study English, but you haven't decided which courses to do. You are going to talk to two students who have been studying there for two months. Look at the table and ask each student for their recommendations. Make brief notes about what they say.

You want advice on:	Student A	Student B
which course to do – part-time or intensive English.		
whether to study in the morning, afternoon or evening.		
which extra classes to do (you want to do at least one).		
the best place(s) to study in your free time.		
whether to join the Conversation Club.		
a good place to go for coffee / food, etc.		

PHOTOCOPIABLE © Addison Wesley Longman Limited 1998

Cutting Edge Intermediate Resource bank

Old student A

You have been studying at the *City Language School* for nearly two months. A new student is going to ask you for recommendations and advice about the school. Read the following information about your experience there before you talk to him / her.

This month you're doing ...
- the intensive English course (*great – you're improving fast, hard work, homework every night*)
- the afternoon class (*friendly students, good atmosphere*)
- extra classes – Vocabulary (*teacher, Laura, is great!*) and Listening (*boring, very difficult*)

Last month you did ...
- the part-time English course (*too slow, didn't improve much*)
- the evening class (*very quiet, only five students in class*)
- extra class – Pronunciation (*waste of time – teacher, Mark, worst in the school!*)

Free-time study
- self-study centre (*good, almost empty in the evening*)
- language laboratory (*okay, machines quite old*)
- library (*quite noisy at lunchtime*)
- Conversation Club (*boring – not enough native speakers*)

Food and drink
- school coffee bar (*excellent coffee, terrible food, good place to meet other students*)
- Happy Café (*opposite school, great pizza!*)

Old student B

You have been studying at the *City Language School* for nearly two months. A new student is going to ask you for recommendations and advice about the school. Read the following information about your experience there before you talk to him / her.

This month you're doing ...
- the part-time English course (*great – you talk a lot, teacher, Chris, is excellent!*)
- evening class (*friendly students, same age as you*)
- extra class – Vocabulary (*great, interesting topics*)

Last month you did ...
- the intensive English course (*didn't like it – too much grammar, homework every night, no fun*)
- morning class (*students mainly men*)
- extra classes – Pronunciation (*teacher, Mark, terrible!*) and Listening (*good, lots of videos*)

Free-time study
- self-study centre (*excellent, crowded at lunchtime*)
- language laboratory (*very old – some machines don't work!*)
- library (*quiet, good place to do homework*)
- Conversation Club (*good fun – lots of speaking practice*)

Food and drink
- school coffee bar (*coffee okay, but expensive*)
- Moon Café (*next to school, wonderful coffee, great food – except for the disgusting pizza!*)

3D How do I get to ...?

Asking for and giving directions

1 Look at the map below. Complete the directions from the station to the Grand Hotel using the words in the box.

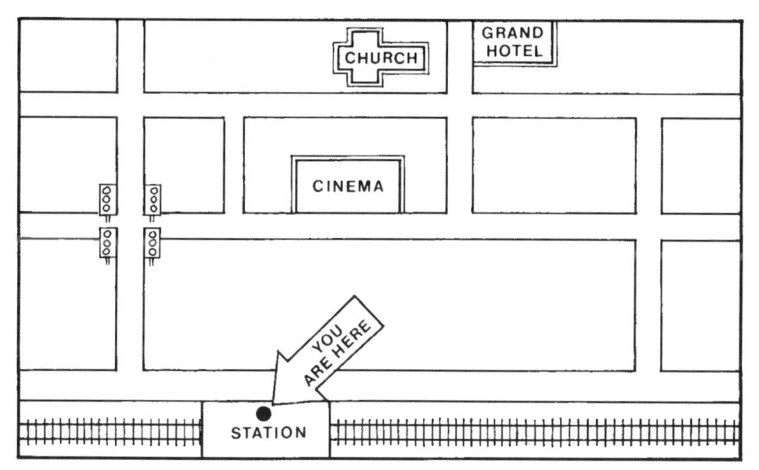

on	on	out	of
past	opposite		to
at	keep		next
turn	see		take

You go (1) .... (2) .... the station and (3) .... left. (4) .... the first right, and (5) .... going until you come (6) .... some traffic lights. Turn right (7) .... the lights, and after a few minutes you'll (8) .... a cinema (9) .... your left. Go (10) .... the cinema and take the (11) .... left. Go straight (12) .... at the next crossroads, and the Grand Hotel is on the right, (13) .... a church.

Useful language

Asking for directions

"Excuse me, how do I get to ...?"

"Excuse me, is there a ... near here?"

Saying you don't know

"I'm sorry, I've no idea."

"I'm sorry, I don't live round here."

Giving directions

"(You) go out of ... and turn left / right."

"(You) take the first / second / next left / right."

"(You) keep going until you come / get to a / the ..."

"After a few minutes you'll see a / the ... on your left / right."

"(You) go past a / the ..."

"(You) go left / right / straight on at the crossroads."

"It's on your left / right, next to / opposite the ..."

2 Look at the map below and give your partner directions to one of the places. **Do not** tell your partner which place it is. When you have finished giving your directions, your partner must tell you where he / she is.

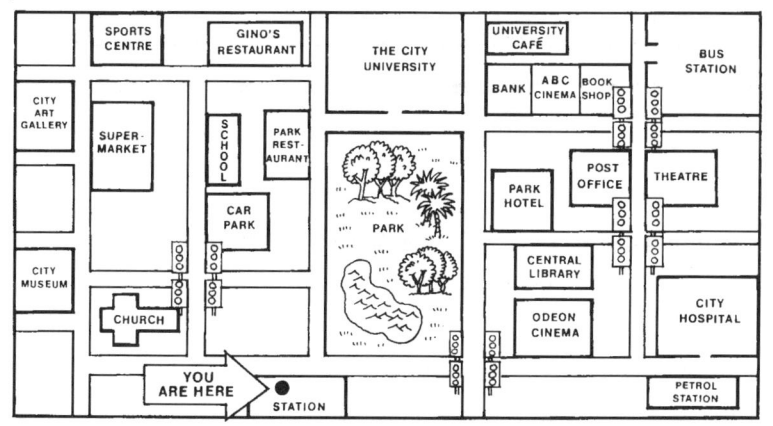

3 Choose a place on the map and ask your partner how to get there.

Cutting Edge Intermediate Resource bank

4A Twin lives
Vocabulary extension (dependent prepositions)

Which preposition?

1 The following phrases all appear in the *Twin lives* text on page 37 of the *Students' Book*. Without looking back at the text, try to complete the gaps with a preposition (*to, for, by,* etc.)

a to be close .... someone
b to spend time .... someone
c to be capable .... (doing) something
d to find the answer .... something
e to interview somebody .... something
f to arrive .... a city or country
g to arrive .... a meeting
h to be dressed .... clothes of a particular style / colour
i to appear .... television
j to be the explanation .... something

2 Find the phrases in the text and check your answers. How many did you get right?

Student A

- Do you know anyone who has appeared .... television?
- What do you think is the explanation .... all the reports of UFOs that we hear about?
- When did you last arrive late .... something?
- Who would you like to interview .... their life?
- Are women capable .... doing everything that men can?

Student B

- Who do you spend most of your free time ....?
- Can you tell me three places where you can find answers .... questions you have about English?
- When was the last time you were dressed .... very smart clothes?
- Who are you closest .... in your family?
- What's the first thing you do when you arrive .... a foreign country?

© Addison Wesley Longman Limited 1998 PHOTOCOPIABLE

Cutting Edge Intermediate Resource bank

4B Find someone who ... lied!

Present Perfect Simple (for experience)

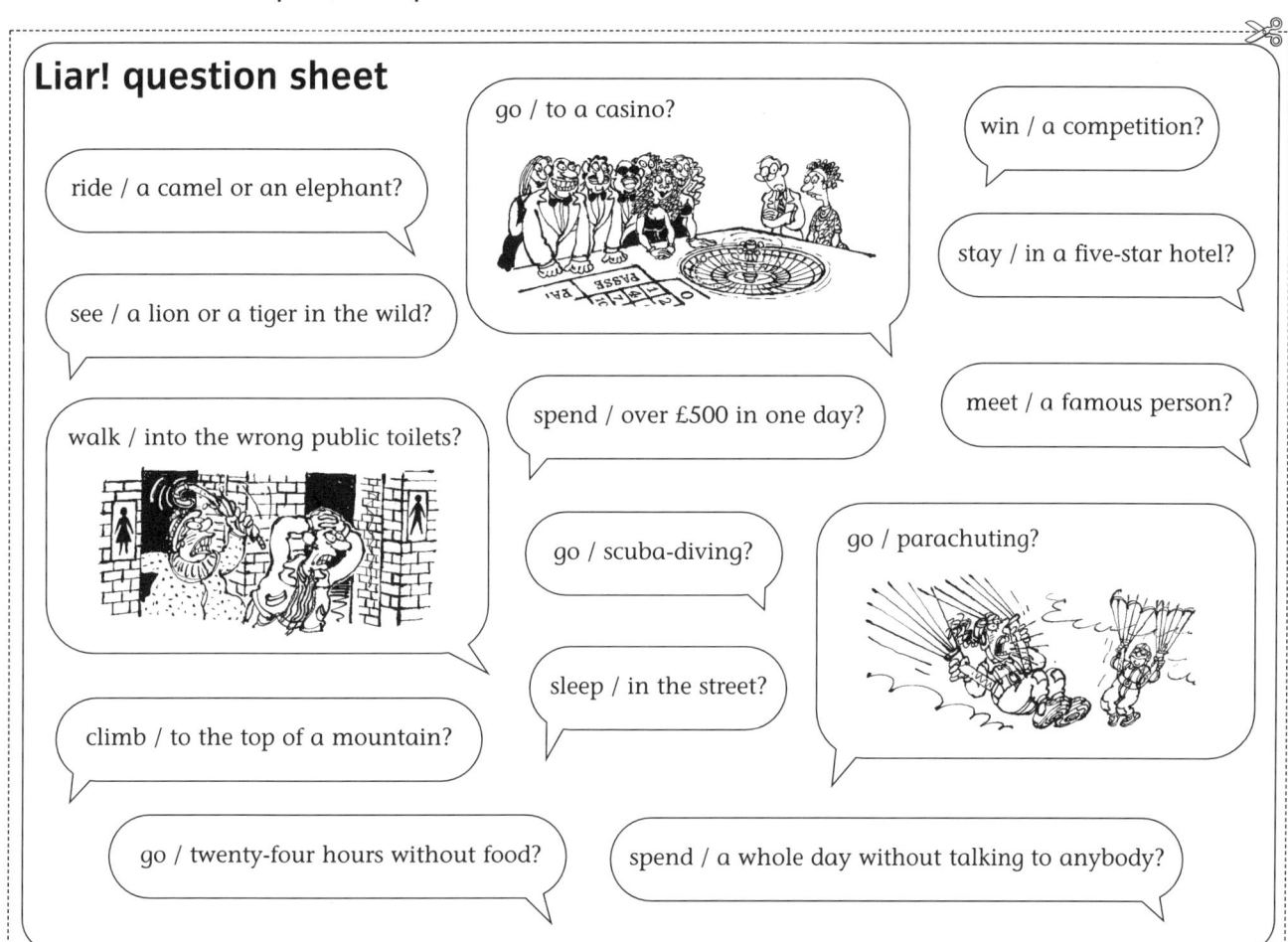

Liar! question sheet

- go / to a casino?
- win / a competition?
- ride / a camel or an elephant?
- stay / in a five-star hotel?
- see / a lion or a tiger in the wild?
- meet / a famous person?
- walk / into the wrong public toilets?
- spend / over £500 in one day?
- go / scuba-diving?
- go / parachuting?
- sleep / in the street?
- climb / to the top of a mountain?
- go / twenty-four hours without food?
- spend / a whole day without talking to anybody?

LIAR!

LIAR!

LIAR!

LIAR!

PHOTOCOPIABLE © Addison Wesley Longman Limited 1998

129

4C How long have you had it?

Present Perfect Simple and Continuous (for unfinished past)

How many students have a best friend?
Question: ....?

Who's known their best friend the longest?
Question: ....?

How many students support a football team?
Question: ....?

Who's been supporting their team the longest?
Question: ....?

How many students use a computer regularly?
Question: ....?

Who's been using a computer the longest?
Question: ....?

How many students are reading a book at the moment?
Question: ....?

Who's been reading their book the longest?
Question: ....?

How many students have got a pet?
Question: ....?

Who's had their pet the longest?
Question: ....?

How many students have got a favourite pair of shoes?
Question: ....?

Who's had their favourite pair of shoes the longest?
Question: ....?

How many students have a leather jacket?
Question: ....?

Who's had their leather jacket the longest?
Question: ....?

How many students own a car or a bike?
Question: ....?

Who's had their car or bike the longest?
Question: ....?

How many students study another foreign language?
Question: ....?

Who's been studying another language the longest?
Question: ....?

How many students live in a flat?
Question: ....?

Who's been living in their flat the longest?
Question: ....?

How many students have a boyfriend / girlfriend?
Question: ....?

Who's been going out with their boyfriend / girlfriend the longest?
Question: ....?

How many students have a favourite restaurant, bar or club?
Question: ....?

Who's been going to their favourite restaurant, bar or club the longest?
Question: ....?

Cutting Edge Intermediate Resource bank

5A How organised are you?

Vocabulary extension (phrasal verbs)

1 The following phrasal verbs all appear in the quiz *How organised are you?* on pages 48–49 of the *Students' Book*. Find each verb and <u>underline</u> it. Then match each one with a definition on the right. Write the number in the box.

a to fill something in
b to hand something in
c to read something through
d to go out
e to get down to (doing) something
f to bump into someone
g to get something out
h to save up (for something)
i to pay off (a debt)
j to take someone out
k to look into something
l to pick someone up

1 to give a person or a bank all the money that you owe them
2 to take something out of a pocket, bag, etc.
3 to write information on a form or official document
4 to go and collect someone (usually in a car)
5 to investigate something
6 to regularly keep money that you usually spend in order to buy something in the future
7 to meet someone you know when you aren't expecting to
8 to read something you have written to see if there are any mistakes in it
9 to take someone to a restaurant, cinema, etc. and pay for them
10 to give something you have written to a person in authority so that it can be read or corrected
11 to leave your house and go somewhere to enjoy yourself
12 to finally begin doing something that requires a lot of attention or energy

2 Complete the gaps in the following sentences with a phrasal verb from above in the correct form.

Find someone who ...	Name
a finds it difficult to .... doing their homework.	
b .... someone they knew last month.	
c hasn't .... any homework for a week.	
d has .... someone .... to a restaurant this year.	
e always .... his / her homework before giving it to the teacher.	
f hates .... forms.	
g has .... someone .... from the station or the airport this year.	
h is .... something special at the moment.	
i has to .... some debts.	
j is planning to .... tonight.	
k has something interesting in their pockets or bag. If they have, ask them to .... it .... and show you.	
l has .... the possibility of studying English somewhere else!	

3 Walk around the class and ask the other students questions about the above. When you find someone who answers 'yes', write their name in the column on the right. Try to find a different student for each question.

PHOTOCOPIABLE   © Addison Wesley Longman Limited 1998   131

Cutting Edge Intermediate Resource bank

5B The great diamond robbery

Future clauses with *if*, *when*, etc.

The largest and most valuable diamond in the world, the Blue Ice diamond, is on display at the National Museum. You are international jewel thieves, who are planning to steal the diamond! You are going to work out a plan – you must not get caught! Below is all the information you need to plan the robbery. First match the letters in brackets to an item on the map of the museum. Then plan your robbery and your escape!

1. The museum is open from 9.30 until 5.30. When the museum is open, four guards stand by the diamond at all times.

2. At 5.30 the front doors (F) are locked, and the keys are kept by one of the security guards. The two windows (W) are locked from the inside. There are two security cameras (S), one at the front of the building and the other in the Diamond Room.

3. When the museum is closed, there are two guards on duty. One guard (A) walks around the building, while the other guard (B) sits in the office watching the pictures from the security cameras on television screens (T). Every hour the two guards change places.

4. There is also an emergency phone (Ph). As soon as the guard picks up the phone, an alarm automatically rings in the police station next door.

5. The Blue Ice Diamond (X) is kept behind a locked glass door (G), which is connected to an alarm. If anyone breaks the glass, an alarm will go off in the police station next door.

6. The key which opens the glass door is kept in a cupboard in the security room (D).

7. Guard A keeps the key that turns off the alarm on the glass door in his pocket (P). (**Note:** you need *both* keys to open the glass door without the alarm going off.)

8. There is one extra guard's uniform in a cupboard in the security room (C).

9. The guards do not have guns, and you are not allowed to take **any** weapons into the museum.

Useful language

If		will / won't	
Unless		can	
After	+ present	might	+ infinitive
When	tense,	will have to	
Once		is / are going to	
Until		will need to	
Before		will be able to	
As soon as			

> Once we're inside, we'll have to hide.

> We'll have to get the keys before we steal the diamond.

> When we get the keys, we'll be able to get the diamond.

132 © Addison Wesley Longman Limited 1998 PHOTOCOPIABLE

Cutting Edge Intermediate Resource bank

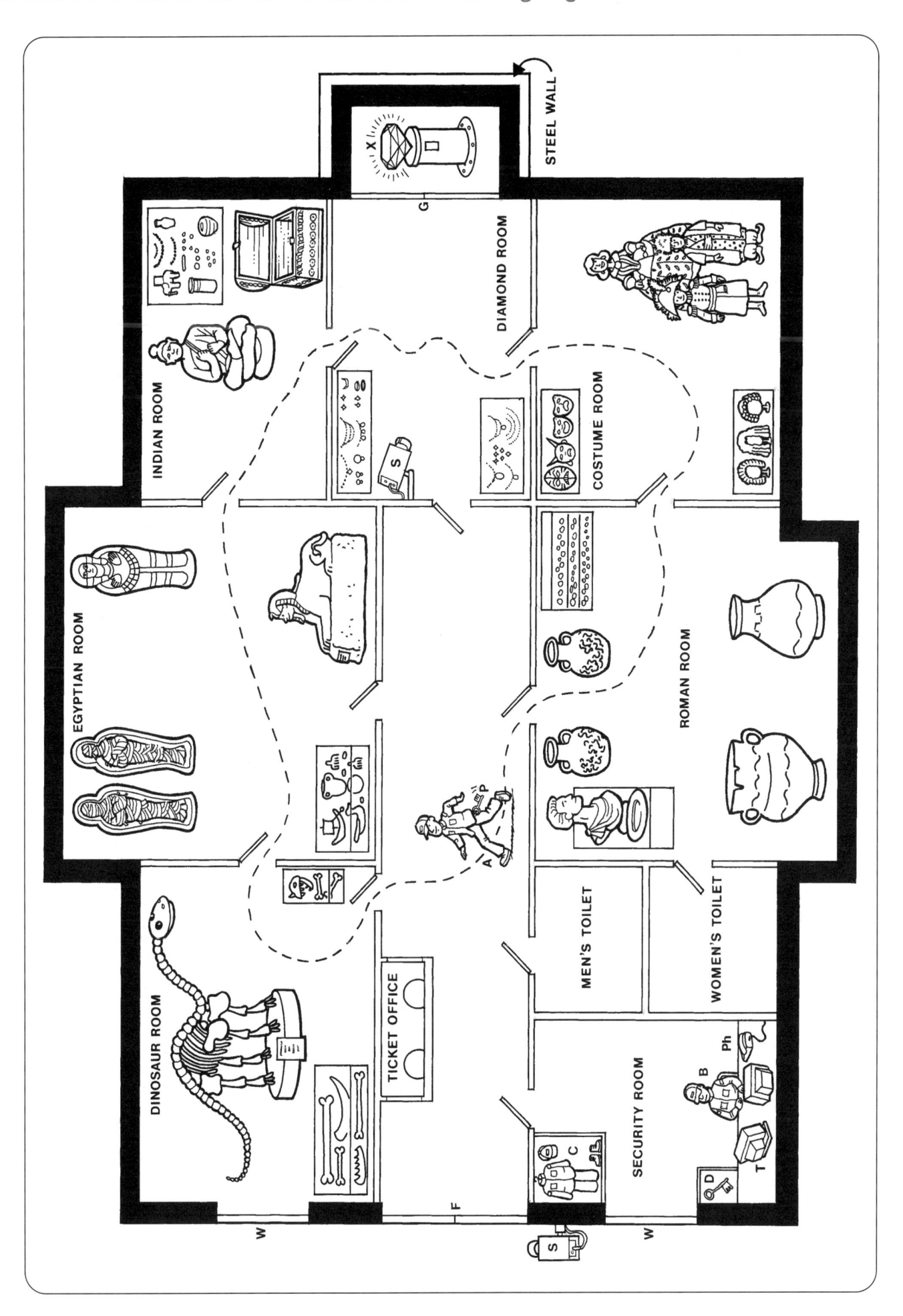

PHOTOCOPIABLE © Addison Wesley Longman Limited 1998

133

Cutting Edge Intermediate Resource bank

5C Vocabulary extension

Talking about work and training

1 Match the following questions with an answer below, paying attention to the words and phrases in **bold**.

a Do you **earn a good salary** working for the newspaper?
b What **qualifications** do you need for the job at the hospital?
c Does Anna have any **previous experience** of reception work?
d Are they going to give you any **training in** how to use the new computers?
e So when did you leave **full-time education**?
f Is Dr Clarkson **experienced in** doing this kind of operation?
g So you're **training to be** a language teacher, is that right?

1 Well, I graduated from university in 1995, then I took a **one-year diploma course** in computing, to get some more **practical skills**.
2 Yes, they're going to send everyone in the office on **a training course** next month.
3 Not yet, I'm still only **a trainee reporter**.
4 Well no, actually I'm already **fully trained** – I finished my training course last month.
5 You need **a degree in** either Maths or Physics.
6 Not really, but she has good **secretarial skills** and a friendly telephone manner.
7 Yes, he's a very **skilled** surgeon – your husband's in safe hands.

2 a) Look at the job advertisement opposite. Who are they looking for? Do applicants need to have experience and qualifications?

We are looking for:
TRAINEE REPORTERS
for a popular radio station

No previous experience necessary
Applicants should have relevant qualifications and good communication skills

Interested? Phone: 0114 234237

b) Work in pairs. Student A is the manager of the radio station and is going to interview applicants for the job of trainee reporter. Student B has sent in an application and has been asked for an interview. Look at the information on the cards below and spend a few minutes preparing what you are going to say.

STUDENT A: INTERVIEWER

Think about the questions you are going to ask Student B. You need to find out about his / her:

- qualifications
- practical skills (for example, typing)
- relevant work experience
- ability to work in a team
- personality (for example, confident, lively)
- communication skills

STUDENT B: APPLICANT

Think about what relevant qualifications, skills and experience you have. Use the following prompts and invent the details yourself.
- you have a degree in English (which university? / what did the course involve?)
- you have some experience of interviewing people (how did you get this experience?)
- you have some secretarial skills (what? / how did you get them?)
- you have trained people to use a computer? (when? / why?)
- you speak two languages (which? / when did you learn them?)
- you think you have the right personality for the job (why?)

c) You are now ready to conduct your interview. Remember:
 - Student A: you really want to find the right person for the job, so find out as much as you can about the applicant!
 - Student B: you really want this job, so answer the interviewer's questions as fully as possible!

6A Passive dominoes

Passive forms

… been described as the greatest actor ever.	In Britain, 28 million letters are …	… delivered every day.	My car is …
… being repaired at the moment.	*Hamlet* was …	… written by William Shakespeare.	The tickets will all be …
… sold before we get there.	Twenty-seven people were …	… arrested after the match.	When we arrived, the children were …
… being put to bed.	Dogs must be …	… kept on a lead while in the park.	Three hundred people have been …
… killed by an earthquake in China.	John's in hospital, but he's …	… being looked after very well.	Quick, get a doctor! She's …
… been shot!	The meeting will be …	… held next Tuesday.	Fifteen people are …
… known to have survived the explosion.	I don't believe it! My car has …	… been stolen!	Old people shouldn't be …
… left on their own.	If the police catch you, you'll …	… be sent to prison.	The staff are going to be …
… told about it at today's meeting.	I went inside although I had …	… been told to wait in the corridor.	*Jurassic Park* was …
… directed by Steven Spielberg.	All bags must be …	… checked before entering the building.	A lot of coffee is …
… produced in Brazil.	Purchases cannot be …	… exchanged without a receipt.	I took some photos of him while he was …
… being interviewed.	When I was a child, I used to be …	… sent to bed early if I was naughty.	Marlon Brando has …

Cutting Edge Intermediate Resource bank

6B Vocabulary extension

Passive verbs often in the news

1 The verbs in the box are often used in news stories. Organise them into groups which are similar in meaning. (Four of the groups should contain three verbs, one group should contain two verbs.) What is the difference between the verbs in each group?

to be damaged	to be murdered	to be burgled	to be arrested	to be killed	to be wounded
to be robbed	to be jailed	to be assassinated	to be injured	to be stolen	to be destroyed
to be hurt	to be held				

2 Circle the correct alternative in the following news stories.

a "Several people were badly (1) *injured / wounded* and one was (2) *murdered / killed* when a bus crashed into a florist's this morning. The bus driver is being (3) *arrested / held* at a local police station for questioning. Witnesses say that he was driving at 60 miles an hour when the accident happened."

b "Eight houses in the same street were (4) *burgled / stolen* in the space of one hour yesterday while all the residents of the street were at a garden party. Police believe that more than £100,000 worth of valuables were (5) *robbed / stolen*."

c "The family of Geri Baines, who was (6) *assassinated / murdered* by her ex-husband a year ago, were angry today when they heard that he had only been (7) *arrested / jailed* for eight years, following a psychiatrist's report."

d "Over 80 paintings were completely (8) *damaged / destroyed* in a fire at the City Art Gallery last night. Another 120 paintings were quite badly (9) *damaged / destroyed* by smoke and will need very careful restoration."

3 Match the following headlines with a newspaper article below. Then complete the gaps with the correct form of a verb from Exercise 1.

- Wigs lead police to prisoners
- Hairdresser's final cut
- Popstar loses hair

1
Two people were slightly (1) .... and equipment was badly (2) .... when a hairdresser, Mari Clarke, 23, went 'crazy' with a pair of scissors in a high-street salon yesterday. Manageress Jacqui Reeves said: 'I feel sorry for Mari. She's been very depressed since her boyfriend was (3) .... for three years for armed robbery.' Ms Clark is being (4) .... for questioning by police.

2
Multi-millionaire popstar Frankie Vale came home from a tour of Europe last night to find that his house had been (5) .... and his collection of valuable antique wigs had been (6) .... Tapes of his new album, which comes out next week, were also (7) .... – pieces of plastic and tape were left all over the floor. 'This was done by someone who is jealous of me, and I know who it is,' said Frankie.

3
Two men who escaped from Winkfield prison last week dressed as women were (8) .... at Manchester Airport yesterday afternoon. Police were alerted when a nearby supermarket was (9) .... by two 'women' – as one of them was escaping 'her' blonde wig came off. A shop assistant was slightly (10) .... when she was pushed to the floor by one of the escaped prisoners.

4 Write a news story using the passive verbs in Exercise 1 for one of the following headlines.

- Flood chaos hits London
- Mass-murderer dies
- Football fans in fight
- Burglars robbed

6C Adjective snap

'Extreme' adjectives

terrific	brilliant	appalling	terrible
ridiculous	furious	hilarious	tragic
fascinated	fascinating	astonished	astonishing
terrified	terrifying	boiling	freezing
good	good	bad	bad
silly	angry	funny	sad
interested	interesting	surprised	surprising
frightened	frightening	hot	cold

Questionnaire

1 Have you ever been somewhere which was really ....?
2 When was the last time you were absolutely ....?
3 Can you think of a very .... book you've read recently?
4 What was the last film you saw that was really ....?
5 Have you ever been really ....?
6 Have you seen anything very .... on the news lately?
7 Have you got any clothes that look absolutely .... on you?
8 Has anything really .... happened to you in the last few weeks?

Cutting Edge Intermediate Resource bank

7A Vocabulary extension

Informal words and phrases

1 The words and phrases in the box are 'neutral' – we can use them in any situation. Match each one with an informal word or phrase in **bold** in the sentences below.

| man | doing | talk (to someone) | two or three | Wait! | unhappy | Don't worry |
| a long time | How are you? | friends | going | What's the matter? | | |

a **Hang on!** I'm not ready yet.
b What are you **up to** next weekend?
c There's a new **guy** in the accounts office – he's really nice.
d You look terrible! **What's up?**
e Can we **have a chat** with you about who to invite to the party?
f Hi! Nice to see you! **How's it going?**
g We had to wait **ages** for a bus this morning.
h You've lost your dog? **Never mind** – I'll help you find him.
i I'm going to see a film with some **mates** from college tonight.
j You look **fed up**. Are you okay?
k Nick and I are **off** to Paris tomorrow – I'm so excited!
l Could you lend me **a couple of** pounds for a sandwich and a coffee?

2 The following dialogue is in the wrong order and the language is not informal enough. Put the lines in the correct order. Then replace the 'neutral' words and phrases with more informal ones so that the dialogue sounds more natural.

a Not too bad, thanks. I'm just phoning to ~~talk~~ *have a chat* really. ☐
b Simon – that man you met on the plane? What's he done? ☐
c No, not really. I went to the cinema with two or three friends from work last night. ☐
d Well, he hasn't phoned for two weeks. ☐
e Good! See you at the bus stop in an hour. ☐
f Hi, Suzie! It's Ruth here. [1]
g Well ... okay, I'd like that. ☐
h Did you? I haven't been to the cinema for a long time ... but, Ruth, you don't sound very happy. What's the matter? ☐
i Oh hello, Ruth. How are you? ☐
j Oh dear ... well, don't worry. Perhaps he'll phone tomorrow. Look, I'm going to the shops this afternoon – why don't you come? ☐
k Okay. Wait a minute – I'm going to turn my music down ... so what have you been doing recently? Anything exciting? ☐
l Oh, I suppose I'm unhappy because of Simon. ☐

3 Work in pairs. Write a dialogue using the informal words and phrases from Exercise 1. Choose one of the following situations or invent one of your own. Act your dialogue out for the rest of the class.

– Student A telephones Student B, a friend he / she has not seen for a long time, and tries to arrange to meet. Student B does not really want to meet and tries to make excuses.

– Student A has just failed his / her driving test. Student B is sympathetic, and tries to help him / her to forget about it.

Cutting Edge Intermediate Resource bank

7B Doonbogs!

Making generalisations

The creatures in the pictures below are called Doonbogs. They live on the planet Strackmuna, over eight billion kilometres from Earth. You are space scientists, and have just spent a year on Strackmuna living with these strange creatures. You've just returned home and now have to write a report on the Doonbogs' way of life for the Earth President.

Look at the letter you received from the Earth President before you left, and the photos you took on Strackmuna. Discuss your ideas with your partner(s), then write your report.

OFFICE OF THE EARTH PRESIDENT

Dear friends,

I wish you luck on your trip to Strackmuna to investigate the mysterious Doonbogs. While you are there, collect information on the following aspects of Doonbog culture:

- how they communicate
- their appearance
- their family systems
- their character
- how they travel
- leisure activities
- money and shopping
- what they eat
- their homes
- how long they live

Also include in your report any other interesting facts you find out about Doonbogs.

Good luck, my brave travellers!

Chief Wiggum

Chief Wiggum,
Earth President

Useful language

"Doonbogs generally / usually ..."

"It is quite common / normal / usual for Doonbogs to ..."

"Most / Some Doonbogs ..."

"Doonbogs tend to / don't tend to ..."

PHOTOCOPIABLE   © Addison Wesley Longman Limited 1998   139

Cutting Edge Intermediate Resource bank

7C What time shall we meet?
Making a social arrangement

Role card A1
You are going to ring an old friend to see if he / she would like to come to your house for a meal sometime next week. You would prefer him / her to come on Tuesday, because you finish work early then (see diary). You haven't seen him / her since he / she split up with his / her partner a few months ago. Make sure he / she knows how to get to your house, and what time to arrive.

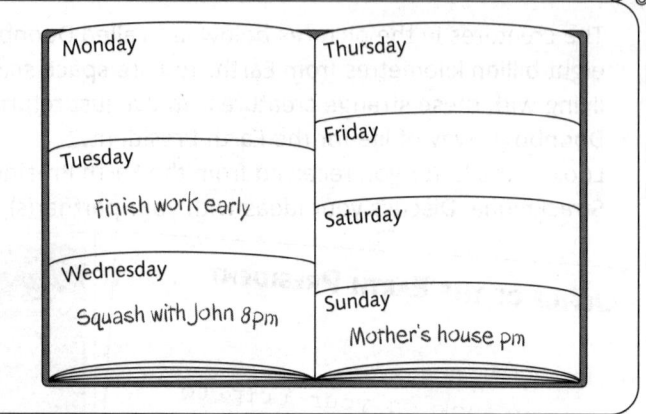

Monday	Thursday
Tuesday — Finish work early	Friday
Wednesday — Squash with John 8pm	Saturday
	Sunday — Mother's house pm

Role card A2
You have recently met a wonderful man / woman, and are spending a lot of time with him / her. Next Tuesday, for example, he / she is taking you to the opera (see diary). You haven't seen a lot of your old friends for a while; you've just been too busy having fun! You are just about to go out to meet your new boyfriend / girlfriend when the telephone rings; it's an old friend of yours.

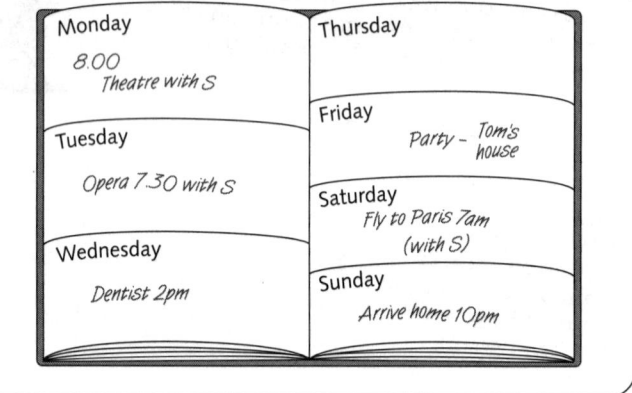

Monday — 8.00 Theatre with S	Thursday
Tuesday — Opera 7.30 with S	Friday — Party – Tom's house
Wednesday — Dentist 2pm	Saturday — Fly to Paris 7am (with S)
	Sunday — Arrive home 10pm

Role card B1
You are going to phone an old colleague of yours. You both used to work at the same travel agent's until your friend left three months ago to start his / her own business. You would like to meet for a coffee or a drink after work, preferably next Friday. The rest of your week is quite busy (see diary). When you talk to your old colleague, make sure you arrange a time and a place to meet.

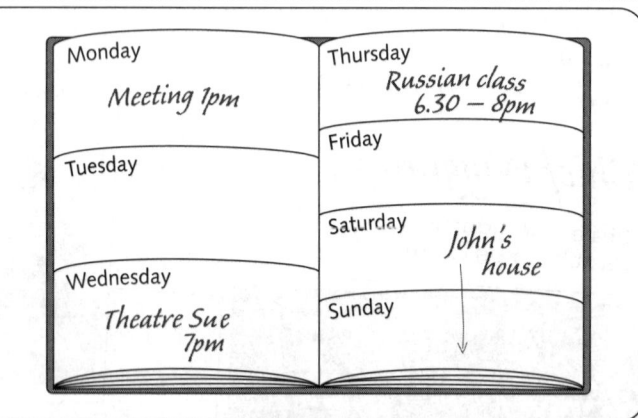

Monday — Meeting 1pm	Thursday — Russian class 6.30 – 8pm
Tuesday	Friday
Wednesday — Theatre Sue 7pm	Saturday — John's house
	Sunday

Role card B2
You have recently left the travel agent's where you worked, and have started your own travel business. You've been working very hard to make it successful, and often work in the evenings. On Friday, for example, you are meeting a very important client (see diary). The telephone rings; it's one of your old colleagues from the travel agent's.

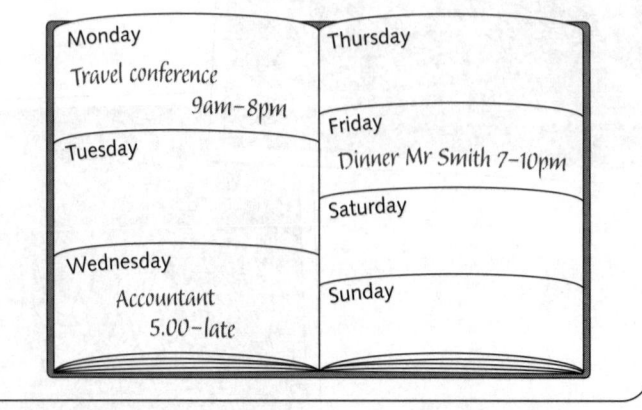

Monday — Travel conference 9am–8pm	Thursday
Tuesday	Friday — Dinner Mr Smith 7–10pm
Wednesday — Accountant 5.00–late	Saturday
	Sunday

Cutting Edge Intermediate Resource bank

Role card C1
You are going to phone a friend and ask if he / she would like to go to the cinema with you sometime next week. You would prefer to go on Monday, as you're quite busy for the rest of the week (see diary). There are three films you'd like to see: *Terror house* (a horror film), *Love in the afternoon* (a romantic film) or *Death trap* (an action film). When you talk to your friend, make sure you arrange a time and a place to meet (see film times).

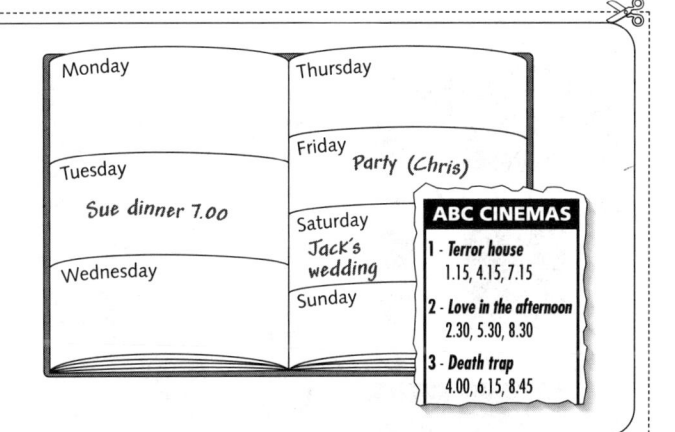

Diary:
- Monday
- Tuesday: Sue dinner 7.00
- Wednesday
- Thursday
- Friday: Party (Chris)
- Saturday: Jack's wedding
- Sunday

ABC CINEMAS
1 - *Terror house* 1.15, 4.15, 7.15
2 - *Love in the afternoon* 2.30, 5.30, 8.30
3 - *Death trap* 4.00, 6.15, 8.45

Role card C2
You have just started a new job in a restaurant, and often have to work in the evenings (see diary). At the moment you are having a coffee with a friend of yours. You've been talking about films you've seen recently. You saw a romantic film called *Love in the afternoon* last week, and thought it was awful. You prefer horror films or action films. The phone rings; it's an old friend of yours.

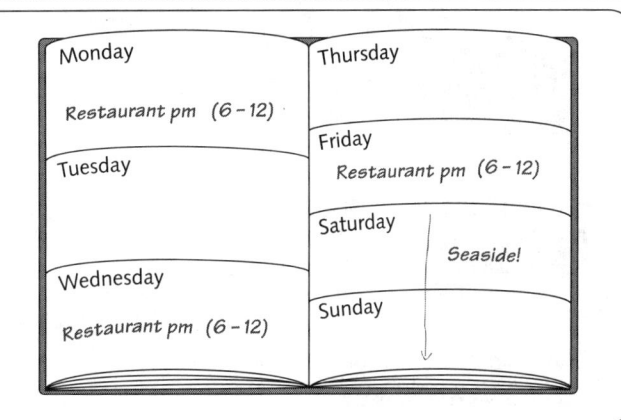

Diary:
- Monday: Restaurant pm (6–12)
- Tuesday
- Wednesday: Restaurant pm (6–12)
- Thursday
- Friday: Restaurant pm (6–12)
- Saturday: Seaside!
- Sunday

Role card D1
You are going to phone your son / daughter and invite him / her to visit you next weekend. Your sister Dorothy and her family are coming then (see calendar), and you'd really like your son / daughter to be there too. You haven't seen him / her since he / she started working in another city six weeks ago. If he / she can't come then, try to organise another date – you want to see him / her as soon as possible.

Calendar – JULY (Today: Tuesday 2)
- Sat 6 / Sun 7: Dorothy + family
- Tue 16: Tom's birthday
- Thu 25: Dentist 2pm

Role card D2
You moved away from home six weeks ago to start a job in a different city. You haven't been home to see your parents since you started work. You would like to visit your parents soon, but you definitely don't want to go when your aunt Dorothy and her awful children are there – they drive you crazy! Your weekends are very busy (see calendar) – next weekend you are planning to go to the countryside with a few friends. The telephone rings; it's your mother / father.

Calendar – JULY (Today: Tuesday 2)
- Sat 6 / Sun 7: Countryside with Phil, Anne
- Mon 8: Meeting 9 am
- Sat 13 / Sun 14: My party!
- Wed 17: Doctor 7pm
- Sat 20 / Sun 21: Jane to stay

PHOTOCOPIABLE © Addison Wesley Longman Limited 1998

141

Cutting Edge Intermediate Resource bank

8A Relative clauses crossword
Defining relative clauses

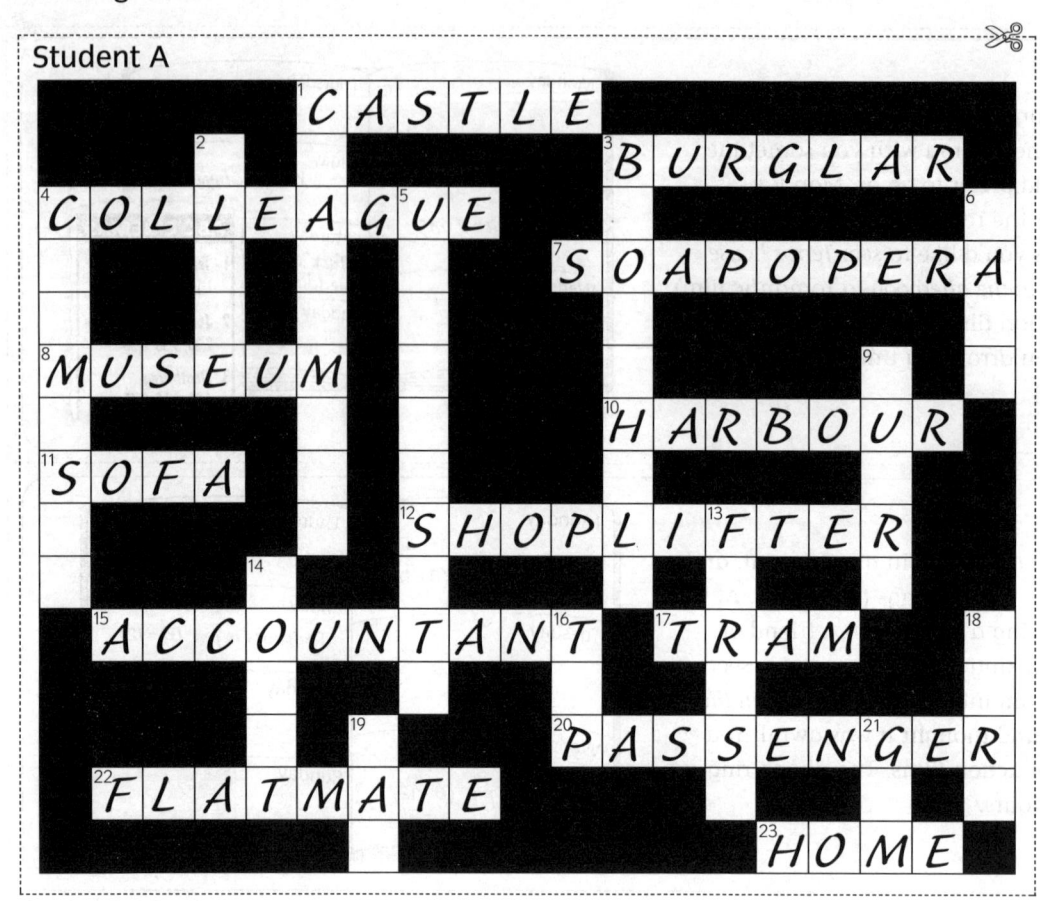

Student A

(Crossword grid with the following filled answers:)
- 1 across: CASTLE
- 3 across: BURGLAR
- 4 across: COLLEAGUE
- 7 across: SOAPOPERA
- 8 across: MUSEUM
- 10 across: HARBOUR
- 11 across: SOFA
- 12 across: SHOPLIFTER
- 15 across: ACCOUNTANT
- 17 across: TRAM
- 20 across: PASSENGER
- 22 across: FLATMATE
- 23 across: HOME

Student B

(Crossword grid with the following filled answers:)
- 1 down: CLASS (CLAS... with C at top)
- 2 down: SLAVE
- 3 down: BOOKSHELF
- 4 down: CHEMISTS
- 5 down: UNIVERSITY
- 6 down: PATH
- 7: OK
- 8 across: M
- 9 down: GUARD
- 10: HE
- 11: S
- 13 down: FOREST
- 14 down: COURT
- 15 across
- 16 down: TIP
- 18 down: JURY
- 19 down: BAR
- 20: P
- 21 down: GYM
- 22: T
- 23: M
- CLASSMATE (2 down area)

142 © Addison Wesley Longman Limited 1998   **PHOTOCOPIABLE**

Cutting Edge Intermediate Resource bank

8B *How to be a successful inventor*
Vocabulary extension (word building)

1 The following words all come from the text *How to be a successful inventor* on pages 80–81 of the *Students' Book*. Find the words in the text and <u>underline</u> them.

a successful *(title)*
b died *(line 7)*
c patient *(line 18)*
d professional *(line 21)*
e designs *(line 27)*
f remembered *(line 30)*
g scientist *(line 34)*
h research *(line 44)*
i invited *(line 46)*
j exhibits *(line 53)*

2 Are the words above verbs, nouns or adjectives? Write them in the correct column of the table. (Make sure you keep the words in the same order as above.)

	verb	noun	adjective	opposite adjective
a	succeed	success		
b				
c				
d				
e		·👤	well-designed	
f				
g		·👤		
h		·👤		
i				
j		·👤		

👤 = the person

3 Complete the rest of the table with the verb / noun / adjective / opposite adjective forms of the words as appropriate. Use an English–English dictionary to help you if necessary. Mark where the stress is on each word.

4 Complete the gaps in the following sentences with a word from the table. If it is a verb, put it in the correct form. (Note that the sentences do *not* follow the same order as the words in the table.)

a Steven made a very .... speech at the wedding. I don't think anyone there will ever forget it.
b This chair is very .... – it makes your back hurt, and your feet don't even touch the floor.
c My brother went to Delhi to do some .... on Indian religions.
d It's very impolite to arrive at a formal party without an ....
e The .... man looked up at his wife and whispered his final words.
f Congratulations, everyone! The conference was a great ....
g Have you seen the new Van Gogh .... at the National Museum? It's wonderful!
h If you want to teach children, you need to have a lot of ....
i In British schools more boys study .... subjects than girls.
j Peter arrived at the sales meeting completely drunk. I thought that was very .... of him.

PHOTOCOPIABLE © Addison Wesley Longman Limited 1998

143

Cutting Edge Intermediate Resource bank

8C Camping holiday

Quantifiers (*a few*, *a lot of*, etc.)

Student A worksheet

Tomorrow you and a friend are going camping in the mountains for three days. Because you are going to camp in a very remote place, you have to carry everything you need with you (except water – there are lots of streams in the mountains).

Unfortunately, both you and your friend packed your rucksacks without talking to each other first. Tell your friend what's in your rucksack, and give your opinion of the things your partner has packed. Together you must **make a list** of what you decide to take with you.

Make sure that you have both got <u>plenty of everything</u>. You don't want to be cold, wet and hungry, and you need to be ready for emergencies!

In your rucksack you've got:

cooking equipment
- a portable gas stove
- four saucepans
- six plates
- four mugs
- ten boxes of matches
- eight spoons and knives

food
- twenty packets of soup
- 3 kg rice
- two big jars of coffee
- ten packets of biscuits
- 1 kg beans
- 1 kg chocolate
- three loaves of bread

clothes
- five T-shirts
- four jumpers
- three pairs of jeans
- six pairs of socks
- a pair of walking boots

other
- six novels
- ten packets of cigarettes
- a sleeping bag
- three tubes of toothpaste
- a camera
- six rolls of film
- washing powder

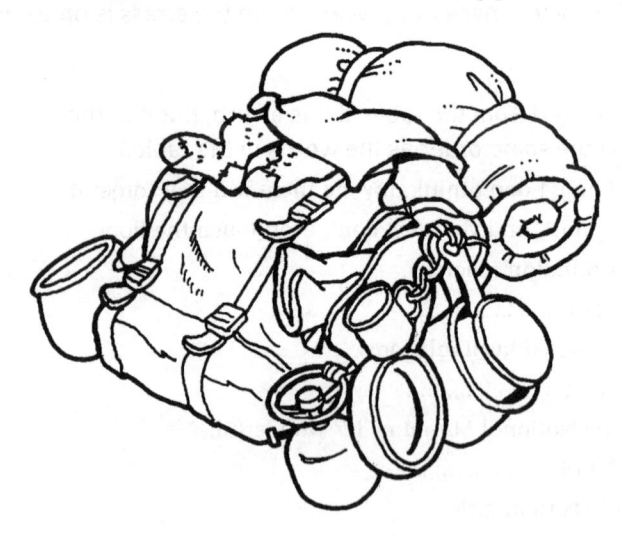

Useful language

"We'll need	plenty of …"
"We've got	a lot of …"
	lots of …"
	loads of …"

"We / You've got	some …"
"We / You have	several …"
	enough …"
	too much …"
	too many …"

	one …"
	one or two …"
"We / You'll only need	a couple of …"
	a few …"
	a little …"

"We / You haven't got	much …"
	many …"
"We / You won't need	any …"
	enough …"

"We've got no …"

144   © Addison Wesley Longman Limited 1998   PHOTOCOPIABLE

Student B worksheet

Tomorrow you and a friend are going camping in the mountains for three days. Because you are going to camp in a very remote place, you have to carry everything you need with you (except water – there are lots of streams in the mountains).

Unfortunately, both you and your friend packed your rucksacks without talking to each other first. Tell your friend what's in your rucksack, and give your opinion of the things your partner has packed. Together you must **make a list** of what you decide to take with you.

You want to make sure that you both take <u>as little as possible</u> – it's very hard to walk with a heavy rucksack!

In your rucksack you've got:

cooking equipment
- two spoons
- one water container
- one big saucepan
- one plate
- one mug
- a lighter
- a small axe (for chopping wood)

clothes
- two T-shirts
- one jumper
- one pair of jeans
- one pair of socks
- a pair of walking boots
- a raincoat

food
- six packets of soup
- 2 kg pasta
- 1 kg rice
- a small jar of coffee
- four packets dried vegetables
- two packets of biscuits
- one loaf of bread

other
- a sleeping bag
- rope (50 metres)
- a torch with spare batteries
- a tent (with 3 tent pegs)
- soap
- a camera
- one roll of film

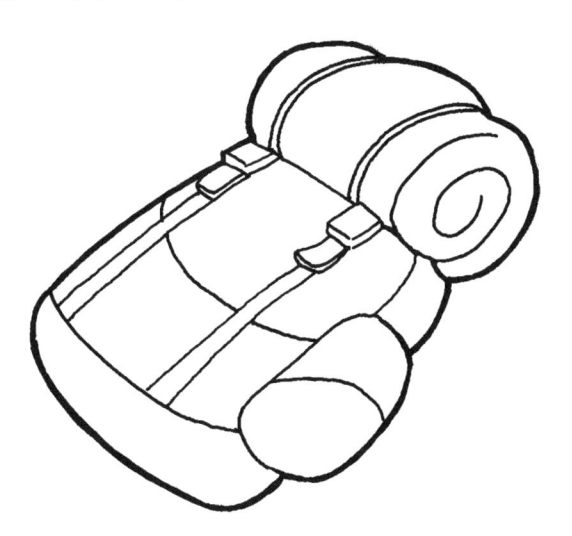

Useful language

"We'll need | plenty of ..."
"We've got | a lot of ..."
| lots of ..."
| loads of ..."

"We / You've got | some ..."
"We / You have | several ..."
| enough ..."
| too much ..."
| too many ..."

"We / You'll only need | one ..."
| one or two ..."
| a couple of ..."
| a few ..."
| a little ..."

"We / You haven't got | much ..."
"We / You won't need | many ..."
| any ..."
| enough ..."

"We've got no ..."

9A Election night special

Hypothetical possibilities with *if* ('second conditional')

Election manifesto for the .... party

Our slogan:- ....

Tax

If we were elected, we would reduce taxes on .... and
...................................., which would mean that ....
....

We would also increase taxes on .... because it would stop people
....

Spending

If we became the next government, we would spend more money on ....
...................................., which would mean that more people would ....
....

We would reduce the amount of money spent on ...., because
....

Education

If .... became Prime Minister, he / she would ....
....
....

Health

The .... party's main health policy would be ....
....
....

Jobs and unemployment

If ...., unemployment would be reduced.

In order to create more jobs, we would also ....
....
....

The Law

If .... was made illegal, ...
....

Other Policies

....
....
....
....

9B How would your life be different?

Hypothetical possibilities with *if* ('second conditional')

- How would your life be different if you .... (*have*) fifteen brothers and sisters?

- How would your life be different if you .... (*have*) four arms?

- How would your life be different if you .... (*can*) see the future?

- How would your life be different if you .... (*know*) you only .... (*have*) a year to live?

- How would your life be different if you .... (*can*) speak twelve languages?

- How would your life be different if you .... (*be*) a famous Hollywood film star?

- How would your life be different if you .... (*can*) talk to animals?

- How would your life be different if you .... (*become*) leader of your country?

- How would your life be different if you .... (*be*) less than one metre tall?

- How would your life be different if you .... (*be*) colour-blind?

- How would your life be different if you .... (*not / need*) to sleep?

- How would your life be different if you .... (*can't*) eat anything except grass?

- How would your life be different if you .... (*be*) telepathic?

- How would your life be different if you .... (*find out*) that your parents .... (*be*) aliens?

- How would your life be different if you .... (*have*) ten children?

- How would your life be different if you .... (*lose*) your memory completely?

PHOTOCOPIABLE © Addison Wesley Longman Limited 1998

Cutting Edge Intermediate Resource bank

9C Hear ... Say!
Ways of saying numbers

Student A

Hear	Say
88	$75
236,000	59%
1.005	1,005
12.75	52,000,000
START ➜	15
2,000 m²	26,035
33.5	13.5
–13°C	99.99%
22.5	–75°C

Student B

Hear	Say
15	64
47.5 km / sec	12.75
13.5	1.005
$75	2,000 m²
26%	14.5
19	236,000
9,069,312	22.5
£27.50	4,444
33	88

Student C

Hear	Say
14.5	9,069,312
59%	**FINISH!**
1,005	26%
52,000,000	19
99.99%	47.5 km / sec
64	33.5
26,035	–13°C
4,444	33
–75°C	£27.50

148 © Addison Wesley Longman Limited 1998 PHOTOCOPIABLE

9D Vocabulary extension

Talking about numbers, amounts and ages without being exact

1 Match a phrase in **bold** from column A with a phrase with the same meaning in column B.

A
a   I waited **a little less than a week** for a letter about the job.
b   Both my parents are **in their forties**.
c   Jake? He's **about fourteen or fifteen**.
d   The suspect says she left the building at **approximately 6pm**.
e   I waited **a little more than a week** for a phone call from Maria.
f   I can't remember exactly, but **I guess there were maybe** 50 people in the club.
g   My sister's boyfriend is **about the same age as me**.
h   The new guy at work is **in his late twenties**.
i   Danny's parents are both quite old – they're in their **late sixties or early seventies**.
j   There were **more or less** 50 people at Tom's wedding.

B
1   She says that she left **at around 6pm**.
2   I waited **a week or so**.
3   They're both **elderly**.
4   He's **about my age**.
5   He's **in his teens**.
6   They're both **middle-aged**.
7   There were **about** 50 people there.
8   I waited **almost a week**.
9   **There were roughly** 50 people there.
10 He's **about 27 or 28**.

2 How much do you know about the people and places around you? In pairs, ask and answer the following questions. If you don't know the exact answer, guess using the phrases from Exercise 1.

Student A
a   How old is your sister's / brother's / mother's best friend?
b   How far is it from your English school to the nearest café or bar?
c   How many students are there in your English school?
d   How much does dinner for two cost in the most expensive restaurant in town?
e   What is the average age of the students in your class?
f   What time do the other people in your family get up in the morning?

Student B
a   What time do the other people in your family go to bed?
b   How many members of staff are there in your English school?
c   How old is the President of the United States?
d   How far is it from your English school to your house?
e   How much does a flight to the UK cost from your country?
f   How tall is the tallest person in your class?

How old is your mother's best friend?

Oh ... I don't know ... but she's definitely middle-aged!

10A Ralph and the guitar case

Past Perfect, Past Simple (Past Continuous)

SKELETON STORY CARDS

A Ralph woke up	**F** Ralph turned off the television and looked around the room.
B His head was aching	**G** He knew that it wasn't his
C He looked at the clock.	**H** Then he remembered
D It was raining outside	**I** Ralph stood up and walked over to the guitar case.
E He sat back down on the bed and turned on the television.	**J** When he looked inside, he couldn't believe his eyes.

EXTRA INFORMATION CARDS

1 and immediately knew something was wrong.	**2** It was five-thirty.	**3** what had happened the previous evening.	**4** A police officer was talking about a bank robbery.
5 He got out of bed and walked over to the window.	**6** and he was still wearing all his clothes.	**7** He had gone to a nightclub,	**8** He realised that he had been asleep for over twelve hours!
9 In the corner there was a guitar case leaning against the wall.	**10** Three hundred thousand dollars had been stolen	**11** where he had met a beautiful singer called Rosanna.	**12** because he had never played the guitar in his life.
13 and people were hurrying home from work.	**14** He quickly picked up the guitar case and ran out of the door.	**15** He laid it on the bed and opened it.	**16** After the show he'd bought her a drink, then another and another.
17 He realised he had drunk too much the previous night.	**18** and two people had been shot.	**19** He couldn't remember what they'd talked about, or how he'd got home.	**20** It was full of $100 bills!

10B Jungle survivors
Reported speech

Back from the dead!

Three years ago a small passenger plane crashed in the middle of the Borneo jungle with twenty-seven people on board. Rescue teams arrived at the scene of the crash three days later. They searched the area, but found no survivors.

Two days ago, however, two people walked into a remote tribal village on the edge of the jungle and said that they were survivors of the plane crash. They told the astonished tribespeople that they had been living in the jungle by themselves since the day of the crash. We have sent two of our reporters to Borneo to interview these amazing people. Look out for an exclusive interview in next week's *Daily Planet*!

Reporter's role card

You are going to interview the survivors of the plane crash. With your partner(s), write down some of the questions you are going to ask. Try to write at least **twelve** questions.

Make sure you include questions to find out the following information:

- personal details
- how they know the other survivor(s)
- the crash and how they survived
- life in the jungle (food, shelter, etc.)
- the dangers they faced
- their health (now and in the past)
- the tribal village and its people
- plans for the future
- how they feel about flying
- how they are getting home

Survivor's role card

You are going to be interviewed by a journalist about what happened to you. With your partner, decide what your story is. Make brief notes to help you in your interview. Use your imagination!

Here are some things you might be asked about:

- personal details (be imaginative!)
- how you know the other survivor
- why the plane crashed
- how you survived the crash
- life in the jungle (food, shelter, etc.)
- the dangers you faced
- your health (now and over the last three years)
- the tribal village and its people
- plans for the future
- how you feel about flying
- how you are getting home

Cutting Edge Intermediate Resource bank

10C Vocabulary extension
Verbs to use instead of *say*

1 Match the verbs in bold in the following sentences with a definition below. Write the correct letter in the box.

a Anne told us that Tony was leaving the school, and **added** that she was very sad about it. ☐
b The doctor **repeated** that Dorothy must remember to take the pills twice a day. ☐
c The children **screamed** for help as the boat carried them further away from the beach. ☐
d The head teacher **announced** at the meeting that the exam results were excellent. ☐
e Martin **explained** that he always took the early train to get to work before eight. ☐
f 'This restaurant is terrible,' Fiona **muttered**, as the waiter took away the burnt steak. ☐
g 'Aren't you ready yet? It's nearly 9 o'clock!' David **shouted** upstairs to Jane. ☐
h 'Are you coming with us?' asked Tricia. 'I can't,' Steve **answered**, 'I've got too much work to do.' ☐
i Just as the play was starting, Marie **whispered**, 'I've got to go outside – I feel really ill.' ☐
j 'Is that really the time?' John **exclaimed**, looking at his watch. 'I must go.' ☐

1 to say something again, because you want to make sure that someone heard or understood you
2 to say something very quietly, because you only want one person to hear you
3 to say something to several people in order to give them information
4 to say something in a very loud voice, because you are angry or want to warn someone of danger.
5 to say something more, after the main thing you said
6 to say something loudly and suddenly, because of surprise or other strong feeling
7 to say something quietly and unclearly, when you are annoyed or complaining about something
8 to say something when someone asks you a question
9 to say something in a very loud, high voice, especially when you are frightened or in pain
10 to make something clear or easier to understand

2 Discuss with a partner why the following sentences are unlikely or impossible.

a 'Please don't tell anyone,' Denise whispered loudly.
b 'Sorry, can you mutter that again? I didn't hear you.'
c 'What would you like for breakfast?' his mum announced.
d Paul had to shout to his friend because they were in the library.
e 'Hello, everyone, I'm home!' added Sara.
f 'Leave me alone!' screamed the man in a low voice.

3 Complete the gaps in the following sentences with a verb from Exercise 1 in the correct form.

a Ssh … I ………………………… because I don't want to wake the children.
b 'Please don't ………………………… – I've got a headache,' said the teacher.
c 'How much?!' Rose ………………………… when she saw the bill.
d 'No – I said that I would not answer any questions,' ………………………… the minister.
e 'First you put the powder in and then you turn it on – okay?' Louis ………………………… .
f 'When did the judges ………………………… that you had won first prize?'
g 'Get out or I'll call the police!' ………………………… the terrified woman.
h Douglas has just left – he was ………………………… something about the phone bill.

4 Work in pairs. Write an extract from a short story based on one of the following ideas, using the verbs given.
• a terrible plane journey: announce, explain, scream, repeat
• a terrible driving lesson: explain, repeat, whisper, exclaim

11A *Freedom of choice?*

Vocabulary extension

---

1 a Find an **adjective** which means *causing a lot of discussion and argument* in the introductory paragraph.
Write it here .... and mark the stress.
b What's the **noun**?
Write it here .... and mark the stress.
c Which of these nouns **cannot** be described by the adjective?
• a plan   • a decision
• a place   • a topic

---

2 a Which of these constructions is correct?
• allow + infinitive with *to*
• allow + someone + infinitive with *to*
• allow + someone + infinitive without *to*
Look in paragraph 1 if you're not sure.
b What construction comes after *help* in paragraph 1?
• help + ... + ...

---

3 a Which **preposition** is used in paragraph 1 with the verb *campaign*?
• to campaign .... *something you want to happen*
b Which preposition do you use with the same verb for something you **don't** want to happen?
• to campaign .... *something*
c What's the word for a person who campaigns?
• an anti-nuclear ....

---

4 a Find a **noun** in paragraph 3 which means *an extremely sad event or situation*.
Write it here .... in the **singular** form and mark the stress.
b What's the **adjective**?
Write it here .... and mark the stress.
c What's the **adverb**?
Write it here .... (be careful of spelling!) and mark the stress.

---

5 a Find a **verb** in paragraph 3 that means *to say officially that something is not allowed* (it's in the present passive in the text).
to .... *something*
b Write the same verb in this sentence in the correct tense and add the correct **preposition**.
Yesterday the court .... *him* .... *driving for a year.*

---

6 a What's the **verb** which means *to make something legal*?
Write it here .... and mark the stress.
Look in paragraph 4 if you're not sure.
b Complete this expression by putting in the correct **preposition**.
to be illegal .... *someone to do something*
c What part of speech (noun, etc.) is *illegal*? ....

---

7 a Which **prepositions** are used with the verb *to vary* in paragraph 5?
• to vary .... + noun + ... + noun
b In this construction, do the two nouns have to be the **same** word? Yes / No
c What's the **adjective** from *vary*?
Write it here .... and mark the stress.

---

8 a Which **preposition** is used with the verb *rely*?
• to rely .... *someone / something*
Look in paragraph 5 if you're not sure.
b What's the **adjective**?
Write it here .... and mark the stress.
c What's the **opposite** adjective?
Write it here .... and mark the stress.

---

9 a Which **preposition** is used with the verb *convict*?
• to be convicted .... *a crime*
Look in paragraph 6 if you're not sure.
b Someone who is guilty of a crime and is sent to prison is often called a *convict*. Mark the stress on the noun and the verb.
• to convict
• convict

---

10 a Which **preposition** is used with the verb *sentence*?
• to sentence someone .... *ten years in prison*
Look in paragraph 6 if you're not sure.
b Which **prepositions** are missing from the following sentence?
He was sentenced .... *six months* .... *shoplifting.*

Cutting Edge Intermediate Resource bank

11B In my opinion …
Agreeing and disagreeing

- COMPUTERS ARE BAD FOR SOCIETY
- GO BACK TWO SPACES!
- PEOPLE WORRY TOO MUCH ABOUT WHAT THEY WEAR
- MEN TAKE SPORT TOO SERIOUSLY
- BOXING SHOULD BE BANNED
- THROW AGAIN!
- SUMMER IS THE BEST SEASON
- PEOPLE SHOULD LIVE TOGETHER BEFORE THEY GET MARRIED
- THE WORLD WOULD BE A BETTER PLACE WITHOUT POLITICIANS
- THERE IS TOO MUCH ADVERTISING IN SOCIETY
- TRAINS ARE THE BEST WAY TO TRAVEL
- VIOLENT TELEVISION PROGRAMMES MAKE PEOPLE MORE VIOLENT
- START
- DOGS ARE BETTER PETS THAN CATS
- ENGLISH IS THE EASIEST LANGUAGE IN THE WORLD
- BLUE IS THE MOST BEAUTIFUL COLOUR
- GO BACK TWO SPACES

154   © Addison Wesley Longman Limited 1998   PHOTOCOPIABLE

Cutting Edge Intermediate Resource bank

OPINION CARDS

MISS A TURN

FINISH!

- TEACHING IS THE MOST DIFFICULT JOB IN THE WORLD
- FOOD IS THE GREATEST PLEASURE IN LIFE
- GO FORWARD ONE SPACE
- WOMEN ARE BETTER DRIVERS THAN MEN
- PARENTS SHOULD NOT BE ALLOWED TO HAVE MORE THAN TWO CHILDREN
- THROW AGAIN!
- THERE IS LIFE ON OTHER PLANETS
- THIS COUNTRY IS THE BEST IN THE WORLD
- YOUR SCHOOLDAYS ARE THE BEST DAYS OF YOUR LIFE
- SPORT IS A WASTE OF TIME
- GO FORWARD TWO SPACES
- PEOPLE WATCH TOO MUCH TELEVISION
- SMOKING SHOULD BE MADE ILLEGAL

PHOTOCOPIABLE © Addison Wesley Longman Limited 1998

Cutting Edge Intermediate Resource bank

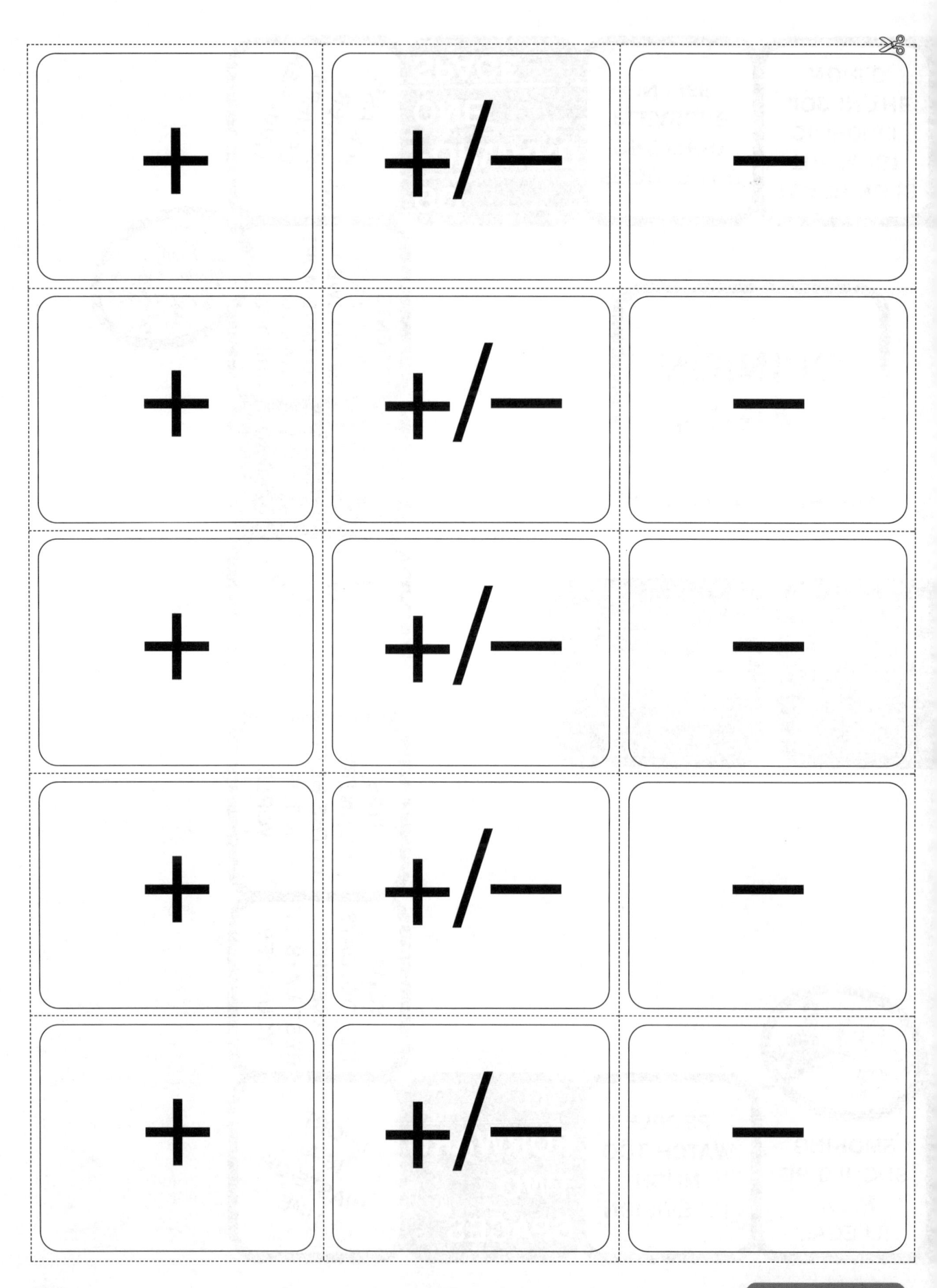

+	+/−	−
+	+/−	−
+	+/−	−
+	+/−	−
+	+/−	−

12A Suzie's story

Past sentences with *if* ('third conditional') and *should(n't) have*

I Suzie wanted to be a musician, so her father gave her a bright pink guitar for her fifteenth birthday.

H Natasha and Jo were musicians too, and so they all decided to form a band, which they called The Convicts.

E She spent so much time practising in her bedroom that she didn't pass any of her exams at school.

L Six months later The Convicts played their first concert. It was a disaster! They were so nervous they forgot all their songs and the audience laughed at them.

P Her father was so angry that he took away her guitar and locked it in a cupboard.

B Natasha and Jo were so upset after the concert that they left the band.

A Suzie was so upset about losing her guitar that she ran away from home.

O Suzie, however, didn't give up. She managed to borrow some money and made a record on her own.

N She started living on the street, and was so hungry that she began stealing food from shops.

C The record was a huge success, and Suzie became famous all over the world.

F One day a policeman saw her shoplifting, and arrested her.

M One day Suzie's father turned on the television to watch a football match and saw his daughter singing her latest song. He couldn't believe his eyes!

J During the arrest Suzie hit the policeman, and was sent to prison for three months.

G He found out that Suzie was playing a concert the following week, and went to buy a ticket.

D While in prison she shared a cell with two women called Natasha and Jo, who became her best friends.

K After the concert he went backstage and found his daughter. With tears in his eyes, he hugged her and gave her a present. It was her bright pink guitar.

PHOTOCOPIABLE © Addison Wesley Longman Limited 1998

Cutting Edge Intermediate Resource bank

12B What should I do?
Giving advice

You're addicted to tomato ketchup. You eat three bottles of ketchup a day!	You've had hiccups for two weeks.
You can't stop watching television. Yesterday you watched television for eleven hours!	You are terrified of vegetables. If you see one, you feel ill.
You have a terrible memory. You forget absolutely everything.	You can't stop sneezing!
You think your cat can talk English. You want to make her famous.	You have terrible nightmares every night.
Your doctor has just told you that you only have twenty-four hours to live.	You can't get to sleep at night. You haven't slept for twelve days.
Your wife / husband believes that he / she is a dog.	You are a shopaholic – you can't stop buying clothes.
You have ghosts in your house.	You have an exam tomorrow and you haven't done any revision.

12C Preposition challenge

Revision of prepositions

Preposition cards

for	for	for	for
in	in	in	in
on	on	on	on
of	of	of	of
about	about	about	about
by	by	by	by

Cutting Edge Intermediate Resource bank

Sentence cards

They've been living in that house .... ages.	I've applied .... lots of different jobs.
It's quite common .... people to worry about dying.	He was awarded first prize .... his beautiful painting of the sunset.
This is the best beach .... the world.	I'm really tired, so I think I'll stay .... tonight.
She was dressed .... a big baggy jumper and jeans.	I have a lot of confidence .... his ability.
My brother insisted .... coming with us.	It wasn't an accident! He did it .... purpose.
Don't leave me .... my own in this old house.	John's in hospital. He's being operated .... tomorrow morning.
Bill's absolutely terrified .... spiders!	I don't think he's capable .... looking after the children.
That woman reminds me .... my grandmother.	Those shoes are made .... plastic, not leather.
He was very angry .... what happened.	I don't know anything at all .... physics.
I'm really worried .... what will happen if they win the election.	He lay on the beach, thinking .... what had happened the previous evening.
I went to the wrong restaurant .... mistake.	I won't be lonely. I like being .... myself.
You can book tickets for the concert .... phone.	Inflation has gone up .... five per cent this year.

160 © Addison Wesley Longman Limited 1998 **PHOTOCOPIABLE**

Test one
TIME: 45 MINUTES

modules 1-4

A Making questions

Look at the answer and write the question in the correct tense from the prompts given.

For example:
you / do your homework last night?
Did you do your homework last night ?
No, I forgot.

1 How much / the train to Edinburgh / cost?
.... ?
It depends. Do you want a single or a return?

2 Where / Sebastian / born?
.... ?
In Uruguay.

3 How long / you / know / your teacher?
.... ?
Since the beginning of September.

4 What / you / look for?
.... ?
My dictionary. I think I left it here yesterday.

5 all your classmates / go / to the party yesterday?
.... ?
Yes, and everyone was late for class today!

6 anyone / see / Mrs Pearson this morning?
.... ?
No, but she doesn't usually come in until 12.00.

7 you / use to speak / Japanese when you were young?
.... ?
Yes, but I've forgotten it all now.

8 it / rain / when you arrived?
.... ?
I don't think so.

9 How long / Sarah and Eduardo / be / married?
.... ?
Only for a few months before he died.

10 Paul / work / on anything special at the moment?
.... ?
Yes, he's got an idea for a new book.

[10]

B Vocabulary: collocations

Cross out the word or phrase which is incorrect

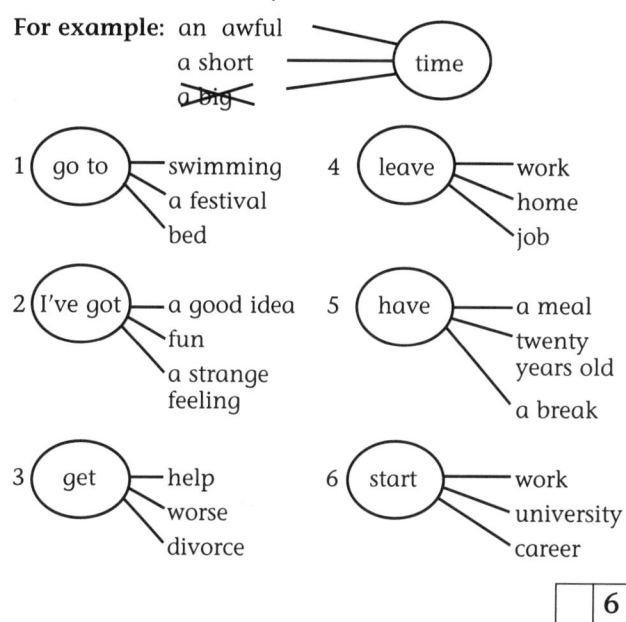

For example: an awful / a short / ~~a big~~ — time

1 go to — swimming / a festival / bed
2 I've got — a good idea / fun / a strange feeling
3 get — help / worse / divorce
4 leave — work / home / job
5 have — a meal / twenty years old / a break
6 start — work / university / career

[6]

C Prepositions

Complete the gaps in the following sentences with the correct preposition (*to*, *by* etc.).

1 Juan's not very good .... spelling.
2 The supermarket's .... the way to the station.
3 Kevin gets .... very well with all his colleagues.
4 The children's grandmother looked .... them while I was in France.
5 Does this photo remind you .... anyone?
6 Deborah brought her children .... as Buddhists.
7 Stratford-on-Avon is famous .... being Shakespeare's birthplace.
8 Tim's very interested .... motorcycles.
9 The new model's very similar .... the old one, but it goes much faster.
10 Hurry up! Uncle Pat will be here .... half an hour.

[10]

PHOTOCOPIABLE   © Addison Wesley Longman Limited 1998   161

Cutting Edge Intermediate Resource bank

D Tense review

Complete the gaps in the following sentences with the correct form of the verb in brackets

1 Before you moved to Washington, how long .... *(you / be)* in Toronto?
2 'Dear Fernando, I .... *(write)* to say thank you for the present you sent me.'
3 Beth .... *(have)* her car for over eight years, and she's still very happy with it.
4 I'm sorry, I .... *(not / agree)* with you.
5 Delgar .... *(spend)* his holiday in France when he produced his first great painting.
6 Kim and I .... *(grow up)* in the south of India in the 1950s.
7 My mother .... *(get)* much better now – the doctor says she can probably get up next week.
8 .... *(you / speak)* to Liz this week? Jan told me she has decided to look for another job.
9 My grandfather's feeling very nervous because he .... *(never / fly)* before.
10 I'm so tired. I couldn't sleep last night because our neighbour's baby .... *(cry)*.

[10]

E Short questions

Respond to the following statements with an appropriate short question.

For example:
A: I hate parties!
B: *Do you* .... ? I love them!

1 A: The children weren't very interested in the programme.
   B: .... ? Why not?
2 A: Bill Denton came to the office today.
   B: .... ? Why?
3 A: Oh no! There aren't any clean knives.
   B: .... ? Try looking in that cupboard.
4 A: My arm really hurts since I fell off my bike.
   B: .... ? Let me have a look.
5 A: Anna's got black hair.
   B: .... ? It was red last week!
6 A: I'm not going to Lorenzo's party tonight.
   B: .... ? Why not?

[6]

F Vocabulary: word stress

Put the words below in the correct column of the table according to their word stress.

| ~~famous~~ recognise achieved travelled |
| retire courageous relative polluted parent |
| colleague arrived festival old-fashioned |

●○	○●	●○○	○●○
famous			

[6]

G Comparatives and superlatives

Complete the gaps with the correct comparative / superlative form of the adjective in brackets.

1 My partner's cooking is far .... *(bad)* than mine.
2 This winter's definitely .... *(wet)* than last year.
3 Prague's one of the .... *(pretty)* cities I've ever been to.
4 Most of my classmates live a lot .... *(far)* away from school than I do.
5 The city centre is much .... *(polluted)* this winter than it used to be.

Complete the gaps with one word.

6 The exam was terrible! Everyone thought it was a .... more difficult than last year's.
7 A: These shoes are slightly too big.
   B: Try these. They're a .... smaller.
8 It's .... far the best house we've seen.
9 I've done some crazy things in my life, but going parachuting was the worst of .... !
10 New York isn't as dangerous .... we thought it would be.
11 Maria found living alone was completely different .... living with her parents.
12 Lisa's more or .... the same size as me.

[12]

H Vocabulary: word building

Complete each sentence with the correct form of the word in capitals.

For example:
Did you know that Eddie is a member of a ....*political*...... party? POLITICS

1. Lake Como is very .... at night. PEACE
2. Einstein will be remembered for his scientific .... ACHIEVE
3. The village is very beautiful, but it's rather .... TOURIST
4. Have you got a good .... for names? REMEMBER
5. .... is getting less popular in the West. MARRY

[5]

I for / since / ago / just

Complete the gaps in the following sentences with *for*, *since*, *ago* or *just*.

1. I've known my best friend Louise .... 1987.
2. My boss has had a bad cold .... a week.
3. Your mum and I used to play together years ....
4. I've been working here .... last summer.
5. The President's .... arrived at the airport.
6. Jane's been doing aerobics classes .... she first came to Warsaw.
7. A: Would you like a sandwich?
   B: No, thank you. I've .... eaten.
8. How long .... did we last see each other?
9. My flatmate's been living here .... a long time.
10. Tolstoy worked on *War and Peace* .... several years.

[10]

J Vocabulary: definitions

Write the missing word to complete the definitions.

For example:
Cars, buses, bicycles, taxis, etc. moving along a street is called ....*traffic*.......... .

1. Your father has just married again. His new wife is your ....
2. Your sister's husband is your ....
3. You have never met or seen the woman who has just entered your office. She's a .... to you.
4. You used to go out with Maria, but you don't any longer. She's your ....
5. When you stop work, usually at about sixty-five, you ....

[5]

K Phrases

Complete the following sentences with *a, an, the* or nothing.

1. Have you got .... time? I've forgotten my watch.
2. Oh no! I've left my homework at .... home.
3. Ukraine is .... second largest country in Europe.
4. Meg phoned. She says she's having .... great time in Menorca.
5. The whole family had .... fun looking at our old holiday photographs.
6. Miss Stone's by far .... most popular teacher in the school.
7. You can have .... breakfast any time between 8.00 and 9.30.
8. Did you speak to Beryl .... last week?
9. Did you know that my step-brother is .... actor?
10. Do you know .... good place to eat round here?

[10]

L Verb patterns

Circle the correct form in the following sentences.

1. I spend a lot of time *sleeping / to sleep / sleep*.
2. Joseph wanted to learn how *playing / to play / play* the piano.
3. I really enjoy *eating out / to eat out / eat out*.
4. They know quite a lot about *programming / to programme / programme* computers.
5. Mr Benson reminded us all *bringing / to bring / bring* sandwiches for the trip.
6. The Winter Palace is really worth *seeing / to see / see*.
7. Don't forget *inviting / to invite / invite* your husband to the office party.
8. Has Abdul found a place *staying / to stay / stay* yet?
9. I don't have enough time *for reading / to read / read* much at the moment, unfortunately.
10. You should definitely *going / to go / go* to Lisbon – it's a great city!

[10]

TOTAL [100]

Test two

TIME: 45 MINUTES

modules 5-8

A Talking about the future

Circle the correct form in the following sentences.

1 I'm sorry, I'm not free at 10.00. *I'll meet / I'm meeting* Tom for a drink then.
2 We'll phone you when we *get / will get* home.
3 Most people think Ireland *will win / is winning* the match next week.
4 Annie wants *that her boss gives her / her boss to give her* more money next year.
5 If *I remember / I'll remember* Gordon's address, I'll e-mail it to you.
6 When *the photos will be / will the photos be* ready?
7 I don't know if there's a flight at that time. *I look / I'll look* on the computer.
8 You won't get any coffee from that machine until the engineer *fixes / is going to fix* it.
9 I didn't realise Mr Cray needs the report now. *I'll do it / I'm doing it* straightaway.
10 Do you think the printer *will work / is working* when we attach it to the new computer?

10

B Vocabulary: collocations

Match a verb in column A with a noun in column B.

A	B
1 go	a an engineer
2 attend	b secretarial work
3 fill in	c grey
4 work as	d hands
5 go on	e a meeting
6 make	f holiday
7 do	g a form
8 shake	h an arrangement

1 .... 2 .... 3 .... 4 ....
5 .... 6 .... 7 .... 8 ....

8

C Passives

In the following news stories put the verb in brackets in the correct passive or active form. Make sure that you use the correct tense.

Three people (1) .... *(take)* to hospital last night after a fire in a house in Newcastle. Immediately afterwards police (2) .... *(arrest)* a young man.

Some children (3) .... *(find)* a bomb on a beach in South Wales yesterday. The bomb (4) .... *(explode)* and one of the children (5) .... *(badly / injure)*.

Ten people (6) .... *(die)* in an air crash in Chile. The accident (7)............................. *(happen)* last night when a plane carrying more than 250 passengers (8) .... *(fly)* into a mountain. It (9) .... *(think)* that the accident (10) .... *(cause)* by engine problems.

10

D Vocabulary: word stress

Put the words below in the correct row of the table according to their word stress.

~~organise~~ satisfaction opportunity qualified amusing experienced interested ridiculous embarrassed punctuality disappointed

o●o o	
●o o	*organise*
oo●o	
o●o o	
oo●oo	

5

Cutting Edge Intermediate Resource bank

E Verb patterns

Complete the gaps in the following sentences with *to leave* or *leaving*.

For example:
Miss Sullivan intended ..*to leave*.. on the 4.30 train.

1 We're hoping .... next weekend.
2 In the UK people tend .... tips of about 10 per cent for waiters.
3 Pete's thinking of .... his wife.
4 Hurry up! The train's about ....
5 You could help us by .... your name and address.
6 I've decided .... my job.
7 I'm planning .... on the evening flight.
8 Would you mind .... your telephone number in case of an emergency?
9 Don't forget .... your keys.
10 It's not polite .... a party without saying 'thank you'.

[10]

F Prepositions

Complete the gaps in the following sentences with the correct preposition (*to*, *by*, etc.).

1 We think Ms Tennant is suitable .... the job.
2 Oh no! I've sent the wrong letter .... mistake.
3 Just a moment – I'll put you .... to the manager's office.
4 In Japan it's common .... people to bow when they meet.
5 Did they come here .... foot?
6 This dress belonged .... Stella's grandmother.
7 My secretary had three days .... work with a terrible headache.
8 Mr Woods hasn't got much experience .... office work.
9 You broke that plate .... purpose! I saw you!
10 I work .... an import–export company in London.

[10]

G Vocabulary: word building

Complete each sentence with the correct form of the word in capitals.

For example:
Was the telephone the most important ...*invention*... of the last century? INVENT

1 There's a lot of .... in this job, but the money isn't very good. RESPONSIBLE
2 I really enjoy watching .... on television. ADVERTISE
3 Have you had an .... to Dan's party? INVITE
4 My aunt's a very .... painter. TALENT
5 Sadly, Sally didn't have the right .... for the job. QUALIFIED
6 Have you seen the .... guide? I want to see if that thriller is on again tonight. ENTERTAIN
7 My brother needs a job with lots of .... VARIED
8 My two-year-old niece is very .... – she never stops running around. ENERGY
9 We got the .... that Sarah didn't really want to come on holiday with us. IMPRESS
10 .... in the city centre is getting worse each year. POLLUTE

[10]

H Defining relative clauses

Complete the gaps in the following sentences with *who*, *which*, *that*, *whose* or *where*.

1 A daffodil is a yellow flower .... grows in the spring.
2 A reliable person is someone .... you can depend on.
3 A chemist's is a shop .... you can buy medicine and things like shampoo and soap.
4 A mobile phone is one .... you can carry around with you.
5 An orphan is a child .... parents are both dead.
6 A punctual person is someone .... is never late.

In two of the sentences above we can leave out the relative pronoun (*who*, *which*, etc.) Which sentences are they?

Sentence (7) .... and sentence (8) ....

[8]

PHOTOCOPIABLE © Addison Wesley Longman Limited 1998

165

Cutting Edge Intermediate Resource bank

I Social English: making requests

Make changes to these requests to make them sound more polite using the word in brackets.

For example:
I want to read your newspaper. *(could)*
Could I possibly read your newspaper ?

1 I must speak to Mrs Kane. *(like)*
   ....

2 Give me some change for £5. *(think)*
   .... ?

3 Look after my cat this weekend. *(possibly)*
   .... ?

4 I want to watch television. *(mind)*
   .... ?

5 Switch off the CD player when you go to bed. *(mind)*
   .... ?

6 I want to have a bath. *(alright)*
   .... ?

[6]

J Vocabulary

Circle the correct word or phrase in the following sentences.

1 Jenny was *shocking / upsetting / shocked* by the news.
2 I think you've forgotten to *plug on / plug up / plug in* the dishwasher.
3 Nick's *getting bald / going bald / losing his hairs*.
4 It's very *worrying / worried / terrific* that the doctors can't find what's wrong with Steve's baby.
5 The meeting *went bad / was badly / went badly*.
6 The President's decision is absolutely *surprised / surprising / astonishing*.
7 *Most of / Almost / Most* the people I work with are well-educated.

[7]

K Quantifiers

Complete the gaps in the following sentences with a word / phrase in the box. (There may be more than one possibility.)

| a few   many   much   enough   too much   a lot of |
| too many   a little   plenty of   not many   several |
| not much   loads of |

1 There's .... traffic in the city centre – sometimes the cars don't move for up to an hour.
2 Have you got .... money for the ticket?
3 I usually see my father .... times a week.
4 Our maths teacher used to give us .... homework.
5 Don't worry. There are .... people who have the same problem as you.
6 Fortunately there isn't .... noise in the hostel after eleven o'clock.
7 Have you got .... minutes? I could show you my photographs.
8 I didn't enjoy the party because there were .... people there.

[8]

L Phrases

Complete the following phrases with *a*, *an*, *the* or nothing.

1 What time did you go to .... bed last night?
2 .... thing I liked best about Tokyo was the nightlife.
3 You didn't get the job? Oh no, what .... shame!
4 After .... work Ralph usually goes swimming.
5 Would Harriet like to go for .... walk?
6 I like my new job, but it's .... hard work physically.
7 Generally people go to .... school for about twelve years.
8 We saw Andrea .... couple of times last year.

[8]

TOTAL [100]

Test three
TIME: 45 MINUTES

modules 9–12

A Grammar: making predictions

Re-write the following sentences using the words / phrases in brackets. You are given the first word of each sentence.

For example:
I don't know if I'll see you tomorrow.
I *may not see you tomorrow* .... (may)

1 I think taxes will go up next year.
   Taxes .... (likely)
2 I think it'll snow tomorrow.
   It .... (may well)
3 I don't think Sylvia will be on the next train.
   Sylvia .... (almost certainly)
4 It's possible that Guy will pass his driving test.
   Guy .... (could)
5 I think Mary will move to Canada.
   Mary .... (probably)
6 I don't think the USA will win the Ryder Cup.
   The USA .... (definitely)
7 I don't think Max will telephone you until tomorrow.
   Max .... (likely)
8 I'm not sure if Andrea will like the present I've bought her.
   Andrea .... (might)

[8]

B Vocabulary

Write the missing word. You are given the first letter of each word.

For example:
It means the opposite of *get better*: d*eteriorate*

1 It means the same as *regulations*: r...................
2 It means the opposite of *liberal* (parents): s...................
3 It means the same as *get better*: i...................
4 It means the opposite of *deny*: a...................
5 It means the opposite of *increase*: d...................
6 It means the opposite of *fall*: r...................
7 It means the opposite of *refuse*: a...................
8 It means the opposite of *pay back* (money): o...................

[8]

C Grammar: sentences with *if*

Complete the gaps in the following sentences with a suitable form of the verb in brackets.

1 A: It's terribly late. What .... (you / do) if you .... (miss) the last train?
   B: I .... (get) a taxi. It isn't too expensive.
2 Our son lives in Florida, but it's very expensive to get there. If it .... (not / cost) so much, we .... (visit) him more often.
3 A: Do they know what caused the crash?
   B: They're saying that if the driver .... (not / be) drunk, the accident .... (not / happen).
4 A: Why don't you phone Angela?
   B: I .... (call) her straightaway if I .... (know) her phone number.
5 Stephanie .... (become) an international athlete if she .... (train) harder when she was younger.
6 I'm going to the shops, so I can get you some aspirin. If the pharmacy .... (be / closed), I .... (go) to the supermarket.
7 I'm sorry Mrs Painter, but if James .... (not / work) much harder between now and June, he .... (not / pass) the exam.
8 A: What .... (you / do) if someone suddenly .... (leave) you loads of money?
   B: I don't know. I .... (probably / spend) it on travelling.
9 Why didn't you tell me about the problem yesterday? If you .... (tell) me immediately, I .... (do) something about it. Now it's too late.
10 I think that if Marcos .... (not / get) so angry that night, he and Ana-Maria .... (still / be) together today.

[11]

PHOTOCOPIABLE © Addison Wesley Longman Limited 1998

Cutting Edge Intermediate Resource bank

D Vocabulary: collocations

For each verb below, choose two words or phrases from the box that can go with it.

> worse   somebody unhappy   your best   a lie
> sorry   your mind   engaged   the right to   well
> goodbye   something possible   a bad time
> your school   the truth

For example:

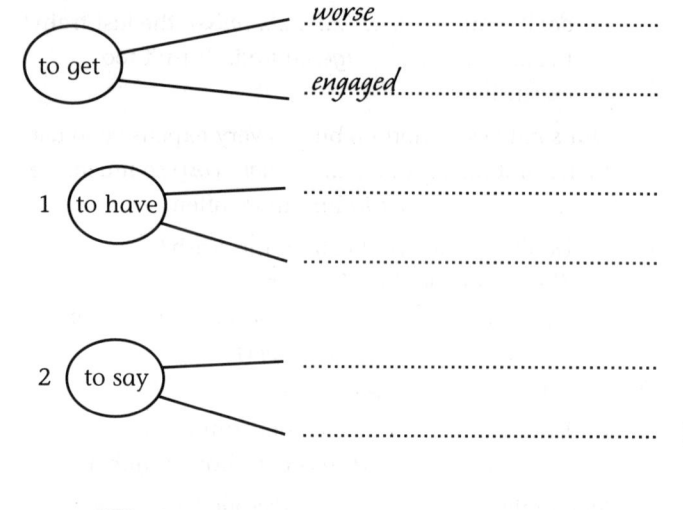

to get — *worse*
to get — *engaged*

1. to have ....
2. to say ....
3. to make ....
4. to change ....
5. to do ....
6. to tell ....

[6]

E Prepositions

Complete the gaps in the following sentences with the correct preposition (*to*, *by*, etc.).

1. .... George's surprise, there was nothing in the box.
2. Mrs Petrie told me .... for eating sweets in class.
3. I'd like to pay .... credit card, please.
4. James wants some time to talk it .... with his wife.
5. The Managing Director agrees with your idea .... theory, but is worried about the cost.
6. If a problem comes .... , please ring us straightaway.
7. Has anyone thought .... a solution yet?
8. The customer outside is insisting .... getting her money back.
9. Would you phone the hotel and ask them to sort .... the problem?

[9]

F Grammar: reported speech

Write the following dialogue in reported speech, making any changes necessary to tenses, word order, etc.

JACK: Hello, Angela.
ANGELA: Why haven't you brought the money?
JACK: I didn't have time to arrange it.
ANGELA: I'll send your boss the photos if you don't give me the money.
JACK: Okay. I can get it by tomorrow. Where are the photos?
ANGELA: They're in a safe place. Don't worry.

Jack said 'hello' to Angie, who ....
....
....
....
....
....
....
....
....

[10]

G Pronunciation: word stress

Put the words below in the correct column of the table according to their word stress.

pretend disadvantage necessary persuade
threaten obey fortunately economic foreign
unemployment obviously promise ignore

o●	●o	oo●o	●ooo
pretend			

6

H Grammar: verb forms

Complete the gaps in the following sentences with the correct Past Simple or Past Perfect form of the verb in brackets. Only use the Past Perfect if it is <u>necessary</u>.

1 When I .... (telephone) my father last week, I .... (not / speak) to him for five years.

2 Eleanor .... (go) to university for four years before she .... (start) work at Microsoft.

3 All of the dinosaurs .... (die) millions of years ago.

4 I .... (got) home at five o'clock yesterday as usual and I .... (find) that someone .... (break into) my flat and .... (steal) my video-recorder.

5 After I .... (leave) school, I .... (join) the army.

6 By the time he was twenty, Mozart .... (write) several of his most popular pieces of music.

6

I Numbers

Write the following numbers in words.
For example:
743,200
seven-hundred and forty-three thousand, two hundred

1 −12°C
   ....

2 2001
   ....

3 87 km²
   ....

4 421,000 km / hr
   ....

5 72.5%
   ....

5

J Grammar: modal verbs

In each of the following sentences there is a mistake in either the meaning or the grammar of the modal verbs (*could, should*, etc.) Correct the mistakes.

For example:
We hadn't to wear school uniform at my school.
We didn't have to wear uniform at my school.

1 You must to have a license to keep a dog.
   ....

2 I know I should have drunk so much beer last night! I feel terrible!
   ....

3 In the last century women can't vote in our country.
   ....

4 Dr Grant told Sue she ought do more exercise.
   ....

5 You don't have to eat food in the library.
   ....

6 Students have to wear any clothes they like.
   ....

7 During the war soldiers didn't allowed to write any letters to their families.
   ....

8 In many countries you haven't to drink and drive.
   ....

9 He shouldn't come to the disco if he didn't want to dance.
   ....

10 We've to solve this problem as soon as possible.
    ....

10

Cutting Edge Intermediate Resource bank

K Vocabulary: word building

Complete each sentence with the correct form of the word in capitals.

For example:
Everyone agreed he'd made the right ....*decision*........ .
DECIDE

1 Sonia's .... is completely impossible!
  BEHAVE
2 Our .... for not doing our homework was to miss football. PUNISH
3 It wasn't very .... to go to the disco the night before the exam. SENSE
4 Carla made a good .... about the Christmas party. SUGGEST
5 You need special .... to play ice-hockey EQUIP
6 The engineers couldn't think of a ....
  SOLVE
7 In my country you have to be twenty-one to vote in an .... ELECT

[7]

L Linking words

Write a suitable linking word or phrase (*What's more*, *although*, etc.) in the gaps. Do not use *and*, *but* or *so*.

For example:
Many people use English on the Internet. ....*Moreover,*...... more people have decided to study English.

1 English is very useful for travelling. .... , it can improve your chances of getting a better job.
2 Students who want to study in the USA have to pass an English listening test. .... , they often still find it difficult to understand what their teachers say.
3 English at the moment seems to be becoming the international language, ... in the future it is thought that Chinese may well become more important.
4 Spanish is also very important on the American continent. .... more and more people in the United States are studying it as their second language.

[4]

M Verb patterns: infinitive or -*ing*

Complete the gaps in the following sentences with the infinitive or -*ing* form of the verb in brackets.

For example:
The shop promised ....*to give me*.......... (give / me) my money back.

1 No one has ever persuaded Jo .... (*eat*) meat.
2 Everyone should be free .... (*read*) whatever they want.
3 Mark's partner suspected him of .... (*have*) an affair.
4 Mrs Ridley didn't know what .... (*do*) about the noise.
5 People shouldn't be allowed .... (*take*) their dogs into the park.
6 Paula suggested .... (*go*) to see a film.
7 You shouldn't have refused .... (*talk*) to Paul.
8 Is it unusual for people .... (*queue*) for buses in this country?
9 The waiter could have denied .... (*take*) the money.
10 If he hadn't threatened .... (*hit*) her, she wouldn't have left him.

[10]

TOTAL [100]

Resource bank key

Learner-training worksheet 2

1 *adj* – adjective; *adv* – adverb; *n* C – countable noun; *n* U – uncountable noun; *v* T – transitive verb; *v* I – intransitive verb

a *n* U   b *n* C   c *v* T   d *n* U   e *adv*
f *adj*   g *v* I   h *v* I

3 a 1   b 2   c 2   d 2   e 2

4 a awoke   b complain about   c looking forward to going   d explain the homework to me

5 a a travel agency, an employment agency, a ticket agency   b a colleague of mine   c boiling hot   d a sales clerk   e it is used in informal situations   f it is used in newspaper stories

6 a cath<u>e</u>dral   b <u>mean</u>while   c per <u>cent</u>   d <u>pop</u>ulated

Learner-training worksheet 3

1 does his homework   2a someone who buys and sells things, especially works of art   b art dealer, antique dealer, car dealer, drugs dealer   3 On   4 dies   5 neighbor   6 in<u>crease</u> / <u>in</u>crease   7 on seeing   8 nephew, uncle, aunt   9 on   10 leapt/leapt

Learner-training worksheet 4

1
a Jack is jealous of his elder brother.
b I suggest that you take / I suggest taking the fast train at 9.45.
c Your schoolwork is showing a big improvement.
d Last month a twenty-year-old man assassinated the President/the Prime Minister/the King, etc.
e After his parents died, Pete's grandparents brought him up.

Discussion point 1: you need information on:
a the preposition that follows *jealous*
b the grammatical construction that follows *suggest*
c the noun form of *improve*
d when you can/cannot use the verb *assassinate*
e the irregular Past Simple form of *bring*

2 1 go shopping   2 do their homework   3 eat out   4 get lost   5 move house   6 say you're sorry   7 have a rest

1A Get to know the *Students' Book*

A Part A – Language, Part B – Task   B page 144
C page 152   D two   E pages 163/164
F Do you remember?   G on the inside cover of the *Mini-dictionary*   H green   I three
J Personal vocabulary (for the tasks)   K blue
L work   M page 74   N Module 12
O Module 10   P Module 9

1C Vocabulary extension

1 a someone at work   b the woman who lives next door   c people I don't know   d people on my course   e the girl I share a flat with   f get talking   g get on well with   h get to know

2 a 3   b 5   c 7   d 6   e 2   f 1   g 4

3B Amazing cities!

3

	verb	noun	adjective	opposite adjective
a		history	historical, historic	
b	disappear	disappearance		
c		democracy	democratic	undemocratic
d	invent	invention, inventor	inventive	uninventive
e	decide	decision	decisive	indecisive
f	lead (led, led)	leader, leadership		
g		crime, criminal	criminal	
h	imagine	imagination	imaginative, imaginary	unimaginative
i	develop	development	developed	undeveloped

4 a undeveloped   b democratic   c imagination   d historic   e disappearance   f indecisive   g criminal   h invention   i led

3D How do I get to . . .?

1 1 out   2 of   3 turn   4 Take   5 keep   6 to   7 at   8 see   9 on   10 past   11 next   12 on   13 opposite

171

Resource bank key

4A Twin lives
a to b with c of d to e about f in
g for h in i on j for

5A How organised are you?

1 a 3 b 10 c 8 d 11 e 12 f 7 g 2
h 6 i 1 j 9 k 5 l 4

2 a get down to b bumped into c handed in
d taken ... out e reads through f filling in
g picked ... up h saving up for i pay off
j go out k take ... out l looked into

5C Vocabulary extension

1 a 3 b 5 c 6 d 2 e 1 f 7 g 4

6B Vocabulary extension

1 *to be damaged/to be destroyed* – if something is *damaged*, physical harm is done to it, but it can still be repaired; if something is *destroyed*, it is harmed so badly that it cannot be repaired or no longer exists
to be murdered/to be killed/to be assassinated – to *murder* someone means that you kill them deliberately and illegally; *kill* is the general word meaning to make someone or something die; *to assassinate* someone means to murder an important, famous and usually political person
to be burgled/to be robbed/to be stolen – *burgle* means to get into a building and steal things from inside; *rob* means to steal property or money from a person, bank, etc.; if you *steal* something, you take something that belongs to someone else
to be arrested/to be jailed/to be held – if the police *arrest* you, they take you to the police station because they think that you have done something illegal; they *hold* you at the police station for a number of hours before charging you with the crime or releasing you; if you are *jailed*, you are put in jail after you have been found guilty of the crime
to be wounded/to be injured/to be hurt – if you *wound* someone, you hurt someone physically, especially by making a cut or hole in their skin with a knife or a gun (for example, in a battle); if you are *injured*, you are physically hurt as a result of an accident or attack (for example, in a car accident); if you *hurt* someone, you cause physical pain to them (for example: *Don't hold my hand so tight – it hurts!*)

2 1 injured 2 killed 3 held 4 burgled
5 stolen 6 murdered 7 jailed 8 destroyed
9 damaged

3 1 Hairdresser's final cut 2 Popstar loses hair
3 Wigs lead police to prisoners

1 injured 2 damaged 3 jailed 4 held
5 burgled 6 stolen 7 destroyed 8 arrested
9 robbed 10 injured

7A Vocabulary extension

1 a Wait! b doing c man
d What's the matter?
e have a chat (with someone) – to talk (to someone)
f How are you? g a long time h Don't worry
i friends j unhappy k going l two or three

2 f, i, a, k, c, h, l, b, d, j, g, e

b that man – that guy
c two or three friends – two or three mates
d two weeks – a couple of weeks
h for a long time – for ages; What's the matter? – What's up?
i How are you? – How's it going?
j don't worry – never mind; going to the shops – off to the shops
k So what have you been doing recently? – So what have you been up to recently?
l unhappy – fed up

8A Relative clauses crossword

				¹C	A	S	T	L	E							
	²S			L					³B	U	R	G	L	A	R	
⁴C	O	L	L	E	A	⁵G	U	E		O						⁶P
H		A			S				⁷S	O	A	P	O	P	E	R	A
E		V			S				K							T
⁸M	U	S	E	U	M				S				⁹G		H
I			A		V				¹⁰H	A	R	B	O	U	R
¹¹S	O	F	A		E				E				A		
T			T			¹²S	H	O	P	L	I	F	T	E	R
S		¹⁴C				I			F		¹³D			
	¹⁵A	C	C	O	U	N	T	A	N	T		¹⁶T		¹⁷T	R	A	M	¹⁸J
		U					Y				I			E			U
		R		¹⁹B				²⁰P	A	S	S	E	N	G	E	R
²²F	L	A	T	M	A	T	E				T			Y		Y
				R				²³H	O	M	E					

172

Resource bank key

8B How to be a successful inventor

3

	verb	noun	adjective	opposite adjective
a	succeed	success	successful	unsuccessful
b	die	death	dead / dying	
c		patience	patient	impatient
d		profession	professional	unprofessional
e	design	designer / design	well-designed	badly-designed
f	remember	memory	memorable	unmemorable
g		scientist / science	scientific	unscientific
h	research	research / researcher		
i	invite	invitation	invited	uninvited
j	exhibit	exhibit / exhibition		

4
a memorable   b badly-designed   c research
d invitation   e dying   f success   g exhibition
h patience   i science   j unprofessional

9D Vocabulary extension

1
a 8   b 6   c 5   d 1   e 2   f 7   g 4   h 10
i 3   j 9

10A Ralph and the guitar case
(there is more than one possible answer)

A Ralph woke up
1 and immediately knew something was wrong.
B His head was aching
6 and he was still wearing all his clothes.
17 He realised he had drunk too much the previous night.
C He looked at the clock.
2 It was five-thirty.
8 He realised that he had been asleep for over twelve hours!
5 He got out of bed and walked over to the window.
D It was raining outside
13 and people were hurrying home from work.
E He sat back down on the bed and turned on the television.
4 A police officer was talking about a bank robbery.
10 Three hundred thousand dollars had been stolen
18 and two people had been shot.
F Ralph turned off the television and looked around the room.
9 In the corner there was a guitar case leaning against the wall.
G He knew that it wasn't his
12 because he had never played the guitar in his life.
H Then he remembered
3 what had happened the previous evening.
7 He had gone to a nightclub,
11 where he had met a beautiful singer called Rosanna.
16 After the show he'd bought her a drink, then another and another.
19 He couldn't remember what they'd talked about, or how he'd got home.
I Ralph stood up and walked over to the guitar case.
15 He laid it on the bed and opened it.
J When he looked inside, he couldn't believe his eyes.
20 It was full of $100 bills!
14 He quickly picked up the guitar case and ran out of the door.

10C Vocabulary extension

1
a 5   b 1   c 9   d 3   e 10   f 7   g 4   h 8
i 2   j 6

2
a It is unusual to whisper <u>loudly</u>.
b You don't <u>ask</u> someone to mutter, because it means to speak unclearly.
c To <u>announce</u> is to give information, not to ask a question.
d It is more usual to <u>whisper</u> in a library, because you have to be quiet.
e She is not <u>adding</u> anything, because this is the first thing she says.
f It is very difficult to <u>scream</u> in a low voice.

3
a 'm whispering   b shout   c exclaimed
d repeated   e explained   f announce
g screamed   h muttering

11A Freedom of choice?

1 a controversial   b controversy (noun)
   c a place
2 a *allow* + someone + infinitive with *to*
   b *help* + someone + infinitive with *to*
3 a for   b against   c an anti-nuclear campaigner
4 a tragedy   b tragic   c tragically
5 a ban   b banned/from
6 a to legalise   b for   c adjective
7 a from/to   b Yes   c variable
8 a on   b reliable   c unreliable
9 a of   b to convict/a convict
10 a to   b to/for

173

Resource bank key

Test one (modules 1–4)

A
1 How much does the train to Edinburgh cost?
2 Where was Sebastian born?
3 How long have you known your teacher?
4 What are you looking for?
5 Did all your classmates go to the party yesterday?
6 Has anyone seen Mrs Pearson this morning?
7 Did you use to speak Japanese when you were young?
8 Was it raining when you arrived?
9 How long were Sarah and Eduardo married?
10 Is Paul working on anything special at the moment?

B
(incorrect words/phrases)
1 swimming 2 fun 3 divorce 4 job
5 twenty years old 6 career

C
1 at 2 on 3 on 4 after 5 of 6 up 7 for
8 in 9 to 10 in

D
1 were you 2 am writing 3 has had
4 don't agree 5 was spending 6 grew up
7 is getting 8 Have you spoken 9 has never flown
10 was crying

E
1 Weren't they? 2 Did he? 3 Aren't there?
4 Does it? 5 Has she? 6 Aren't you?

F (half a mark each)
●o travelled, parent, colleague
o● achieved, retire, arrived
●oo recognise, relative, festival
o●o courageous, polluted, old-fashioned

G
1 worse 2 wetter 3 prettiest 4 further/farther
5 more polluted 6 lot 7 bit 8 by 9 all
10 as 11 from 12 less

H
1 peaceful 2 achievements/achievement 3 touristy
4 memory 5 marriage

I
1 since 2 for 3 ago 4 since 5 just 6 since
7 just 8 ago 9 for 10 for

J
1 step-mother 2 brother-in-law 3 stranger
4 ex-girlfriend 5 retire

K
1 the 2 – 3 the 4 a 5 – 6 the 7 – 8 –
9 an 10 a

L
1 sleeping 2 to play 3 eating out
4 programming 5 to bring 6 seeing 7 to invite
8 to stay 9 to read 10 go

Test two (modules 5–8)

A
1 I'm meeting 2 get 3 will win 4 her boss to give her 5 I remember 6 will the photos be 7 I'll look
8 fixes 9 I'll do it 10 will work

B
1c 2e 3g 4a 5f 6h 7b 8d

C
1 were taken 2 arrested 3 found
4 exploded 5 was badly injured 6 have died
7 happened 8 flew 9 is thought 10 was caused

D
o●o amusing, embarrassed
●oo qualified, interested
oo●o satisfaction, disappointed
o●oo ridiculous, experienced
oo●oo opportunity, punctuality

E
1 to leave 2 to leave 3 leaving 4 to leave
5 leaving 6 to leave 7 to leave 8 leaving
9 to leave 10 to leave

F
1 for 2 by 3 through 4 for 5 on 6 to
7 off 8 of 9 on 10 for

G
1 responsibility 2 advertisements/adverts/ads
3 invitation 4 talented 5 qualification(s)
6 entertainment 7 variety 8 energetic
9 impression 10 pollution

H
1 which/that 2 who/that 3 where 4 which/that
5 whose 6 who 7 sentence 2 8 sentence 4

I
1 I'd like to speak to Mrs Kane, please.
2 Do you think you could give me some change for £5?
3 Could you possibly look after my cat this weekend?
4 Do you mind if I watch television?
5 Would/Do you mind switching off the CD player when you go to bed?
6 Is it alright if I have a bath?

J
1 shocked 2 plug in 3 going bald 4 worrying
5 went badly 6 astonishing 7 Most of

K
1 too much/a lot of 2 enough 3 a few/several
4 too much/a lot of/plenty of/loads of 5 a lot of/plenty of/several/loads of 6 much/too much/a lot of 7 a few 8 too many

L
1 – 2 The 3 a 4 – 5 a 6 – 7 – 8 a

174

Resource bank key

Test three (modules 9–12)

A
1 Taxes are likely to go up next year.
2 It may well snow tomorrow.
3 Sylvia almost certainly won't be on the next train.
4 Guy could pass his driving test.
5 Mary will probably move to Canada.
6 The USA definitely won't win the Ryder Cup.
7 Max isn't likely to phone you until tomorrow.
8 Andrea might not like the present I've bought her.

B
1 rules   2 strict   3 improve   4 admit   5 decrease
6 rise   7 agree/accept   8 owe

C
1 will you do; miss; 'll get
2 didn't cost; 'd (would)/could/might visit
3 hadn't been; wouldn't/mightn't have happened
4 'd (would) call; knew
5 could/would/might have become; 'd (had) trained
6 's (is) closed; 'll go
7 doesn't work; won't pass
8 would you do; left; 'd (would) probably spend
9 'd (had) told; could/would/might have done
10 hadn't got; 'd (would) still be/'d (would) have still been

D
1 the right to, a bad time   2 sorry, goodbye
3 somebody unhappy, something possible   4 your mind, your school   5 your best, well   6 a lie, the truth

E
1 To   2 off   3 by   4 over   5 in   6 up   7 of
8 on   9 out

F *(1 mark for each phrase underlined)*
... <u>asked him why he hadn't brought</u> the money. Jack <u>said he hadn't had</u> time to arrange it. She <u>said she would send his boss</u>* the photos if <u>he didn't give her</u> the money. Jack <u>said okay</u>, he <u>could get</u> it by <u>the next day</u>. He <u>asked her where the photos were</u>. She <u>said they were</u> in a safe place and <u>told him not to worry</u>.

* also possible: She threatened to send

G
o● persuade, obey, ignore
●o threaten, foreign, promise
oo●o disadvantage, economic, unemployment
●ooo necessary, fortunately, obviously

H
1 telephoned; hadn't spoken   2 went; started   3 died
4 got; found; 'd (had) broken into; 'd (had) stolen
5 left; joined   6 had written

I
1 minus twelve degrees Celsius/Centigrade
2 two thousand and one
3 eighty-seven square kilometres
4 four hundred and twenty-one thousand kilometres per/an hour
5 seventy-two point five per cent/seventy-two and a half per cent

J
1 you must have/you have to have/you've got to have
2 shouldn't have drunk
3 couldn't vote/weren't allowed to vote
4 ought to do/should do
5 mustn't eat/can't eat/aren't allowed to eat
6 can wear/are allowed to wear
7 weren't allowed to write
8 mustn't drink/can't drink/aren't allowed to drink
9 shouldn't have come/doesn't want to dance
10 We've got to solve/We have to solve/We must solve

K
1 behaviour   2 punishment   3 sensible
4 suggestion   5 equipment   6 solution   7 election

L
1 What is more/Moreover/Besides   2 However/Despite this   3 although   4 As a result/For this reason/Therefore

M
1 to eat   2 to read   3 having   4 to do   5 to take
6 going   7 to talk   8 to queue   9 taking   10 to hit

175

Pearson Education Limited
Edinburgh Gate, Harlow,
Essex, CM20 2JE, England
and Associated Companies throughout the world

www.longman.com/cuttingedge

© Addison Wesley Longman Limited 1998
All rights reserved; no part of this publication
may be reproduced, stored in a retrieval system,
or transmitted in any form or by any means, electronic,
mechanical, photocopying, recording or otherwise,
without the prior written permission of the Publishers.

First published 1998

Tenth impression 2004

Set in Congress Sans and Stone Informal

Printed in Spain by Mateu Cromo, S.A. Pinto (Madrid)

ISBN 0582 302080

Authors' acknowledgements
We would like to express our gratitude to the following writers, whose work has influenced us in different areas: John Eastwood, Michael Lewis, Peter Skehan and Jane Willis.

The Publishers would like to thank Will Moreton, Chester Formacion, Madrid for activity 9C on page 148.

Design: teacher's notes by Glynis Edwards, photocopiable and other pages by Jennifer Coles.

Illustrated by Pavely Arts, Kathy Baxendale, Graham Humphreys/The Art Market, Ed McLachlan, Graham Smith/The Art Market.

Photocopying
The Publisher grants permission for the photocopying of those pages marked 'photocopiable' according to the following conditions. Individual purchasers may make copies for their own use or for use by the classes they teach. School purchasers may make copies for use by their staff and students, but this permission does not extend to additional schools or branches. Under no circumstances may any part of this book be photocopied for resale.